7161

EMILY DICKINSON'S READING

1836-1886

EMILY DICKINSON'S
READING

1836–1886

Jack L. Capps

HARVARD UNIVERSITY PRESS

Cambridge, Massachusetts

1966

The poems and letters of Emily Dickinson quoted here in whole or in part are reproduced with the permission of the publishers. Harvard University Press: The Poems of Emily Dickinson, edited by Thomas H. Johnson, copyright, 1951, 1955, by the President and Fellows of Harvard College; The Letters of Emily Dickinson, edited by Thomas H. Johnson and Theodora Ward, copyright, 1958, by the President and Fellows of Harvard College. Little, Brown and Company: poems first published in The Single Hound, copyright, 1914, 1942, by Martha Dickinson Bianchi; poems first published in Further Poems of Emily Dickinson, copyright, 1929, 1957, by Mary L. Hampson; poems first published in Unpublished Poems of Emily Dickinson, copyright, 1935, by Martha Dickinson Bianchi; all reprinted in The Complete Poems of Emily Dickinson, edited by Thomas H. Johnson (1960). Houghton Mifflin Company: Emily Dickinson Face to Face, copyright, 1932, by Martha Dickinson Bianchi; The Life and Letters of Emily Dickinson, copyright, 1924, 1952, by Alfred Leete Hampson.

Poems by Emily Dickinson included in this volume are reprinted by permission of the President and Fellows of Harvard College and the Trustees of Amherst College from THE POEMS OF EMILY DICKINSON, edited by Thomas H. Johnson, The Belknap Press of Harvard University Press, Cambridge, Mass., copyright, 1951 and 1955, by the President and Fellows of Harvard College.

Distributed in Great Britain by Oxford University Press, London

Publication of this book has been aided by a grant from the
Ford Foundation

Library of Congress Catalog Card Number 66-14439

Printed in the United States of America

Preface

Emily Dickinson's voluntary seclusion has often been mistakenly equated to intellectual isolation. Those who accept this premise consider her verse primarily the product of an agile, Transcendental mind articulating quasi-mystical experience, and they maintain that she was in no one's poetic debt. Such positions are not without support. Surely her Christian faith was unencumbered by the apparatus of church or dogma; she perceived the greatest of truths through the simplest of beauties; and in her finest poems she saw life steadily and she saw it whole. But to limit her horizons to the house and garden of the Dickinson homestead is to underestimate grossly the capacity of her imagination. Although she says of her poetry, "This is my letter to the World/That never wrote to Me," she also declares that "There is no Frigate like a Book/To take us Lands away." From Amherst she could thus venture to "Lands away" without crossing any field, for she was both an omnivorous reader and a prodigious correspondent. Her reading and correspondence introduced her to much of the world's great literature, brought her into contact with the major events of nineteenth-century Europe and America, and kept her informed about everyday life in Amherst.

So it should not be surprising to find in a careful examination of Emily Dickinson's reading that a considerable amount of her poetry can be related to a variety of external sources. By fixing as accurately as possible the limits and content of her reading, her relationship to literary movements and figures can be more clearly established, and there emerges a picture of a working poet supplementing limited personal experience with the vicarious experience available in letters, books, and periodicals. Knowing what she read is all the more significant because an entire poem frequently turns upon an enigmatic allusion that becomes meaningful when related to her reading.

In preparing this book I have had the generous assistance and cooperation of a number of associates. First of all, I am happy to express my gratitude to Dr. Hennig Cohen of the University of Pennsylvania for the advice and encouragement that guided this project from its inception. I also wish to indicate my sincere appreciation to members of the English Department at West Point for their invaluable help and indulgence: particular thanks are due Brigadier General Russell K. Alspach, Lieutenant Colonel Wilfred C. Burton, and Mrs. Beatrice Coleman.

I have relied heavily upon the authoritative editions of Dickinson's poems and letters compiled by Dr. Thomas H. Johnson of the Lawrenceville School, and I am further indebted to Dr. Johnson for his reading of the manuscript. Lacking his contribution of criticism and suggestion, this would have been a lesser book.

It is a pleasure to acknowledge the assistance of a number of librarians who have been most helpful. Miss Geraldine Armstrong and Mr. John Parker of the United States Military Academy Library made themselves constantly available to provide essential books and materials. Miss Carolyn E. Jakeman of the Houghton Library contributed importantly by aiding in my examination of the Dickinson Collection at Harvard. Also of importance were the contributions of Mr. Charles R. Green of The Jones Library, Amherst; Miss Flora B. Ludington of the Williston Memorial Library, Mount Holyoke College; Mr. Donald C. Gallup of the Yale University Library; and Mr. Newton F. McKeon of the Converse Library, Amherst College.

Finally, I should like to thank my wife, Marie, without whose understanding and enthusiasm this book could neither have been begun nor completed.

J. L. C.

West Point, New York
October, 1965

CONTENTS

EMILY DICKINSON'S READING

1836-1886

Introduction

A sound basis for study now exists in Thomas H. Johnson's editions of the poems and letters of Emily Dickinson. These texts make it possible to analyze how the mind of a poet who lived in almost complete isolation worked. In such an analysis, one persistent problem is the question of sources. Were the sources of Emily Dickinson's poetry native only to the confines of the homestead in Amherst? Could she by her late twenties, when she had selected her own society and "shut the door," have accumulated the breadth of experience and knowledge evident in the sustained poetic utterance that followed? If one accepts her isolation as complete — and the physical limits of her seclusion have been well documented — that portion of her works dated after 1861 becomes the product of unaugmented mystical genius. Arguments to the contrary notwithstanding, withdrawal from society did not reduce Emily Dickinson's world to the limits of the grounds surrounding the family home. Her contact with the world was selective, but the world was by no means completely excluded. There is ample evidence throughout both the poems and the letters to indicate her continuous awareness of events outside the household. As the alert and cultivated daughter of a stern, pragmatic New England Congressman, she knew the spirit of her times; but by maintaining the prerogatives of a cloistered existence she achieved an uncluttered perspective that would otherwise have been impossible.

The familiar lines, "This is my letter to the World/That never wrote to Me,"[1] should be considered an overstatement. Not only did much of what the world wrote come to Emily Dickinson, but she enthusiastically read a great deal of it. And she was not unaware of the exciting force of her reading. Near the height of her poetic activity she declared,

> Strong Draughts of Their Refreshing Minds
> To drink – enables Mine
> Through Desert or the Wilderness
> As bore it Sealed Wine –
>
> To go elastic – Or as One
> The Camel's trait – attained –
> How powerful the Stimulus
> Of an Hermetic Mind –

The stimulus, whatever its source, was often a fleeting one, as these stanzas from a later poem illustrate:

> A Cloud withdrew from the Sky
> Superior Glory be
> But that Cloud and it's Auxiliaries
> Are forever lost to me
>
> Had I but further scanned
> Had I secured the Glow
> In an Hermetic Memory
> It had availed me now.

Taken together, these two poems suggest not only the peregrinations of a perceptive mind but also the significant pressures generated by the knowledge and experience accumulated in an "Hermetic Memory."

To be sure, Emily Dickinson entertained some very grand concepts regarding the breadth of knowledge required of a poet:

> I reckon – when I count at all –
> First – Poets – Then the Sun –
> Then Summer – Then the Heaven of God –
> And then – the List is done –

But, looking back – the First so seems
To Comprehend the Whole –
The Others look a needless Show –
So I write – Poets – All –

She included herself in this category of poets and firmly announced, "My Business is Circumference." [2] Perceiving the awesome extent of "circumferential" knowledge, she must also have realized the immensity of the task of expressing it. She reviewed a wealth of words, ideas, and images in order to choose the particular words capable of accomplishing the compression characteristic of her verse and outlined the tedium of the selection process when she wrote:

Shall I take thee, the Poet said
To the propounded word?
Be stationed with the Candidates
Till I have finer tried –

The Poet searched Philology
And was about to ring
for the suspended Candidate
There came unsummoned in –

That portion of the Vision
The Word applied to fill
Not unto nomination
The Cherubim reveal –

When conscious search for the exact expression went unrewarded, the answer occasionally came from the far reaches of memory or imagination. Hers was a difficult task, for, as George Frisbie Whicher has pointed out, "to grasp the soul at white heat she needed more than ever the tongs that wit supplied. Complete integrity in what lay too deep for tears was possible only by indirection." [3] She acknowledged the necessity for such

3

indirection, commenting that "The thought beneath so slight a film –/Is more distinctly seen" and advising, "Tell all the Truth but tell it slant –/Success in Circuit lies." She seems constantly to have explored labyrinthine paths, seeking out those points of view that would present her subject in singularly advantageous attitude. Her explorations were neither naive nor aimless. She was familiar with the trophies of other literary adventurers; she knew what she was looking for and had the judgment to realize when she had found it. Sometimes, encountering a pregnant thought poorly expressed, she reshaped and refined it; at other times, she embraced a word or phrase from an accepted master and continued to use it in his special sense.

But suggestion that Emily Dickinson derived some of her verse from sources other than her own mind and environment, especially if those other sources were literary ones, has long been regarded as heresy. In his biography, Whicher discussed Dickinson's "Books and Reading" in an entire chapter and came to the conclusion that "Emily Dickinson's poetry is not derivable from her reading." [4] Thirteen years later, Richard Chase was of the same opinion: "Neither in her thought nor in her style is Emily Dickinson influenced in any particular way by literary sources." [5] Yet, even before the definitive editions of the poems and letters appeared, there had been a number of independent studies relating Dickinson poems, in a limited way, to the works of other writers — "Emily Dickinson and Sir Thomas Browne," "Elizabeth Browning and Emily Dickinson," "Emily Dickinson and Isaac Watts" — to name only a few. Other sources have been suggested; nearly every biographer mentions one or two, and the Johnson editions identify a number of the allusions and quotations that she used. This indicates that significant literary sources for Dickinson poems do exist, and that the opinions of Whicher and Chase can be reconsidered. There can be little doubt that an increased knowledge of her sources would further the understanding of both Emily Dickinson and her poetry.

Many of her obscure allusions can be fully appreciated only when their source is comprehended; and, insofar as literary biography is concerned, examination of her reading can be expected to reveal her attitude toward other authors and to establish more definitely the relationship between their works and her own.

The poet herself offers very little assistance in this respect. Writing to Thomas Wentworth Higginson in August 1862, she professed complete literary independence, "I marked a line in One Verse – because I met it after I made it – and never consciously touch a paint, mixed by another person." [6] She was capable, however, of taking another's paint and mixing it herself. One may agree with Roy Harvey Pearce that "Emily Dickinson's situation, temperament, and genius made [the basic style of her poems] peculiarly and directly her own," but when he continues, "As poet she was strong enough to need nothing else," [7] it is difficult not to complain that "nothing" is a very strong word. Whether she would have been so successful with "nothing else" we shall never know, for the truth is that, while the poems may be accepted as unique products shaped by her catalytic intuition and craftsmanship, she acquired the raw material for them in a number of ways from a number of different sources. Aside from personal observation and experience, she acknowledged habitual reference to her "lexicon"; and her frequent quotations from the King James version, for instance, indicate its importance in her writing. The relation of her metrics to traditional hymn meter has been pointed out and is generally accepted. The bookish atmosphere in which she was reared and the frequency with which biographers and critics turn up similarities between Emily Dickinson's writings and literary works to which she may have had access, sustain the question of her use of literary source material. Incorporation of such material is not always obvious, primarily because her assimilation was nearly always complete. "Lay this Laurel on the One" is an example of this process. She indicated to Higginson that she wrote it

5

after rereading his twenty-eight-line poem "Decoration." [8] He acknowledged her four-line, twenty-one-word version by remarking, "It is the condensed essence of [my poem] and so far finer." [9] Certainly the Dickinson poem can stand on its own merits, but the awareness of its genesis in the longer Higginson elegy gives a more profound understanding of it and a measure of her accomplishment. The relationship of these two poems gives, in addition, an indication of Emily Dickinson's search for kindred minds suitable to share her emotional or intellectual experiences. In sending "Lay this Laurel on the One" to Higginson she confided, "It comforts an instinct if another have felt it too." [10] Her acceptance of such companionship, however, was tentative:

> Experiment to me
> Is every one I meet
> If it contain a Kernel?
> The Figure of a Nut
>
> Presents upon a Tree
> Equally plausibly
> But Meat within, is requisite
> To Squirrels and to Me

Only those who proved themselves in this appraisal interested her.

Emily Dickinson had a high regard for established literary masters, but her taste in contemporary literature was often erratic. Nevertheless, by absorbing a variety of detail from those correspondents whom she accepted and from the authors whom she read, she could reinforce the strength, determine the direction, and select the material needed to cope with her own discoveries. We should suspect that her intellectual contacts not only suggested routes and horizons but also possible approaches to what she termed "flood subjects": nature, life, death, and immortality.

Chronological tabulation of certain specific references and allusions in the poems reveals an interesting pattern. Consider, for example, the place names she used, knowledge of which was almost entirely derived from reading and study. On the average, place names occur in one of every six poems dated 1862; they occur one in twenty in 1864, and none occurs in 1867. They reappear in later years, though in much smaller numbers. It would appear that Dickinson's vicarious travels decreased as her seclusion deepened. On the other hand, that one-third of the poems dated generally between 1862 and 1866 accounts for only one-fifth of the total number of apparent literary allusions in all the poems. Few allusions recur in the poems for any reference once employed seems to have been considered exhausted.

In addition to contributing to the understanding of her literary kinship and her development as a person and a poet, a knowledge of Emily Dickinson's reading can do much to resolve problems of explication that have resulted from her penchant for esoteric and arcane reference. Whicher noted that, "her obscurities are less frequent and less baffling than those of Donne, or Browning, or George Meredith, or Gerard Manley Hopkins, and no less than theirs are worthy of patient interpretation." [11] For example, the line "Fresh as a Cargo from Batize" in "After the Sun comes out" has limited meaning until one determines what and where "Batize" may be. John L. Stephens' *Incidents of Travel in Central America, Chiapas, and Yucatan,* a two-volume travel book available in the Dickinson family library, provides a clue. The first chapter discusses in some detail the port of Balize [12] in what is now British Honduras. Emily's handwriting is such that one could easily mistake the combination of an adjacent "l" and dotted "i" for a "t"; or possibly it is simply a misspelling on her part. In either case, the examination of her reading identifies the word "Batize," and Stephens' discussion suggests the breadth of image that the word was meant to convey. *Incidents of Travel* presents Balize as port known primarily for its export of mahogany logs, and thus a "cargo from Batize" was probably raw material for the hands and tools of New England cabinetmakers. The potential value of such a cargo adds a new dimension to the poem in which the phrase occurs; but determining a satisfactory analogue for "Batize" would have been unlikely without knowledge of the poet's familiarity with the Stephens work.

Although a listing of Emily Dickinson's reading would be highly desirable for the purposes of interpretation and literary history, a complete listing is, of course, an impossibility because many sources are no longer ascertainable. Library charge slips have disappeared, and even the usefulness of the Dickinson family library now at Harvard is limited by the fact that books from the Austin Dickinson and Edward Dickinson households have been mixed and, in most cases, dates of acquisition and individual ownership are uncertain. After her death, Emily's private papers other than the poems were burned by her sister, Lavinia. As useful as these papers would be in other respects, it is entirely unlikely that Emily had tabulated her reading in them. In spite of such difficulties as these, much concerning her reading can be determined from her letters and poems. References and quotations in the letters help to disclose her reading habits and occasionally reveal reading interests of the moment. It is fortunate that she was so scrupulous in designating quoted words: the author is seldom identified, the quotation may be from memory and inexact, but the quotation marks are usually there. Her letters and poems thus provided the initial basis for the list of her reading that appears in the Appendix. Additional entries were derived from supplementary data found in the Houghton Library holdings, Dickinson family correspondence, and a variety of lesser sources. A title appears on the list only when there is substantial evidence that Emily was to some degree familiar with the work. Shorter items, such as essays and poems, are listed individually when they may have been read in either an anthology or a periodical. In those cases in which the exact edition can be fixed, the bibliographical entry is complete. While close correlation of the entire fifty years of Dickinson reading to the Dickinson canon is a task only suggested and begun here, the accumulated evidence is sufficient to conclude not that Emily Dickinson necessarily sought out and relied upon literary sources but that such sources can be profitably related to her poems.

≥ I ≤

Emily Dickinson on Books and Reading

> I am glad there are Books.
> They are better than Heaven for that is
> unavoidable while one may miss these.
> — *Emily Dickinson to F. B. Sanborn, c. 1873*

Several biographers have given considerable notice to the fact that in O. A. Bullard's 1840 portrait of the three Dickinson children Emily is holding an open book. It is unfortunate for my book that little importance can be attached to this coincidence other than that Mr. Bullard, like many artists, found it difficult to paint his subjects' hands. There is no doubt, however, that books formed a vital part of Emily Dickinson's life. By feeding her astonishing memory and imagination, they prevented her from living the narrow, desiccated life of a recluse. Her life was full: she found, as she told Higginson, "ecstasy in living."[1] In the combination of forces that made her a poet, her assorted reading materials appear as one of the few tangible elements that can, to a considerable degree, be reassembled for study. For this reason her reading habits, the attitudes that she expressed regarding reading, and her evaluation of what she read are particularly significant.

Without question, Emily's father exerted the greatest influence upon her reading. Exactly when she learned to read we do not know, but it was Edward Dickinson who saw to the beginnings of her early schooling and dutifully reported to his wife, who was in Boston on Monday, September 7, 1835, that "The Children went to school today—and now are snug in bed—."[2] When away from Amherst as a member of the Massachusetts legislature, he continually charged his children to "keep school and learn." In February 1838, he enclosed the following note in a letter to his wife: "My Dear little Children—I send you some of Parley's Magazine—They have some interesting stories for you to read. I want to have you remember some of them to tell me when I get home . . ."[3] That the Puritan association of sin and ignorance was in his mind is indicated in another letter that tells of his visit to the Charlestown prison, where he had tried to teach one of the inmates to read. At the end of the account he carefully instructed his wife to "tell the children that the poor ignorant fellow took a pin, & pointed to each letter, & called it by name, but could not pronounce words."[4] Such moral training by mail typifies the strict control that Edward Dickinson exercised over his household whether he was in Amherst or Boston. He was a devoted, if severe parent who discharged what he conceived to be his fatherly obligations with diligence and dispatch. He was no less conscious of his moral and civic responsibilities. As a lawyer, church leader, and Congressman, he was both literally and figuratively a representative New Englander. He had been educated in the classical tradition (Yale, 1823), and there remain in the Dickinson Collection at Harvard a sufficient number of books identifiable as his to establish the quality of his taste. Emily grew up among the books his library provided. Some of the works bearing his signature are Pope's *Homer, Don Quixote, Paradise Lost,* twelve volumes of *The Spectator, The Works of Lord Byron* in four volumes, Cowper's *Poems,* Crabbe's *English Synonymes, Franklin's Essays and Letters,* and an eight-volume edition of Shakespeare. Although Emily reported to Higginson that her father read *"lonely* and *rigorous* books," she mentions very candidly to another friend that "the letters of suspected gentlemen form quite a valuable addition to our family library, and father pursues the search with a mixture of fun and perseverence, which is quite diabolical!" [5]

In spite of the fact that Higginson inferred from Emily's remarks that her father wanted the family to read only the Bible, [6] it was Edward Dickinson who continually stimulated his children's interest in contemporary as well as classical reading by his admonitions regarding their choice of authors. Most current books were proscribed, and Emily, like all children, was fascinated by any forbidden fare.

One day her brother brought home Kavanagh hid it under the piano cover & made signs to her & they read it: her father at last found it & was displeased. Perhaps it was before this that a student of his was amazed that they had never heard of Mrs. [Lydia Maria] Child & used to bring them books & hide in a bush by the door. They were then little things in short dresses with their feet on the rungs of the chair. After the first book she thought in ecstacy "This then is a book! And there are more of them!" [7]

In examining this romantic little drama, one must bear in mind that it was reported by Higginson in August 1870, immediately following the second afternoon of his first visit with Emily Dickinson. Higginson was frankly in awe of Emily, who doubtless sensed his attitude and for his benefit seems to have been led to overplay her breathless role. This interview must have confirmed Higginson's impression of the dour characteristics of her father, whom he had met only the morning before. He judged Edward Dickinson to be "thin dry & speechless" and assumed after meeting him that he "saw what her life had been." [8] In arriving at this conclusion, Higginson failed to consider that the elder Dickinson might have little to say to a professional writer who had left the ministry to turn abolitionist agitator and army officer, and whose purpose in visiting Emily had not been clearly declared. Even after his visit, Higginson was far from seeing "what her life had been." It is unlikely, for instance, that Edward Dickinson played "cat and mouse" with the children and their borrowed books; and Emily had informed Higginson eight years before his trip to Amherst that "[father] buys me many Books — but begs me not to read them — because he fears they joggle the Mind."[9] Her father, in fact, purchased the volumes he considered appropriate for a parent to recommend, and inscribed them to his daughter. They included her Bible, which he gave her in 1844, Huntington's *Christian Believing and Living*, and Sprague's *Letters on Practical Subjects to a Daughter*. He showed he was aware of Emily's interests when he gave her Herndon and Gibbon's *Exploration of the Valley of the Amazon*, and Mrs. Badger's magnificently illustrated folio volume of *Wild Flowers*. He also provided books that would "joggle the Mind," but left them uninscribed. Because Edward Dickinson was not a man to spend money foolishly, that is, for books that were not to be read, it is safe to assume that he meant the uninscribed works for family consumption; and the family library contained a number of titles and authors that he spoke of disparagingly but did not remove. He must have sensed that Emily was precocious to the point of understanding beyond her years for he continually directed her to mature works that he considered worthwhile. In April 1853, Emily wrote Austin at Harvard that their father had just given her "quite a trimming about 'Uncle Tom' and 'Charles Dickens' and these 'modern Literati' [because they were] *nothing*, compared to past generations, who flourished when *he was a boy*." It is doubtful that Edward Dickinson expected this oration against the "modern Literati" to intimidate his daughter, for she immediately sensed that she was only temporarily "in disgrace."[10]

Few people understood Edward Dickinson so well as Emily did; and he, in turn, was one of an even smaller group who understood her. Over the years there developed between them a fondness that overt affection would have destroyed but one that flourished under seal. When he fed the birds in winter or called attention to the sunset by ringing the church bell, she sensed in him the gentle and romantic nature that others overlooked and that he seldom openly displayed. She followed his example of hesitancy regarding profession of Christian faith until church membership for her was an impossibility. She learned his legal terms and used them to such an extent in her poems that one can only conclude she must have occasionally read his law books.[11] Though she unconsciously emulated her father, Emily Dickinson's femininity made her incapable of assuming the granite façade that concealed and protected her father's emotions; instead, she found similar refuge in her seclusion. Neither of them attempted to invade the privacy of the other; and Emily's love for her father and her admiration for his unyielding reserve increased until, in abject sorrow at his death, she wrote: "His Heart was pure and terrible and I think no other like it exists." [12] Perhaps none did, except her own.

Emily placed a high value on her father's opinions; and, insofar as her reading was concerned, those opinions contributed to a sustained interest in master works, even though his criticism proved ineffective in diverting her from contemporary literature. In addition to the influence of Edward Dickinson, her reading was affected by formal schooling. She had the serious dedication to scholastic achievement that was becoming to a member of the third generation of Dickinsons to be actively connected with the administration of Amherst College. She admired her teachers immensely and went about academic chores with a zeal worthy of her Puritan heritage. Her education was one befitting the daughter of a leading citizen of Amherst: first the local "Primary School," which she entered at five, then Amherst Academy and Mount Holyoke.[13] In the surviving letters, Emily never mentions her primary school experience. In one written at age twelve, during her second year at the Academy, however, she describes to Jane Humphrey the unsuccessful efforts of one of her classmates in the Wednesday afternoon Speaking and Composition Class and then goes on to say, with the fresh eagerness of a young pupil, "Besides Latin I study History and Botany [and] like school very much indeed." [14] Daniel Fiske, preceptor at the Academy during her third year, recalled that she was "very bright, but rather delicate and frail," and that "her compositions were strikingly original; and in both thought and style seemed beyond her years." [15]

Emily's delicate health was responsible for frequent absence from classes, and one has only to consider the frequent death notices of children during the Amherst winters to understand why her parents' apprehension was great enough to cause them to keep her from school. Absences notwithstanding, by the spring of 1847, Emily was in her final term at the Academy and was preparing for admission to Mount Holyoke by "studying Algebra, Euclid, Ecc[lesiastical] History & reviewing Arithmetic again, to be upon the safe side of things [the] next autumn." That November she confided in her friend Abiah Root, "I am really at Mt Holyoke . . . contented & quite happy." [16] And yet her happiness was not without qualification, for she added in the same sentence: "if I can be happy when absent from my dear home & friends." During the entire stay in South Hadley her enthusiasm for higher education never overcame her attachment to the Dickinson hearth in Amherst. Ostensibly, it was chronic physical illness that interrupted her studies and finally precipitated her failure to complete the two-year curriculum, but both the illness and the departure seem to have been aggravated by her inability to accept the entire atmosphere of life in the seminary. The homesickness so apparent in her first letters from school never really subsided and was made bearable only by intense devotion to her studies and the visits which she made to Amherst and which members of the family made to South Hadley. She seems to have viewed the conviviality of her contemporaries in the seminary with some annoyance. During her first three weeks, a menagerie appeared in town and she contentedly reported that "almost all the girls went & I enjoyed the solitude finely." Although she warmly accepted her room-mate, Emily Norcross, a cousin from Monson, she seems to have found no other close friends. She reported, "No Abby. or Abiah or Mary," and by adding unenthusiastically, "but I love many of the girls," [17] she implied their lack of the one important quali-fication that Lavinia was also to expect of her schoolmates at Ipswich: "They are not *Amherst girls*." [18] The Amherst standard was unconsciously applied to everything outside the home com-munity for, in the Dickinson view heaven was heaven only so far as it approximated Amherst.

One contributing cause of Emily Dickinson's dissatisfaction with her situation at Mount Holyoke was the restriction that it imposed upon her reading. She pointed out to Abiah Root, "I have little time to read when I am here, but while at home I had a feast in the reading line." This particular period at home had been brought about by a seven-week illness during which she had kept up her studies, and had read, in addition, Long-fellow's *Evangeline*, Tennyson's *The Princess*, Thomas Moore's *The Epicurean*, Marcella Smedley's *The Maiden Aunt*, and two novels by Martin Tupper.[19] Just three weeks after her enroll-ment at the seminary she complained to Austin, "I have been trying to find out ever since I came [who the candidate for President is] & have not yet succeeded. I dont know anything more about affairs in the world, than if I was in a trance." [20] She missed the familiar newspapers and family discussions of current affairs. The irritation of not being able to read as widely and as freely as she liked, along with her parochial appraisal of her schoolmates, complicated what was her most serious diffi-culty at Mount Holyoke: an intellectual integrity that made it impossible for her to profess open, unreserved Christian faith and thereby identify herself with the remainder of the student body. This situation isolated her from the group without giving her the solitude she valued. When she wrote Abiah in May 1848 that her father had decided not to send her to Mount

Holyoke for the second year, her only regret was: "I fear I have not improved [the advantages I have had] as I ought."[21] By late summer she was ready to return home; there were books and scholars readily accessible in Amherst, and in the Dickinson household one's individuality was assured within the protective framework of stern, yet clearly defined, family tenets.

Final return to Amherst from South Hadley meant resumption of reading adventures and renewed association with old friends who had never been replaced, and Emily seems to have flourished in the more familiar surroundings. From this time until shortly after the family moved back into the Dickinson homestead, she lived the busy life of a well-to-do, socially acceptable young lady residing in a New England college town. Not the least of the pleasures she could once more enjoy was the reading, which she obviously relished and discussed with such stimulating friends as Ben Newton, James Kimball, George Gould, and Leonard Humphrey. The most important of the group was Ben Newton, who had come into her father's law office as a student in 1847. Ten months after his death in March 1853, Emily wrote to Edward Everett Hale, "Mr Newton became to me a gentle yet grave Preceptor, teaching me what to read, what authors to admire, what was most grand or beautiful in nature, and that sublimer lesson, a faith in things unseen."[22] It is to such a person that "Your Riches – taught me – Poverty" is addressed. The poem expresses the awe of an amateur enlightened by a seasoned master, and she sent a copy of it to her sister-in-law on a date very near the ninth anniversary of Newton's death. Her added note, "Dear Sue – You see I remember –,"[23] gives credence to the view that Newton was the benefactor whose stimulating revelation is being acknowledged.[24] Further evidence of his influence is the inscribed copy of Emerson's *Poems* (1847) that he sent to Emily in January 1850 after he had moved from Amherst to Worcester. She prized the volume highly and recalled it when she wrote:

A Book I have – a friend gave –
Whose Pencil – here and there –
Had notched the place that pleased Him –
At Rest – His fingers are –

Now – when I read – I read not –
For interrupting Tears –
Obliterate the Etchings
Too Costly for Repairs.[25]

Unfortunately, none of the letters exchanged between the two have survived.

Leonard Humphrey, George Gould, and James Kimball were also friends with congenial literary interests, though none appears to have been so influential as Ben Newton. The three were part of a literary club to which Emily belonged, and in the years immediately following her return from Mount Holyoke, the group almost certainly included in their reading the novels of Scott, Dickens, and Eliot, shorter pieces by Poe, Irving, and Hawthorne, as well as romantic British poetry and didactic American verse. How completely they explored these items and how thoroughly they shared them one can only surmise. Leonard Humphrey had been the principal of Amherst Academy during Emily's last year there; and, while she may have valued his opinions, it is doubtful that she was as close to him as she was to either George Gould or James Kimball, who were nearer her own age. Gould had been a member of the editorial board of the Amherst student magazine, *The Indicator*; and it was Kimball who presented Emily with a copy of Oliver Wendell Holmes's poems, inscribed, "From J.P.K. 'Philopena.'" By the spring of 1851, even though Humphrey was dead and Kimball and Newton had moved away, Emily kept up her interest in the reading group; and in June of that year she wrote to Austin, "Our Reading Club still is, and becomes now very pleasant." [26] The club appears to have been in existence for a number of seasons;

and, according to Whicher, "the book store run by the kindly, intellectual John S. Adams served as a rallying point [for the literary society of the town]." [27] Emily showed her familiarity with Mr. Adams' establishment in the following note to her prospective sister-in-law, Susan Gilbert:

Longfellow's "golden Legend" has come to town I hear — and may be seen *in state* on Mr. Adams' bookshelves. It always makes me think of "Pegasus in the pound" – when I find a gracious author sitting side by side with "Murray" and "Wells" and "Walker" [textbooks] in that renowned store — [28]

In November 1855 the Dickinsons moved back into the family home, after having lived for fifteen years in a large frame house on Pleasant Street, Amherst. By then, Emily had made her one trip to Washington and Philadelphia, her mother's health had begun to fail, and the pattern of life usually associated with her adult years began to take shape.

> I was the slightest in the House –
> I took the smallest Room –
> At night, my little Lamp, and Book –
> And one Geranium –

The following July, Austin and his bride, Susan Gilbert, moved into the new house that Edward Dickinson had built for them just across the hedge from the homestead. Emily and Sue had been friends for a number of years; they occasionally had stayed together in the Dickinson home on Pleasant Street when the remainder of the family was away from Amherst in Boston, Washington, or elsewhere. Sue shared Emily's literary enthusiasm, and examination of the family library and correspondence reveals habitual exchange of books and periodicals between the adjacent Dickinson households. The exchange took place primarily between the sisters, Emily and Lavinia, and Sue, and became increasingly important as Emily's seclusion approached

complete withdrawal from society. However many corporeal
visitors were excluded, books were always admissible:

> Unto my Books – so good to turn –
> Far ends of tired Days –
> It half endears the Abstinence –
> And Pain – is missed – in Praise –
>
> *   *   *   *   *   *
>
> I thank these Kinsmen of the Shelf –
> Their Countenances Kid
> Enamor – in Prospective –
> And satisfy – obtained –

Thus, it is not surprising to find that Emily Dickinson writes so
impressively in praise of books. The "Kinsmen of the Shelf"
were transport:

> There is no Frigate like a Book
> To take us Lands away.

They were intellectual release:

> And this Bequest of Wings
> Was but a Book – What Liberty
> A loosened spirit brings – 29

They were, at least until opened, unconditionally acceptable:

> The Pedigree of Honey
> Does not concern the Bee –
> A Clover, any time, to him,
> Is Aristocracy –

The devotion of a considerable amount of time to a wide
variety of reading was a fundamental part of the established
routine of Emily Dickinson's mature years. She explained it this
way, "Little – wayfaring acts – comprise my 'pursuits' – and a

few moments at night, for Books – after the rest sleep." [30] She frequently read letters and newspapers aloud to her father or to Lavinia. Only rarely did she allow anything to encroach upon her reading habits. In 1865, between two trips to Boston for treatment of a chronic eye ailment, she informed the Norcross sisters that it was difficult to write much in bed but that she had been reading scenes from the first part of Shakespeare's *Henry VI*. This was contrary to the doctor's advice, but she "read them in the garret, and the rafters wept." [31] Once, in late May 1874, with nephew Ned ill and her father away in Boston on what was to be a final fatal visit, she confided in Higginson, "I have read but a little recently – Existence has overpowered Books." [32] She was seldom thus overcome; her exploration of books was always resumed, encouraged by the rewards of her previous adventures and urged on by her feeling that

> It's far – far Treasure to surmise –
> And estimate the Pearl –
> That slipped my simple fingers through –
> While just a Girl at School. [33]

In her letters, discussion of things read and to be read occurs far more frequently and is much more lively than her occasional mention of the political, religious, or academic issues that were so important to the remainder of the household. In his reply to Dickinson's initial letter, Higginson asked what she read. She courteously answered that she read his chapters in *The Atlantic Monthly* and included this sample of her taste: "For Poets – I have Keats – and Mr and Mrs Browning. For Prose – Mr Ruskin – Sir Thomas Browne – and the Revelations." [34] Because her acquaintance with Higginson was not yet firmly established, she may have been influenced to cite names he mentioned in his "Letter to a Young Contributor," [35] the article that motivated her letter. If she was influenced by his preferences, the influence was slight. She denied knowledge of Whitman (because she had been told "he was disgraceful"),[36] even though Higginson had recommended Whitman when he inquired about her reading; furthermore, Higginson had discussed in his article a number of writers whom Emily Dickinson knew as well or better than the ones whose names she repeated. Thus, the sample she gave was probably a reflection of her current reading rather than an attempt to impress Higginson. Her remark that "for several years her Lexicon was her only companion," is part of her reply and is further evidence of the fascination words held for her. Important as the dictionary must have been to Emily Dickinson, it is difficult to accept Mme. Bianchi's statement that "she read it as a priest his breviary — over and over, page by page, with utter absorption." [37]

Dickinson's apparently omnivorous literary taste and her fallible critical evaluations cast some doubt on her standards of criticism. Her enthusiasm for Ik Marvel's "reveries," Helen Hunt's poems, and sentimental newspaper verse are enough to discount her direct appraisals. She could obligingly express to Higginson "remorse for the brevity" of his *Short Stories of American Authors,* "sweetly commend" Holmes's *Life of Emerson,* and note that "one does not often meet anything so perfect" as Lowell's "A Good Word for Winter." [38] But it is hard to take these comments seriously in terms of the standard she gave Higginson in 1870: "If I read a book [and] it makes my whole body so cold no fire ever can warm me I know *that* is poetry. If I feel physically as if the top of my head were taken off, I know *that* is poetry." She seldom encountered literature that could produce this response, and in the same interview indicated how rare the experience was: "When I lost the use of my Eyes it was a comfort to think there were so few real *books* that I could easily find someone to read me all of them." [39]

In a later letter to Higginson she makes it clear that in her estimation no one approached Shakespeare as an author of "real *books*":

I did not read Mr Miller because I could not care about him –
Transport is not urged –
Mrs Hunt's Poems are stronger than any written by Women since
Mrs – Browning, with the exception of Mrs Lewes [George Eliot]
. . . "Bells and Pomgranates" I never saw but have Mrs Browning's
endorsement. While Shakespeare remains Literature is firm – [40]

She considered Shakespeare's characters as personal acquaint-
ances and expected her more intimate correspondents to do the
same. When she mentioned Desdemona, Cato's Daughter, or
Dunsinane, the reader was expected to understand the implications of the communication as completely as if they were spelled
out in ordinary nouns and adjectives. Next to the King James
version of the Bible, which was by far her most common reference, Shakespeare's works appear as her most frequent source
of allusions.

If the purely statistical procedure of "allusion counting" is
used as a means of determining Emily Dickinson's critical opinion of a given author, the frequency with which lines and
phrases from Longfellow and Higginson occur places those two
authors improbably close to Shakespeare. It would be unfair
and inaccurate to infer from this that she was so fallible a judge,
for she was solely a creative artist with little capacity for expressing critical assessments. Yet, if her relation to other authors
is to be established, her opinion of their works is of fundamental
importance. Since her opinions, except those pertaining to the
Bible and Shakespeare, are not reliably reflected either in her
direct statements or in the frequency of her reference to the
author, perhaps her true evaluation lies not in what she says
about an author's work but rather in what she does with it. In
her reading she was seeking ideas with poetic potential; those
which were poorly expressed she could accept because she realized that "Your thoughts dont have words every day/They come
a single time." If an author whom she read had rushed into
print without waiting for the proper words to come that "single

time," Emily Dickinson willingly retained his idea as the basis for her expression on the day when those proper words might come to her. And she could afford to wait. The ensuing process was a combination of the perceptive selection procedure outlined by Hawthorne in discussing the sources of *The Scarlet Letter* and the literary gestation described by Henry James in his Preface to *The American*. In the meantime, the Bible and Shakespeare were ready for instant use.

It appears, then, that, as Emily Dickinson went through life, she was shopping in the literary market place. She looked at everything, took what she wanted, but did not presume to criticize. She continually tucked away appropriate items for her friends: her letters abound with these acquisitions. She collected a variety of materials; when she encountered promising words and phrases, she took them along against the day when they would satisfy one poem's demands; and, occasionally, she found a literary bargain that she could eventually rework to advantage. Thus, through her reading she acquired new ideas and accumulated the vocabulary that went with them. It was a profitable occupation that she thoroughly enjoyed, for it broadened her perspectives and provided substance for her poetic effort. She was conscious of the importance of her reading, and in the following stanzas she expressed not only gratitude and respect for her literary sources but also an identification of herself with them.

> A precious – mouldering pleasure – 'tis –
> To meet an Antique Book –
> In just the Dress his Century wore –
> A privilege – I think –
>
> His venerable Hand to take –
> And warming in our own –
> A passage back – or two – to make –
> To Times when he – was young –

His quaint opinions – to inspect –
His thought to ascertain
On Them[e]s concern our mutual mind –
The Literature of Man –

ⅺ II ⅺ

The King James Version

There's a verse in the Bible, Emily, I don't know
where it is, nor just how it goes can I remember,
but it's a little like this —
    — *Emily Dickinson to Emily Fowler Ford, 21 December 1853*

In any study of Emily Dickinson the King James version of the
Bible is a basic reference, for its pervasive influence upon both
her life and letters is readily apparent. This influence should be
expected of any New Englander born early in the second quarter
of the nineteenth century and educated in the latter-day puri-
tanism of the Massachusetts hinterland. Details of the conservative atmosphere in the Connecticut River Valley have been frequently used to supplement the limited number of demonstrable
facts concerning Emily Dickinson's early life. Those biographers
who have followed this procedure of extrapolation have properly
interpreted the significance of her detailed familiarity with the
Scriptures. Bible reading and study were part of her existence:
at home, at church, and at school she was subjected to the pressures of individual and collective searches for evidence of hope
and grace. Evangelistic local ministers reviewed often and carefully the prospects of redemption for their intense congregations,
and profession of faith was a matter requiring the most serious
deliberation. Emily along with the others was exhorted to seek
salvation in the Scriptures, in introspective spiritual evaluation,
and in open profession of faith as a church member. Her mother

joined the church the year after Emily's birth; her father, however, did not join until almost twenty years later. His long delay is in no way indicative of indifference in religious matters; it is instead evidence of his hesitancy to declare his faith until his self-doubts were firmly resolved. His own deliberations explain in great measure his insistence that the children pay strict attention to their own spiritual development and that they read regularly the copies of the Bible that he dutifully inscribed and presented to them. His advice in spiritual matters continued long after they were grown. Emily was thirty-three when he cautioned her to "read at devotions the chapter of the gentleman with one talent" because it would be "wiser employment" than the lighter reading in which he had found her engaged.[1] Edward Dickinson thus assured himself that in his home the Bible remained pre-eminent in the family's reading, and that none of his household would fall into spiritual indifference.

In the schools that Emily attended, the instruction was designed to assure the body's survival in the present, the mind's continued development in the future, and the soul's life in the hereafter. Ecclesiastical history was part of the curriculum at Amherst Academy, where she was a student from 1840 to 1847. And there is little doubt that religious instruction was implicit in the other courses there, for the majority of the successive principals and instructors were products of Amherst College and Mount Holyoke Female Seminary, schools that took pride in the dedication and zeal of the missionaries, ministers, and teachers that they produced. When Emily enrolled at Mount Holyoke, the state of her spiritual well-being was almost immediately made a subject of serious concern, for she was not a church member, and such students were singled out for particular attention in the form of special sermons, prayers, and consultations. The devotional exhortations by the competent and zealous headmistress, Mary Lyon, though based on Scriptures already thoroughly familiar, failed to move Emily Dickinson. The atmosphere of propriety in which Emily had been reared in Amherst inhibited her ability to experience the sensation of "conversion" that her preceptors led her to expect. The urgency of the issue, however, did impress her deeply, and she confided her concern to her Amherst friend, Abiah Root:

I tremble when I think how soon the weeks and days of this term will all have been spent, and my fate will be sealed, perhaps. I have neglected the *one thing needful* when all were obtaining it, and I may never, never again pass through such a season as was granted us last winter. Abiah, you may be surprised to hear me speak as I do, knowing that I express no interest in the all-important subject, but I am not happy, and I regret that last term, when that golden opportunity was mine, that I did not give up and become a Christian.[2]

One of Emily's difficulties was inherited from her father: an unyielding devotion to truth, an absolute integrity that would never permit her to profess a thing that she did not sincerely believe. While reservations dictated by her Puritan principles may account for her refusal to add her name to the church rolls, the same principles led her to continue to search for evidence of salvation and grace by scrutinizing the Scriptures in the best Puritan tradition. And, in later years when her faith was firmly realized, she was in no way inclined to expose to the world either her beliefs or her brash familiarities with the deity. Three years before her death, in a letter written to Mrs. J. G. Holland, she reveals a lifelong, inquisitive interest in the Bible, an inquiry never concluded to her complete satisfaction: "The Fiction of 'Santa Claus' always reminds me of the reply to my early question of 'Who made the Bible' — 'Holy Men moved by the Holy Ghost,' and though I have now ceased my investigations, the Solution is insufficient —."[3] Her affinity for the idiom of the King James version accounts for the fact that her style and tone are not so easily compared to the writing of her American contemporaries as they are to that of seventeenth-century English divines, whose language was both chronologically and professionally close to that of the newly translated Bible and whose works usually depended heavily upon it as a model. Emily Dickinson relished the antique flavor of the King James version and treated the Bible with the informal familiarity that characterized her references to God. "Guess I and the Bible will move to some old fashioned spot where we'll feel at Home," she wrote Mrs. Holland.[4] Fortunately, Amherst proved to be sufficiently "old fashioned" to allow her the continued companionship of the Bible without having to move. And, as a result of her undiminished preference for the Scriptures, biblical quotations in her letters and poems far exceed references to any other source or author.

Of the thirty-eight books of the Bible to which Emily Dickinson referred one or more times in her poems and letters, the Gospels, Revelation, and Genesis are most often cited. The most important New Testament sources, in order of frequency of reference, are Matthew, John, Luke, Revelation, and I Corinthians. Revelation and three of the Gospels (Matthew, Luke, and John) account for well over half her biblical allusions, and she makes more references to Matthew than to the other two Gospels combined. In addition to Genesis, the most frequent sources of her references to the Old Testament are Deuteronomy, The Psalms, and Isaiah, in that order. If one considers her poet's concern with creation, prophecy, death, and immortality, her preferences are not surprising. The biblical narratives to which she was exposed in her childhood were securely embedded in her consciousness. She was therefore able to use a variety of biblical names and quotations with ease. In her poems and letters, some of the variations from the exact text are introduced for specific effect or emphasis, while others are slight misquotations that indicate she was writing from memory.[5]

When Emily Dickinson uses the word "Genesis" alone, it is associated primarily with the first three chapters of the book, those describing the Creation, the garden, and the expulsion of

Adam and Eve. These are the images that she recalls when she writes of "A Vagabond from Genesis" or "Genesis' new house." [6] She combines the force of all three to sharpen the element of chance implied by this four-line poem:

> Paradise is of the option.
> Whosoever will
> Own in Eden notwithstanding
> Adam and Repeal.

To Emily Dickinson, Eden is one of the most meaningful of symbols. It implies the supernal bliss of the prelapsarian existence, and she uses it in this sense in such passionate poems as "Wild Nights – Wild Nights!" ("Rowing in Eden –/Ah, the Sea!") and "Come slowly – Eden!" Ecstasy, as presented in these poems, is heightened by the remembrance of pain past and the anticipation of pain future. She writes elsewhere, "Pang in the Past of Peace"; and in her Eden, impending expulsion intensifies the joy. She wishes it were not so, for "'Tasting the Honey and the Sting,' should have ceased with Eden." [7] But the sting remains, and the dramatic alternation of pain and joy persists. Dickinson advises that little more than this can be crowded into life:

> A modest lot – A fame petite –
> A brief Campaign of sting and sweet
> Is plenty! Is enough!
> A *Sailor's* business is *the shore!*
> A *Soldier's – balls!* Who asketh more,
> Must seek the neighboring life! [8]

One must attempt to experience fully the existential moment, for in reality "Eden is that old-fashioned House/We dwell in every day," and ecstatic fulfillment is there, waiting only to be beheld. The error of Adam and Eve was their attempt to discover more. Their misfortune impressed Emily, who observed that, "in all the circumference of Expression, those guileless words of

Adam and Eve never were surpassed, 'I was afraid and hid My-self.'" [9] This same lament from Genesis suggests the theme of the following poem:

> Embarrassment of one another
> And God
> Is Revelation's limit,
> Aloud
> Is nothing that is chief,
> But still,
> Divinity dwells under seal.

The opening lines describe the Adamic shock not only of recognition of nakedness but also the shock of confession of knowledge. The discovered knowledge, per se, is of little value; for, as the final lines remind us, possession of divine knowledge is self-defeating. Divinity, unsealed and fully comprehended, loses its enchantment and thereupon ceases to be divine. This is but one version of Emily Dickinson's frequent warning that certain emotions vanish when subjected to analysis or total discovery and that they can be best conserved by a restraining awe.

Banishment to the "east of Eden" seems also to have been a mystery that appealed to her. Variants of the phrase appear in a number of poems. The first is contained in a good-humored spoof on sleep, which she addressed to her father: "The breaking of the Day . . ./That shall Aurora be–/East of Eternity." [10] A version closer to the biblical phrase appears in an elegy for a dead schoolgirl in which the line "Far – as the East from Even" compounds two diverse images of separation: that of the expulsion from Eden and the polarity of the morning and evening of a single day.

> One little maid – from playmates –
> One little mind from school –
> There must be guests in Eden –
> All the rooms are full –

Far – as the East from Even –
Dim – as the border star –
Courtiers quaint, in Kingdoms
Our departed are.[11]

In another poem, Dickinson places Jacob's wrestling "A little East of Jordan," a location appropriate to the besting of an angel by presumptuous mankind. And a reader's recollection of the expulsion of Adam and Eve gives increased importance to the outcasts in

The lonesome for they know not What –
The Eastern Exiles – be –
Who strayed beyond the Amber line
Some madder Holiday –

And ever since – the purple Moat
They strive to climb – in vain –

To consider the "Eastern Exiles" in this poem as simply the analogues of Adam and Eve would limit interpretation that should be broadened to include the whole drama of the expulsion. In the following two poems, however, the reference to the fall is more explicit:

Bliss is frugal of her Leases
Adam taught her Thrift
Bankrupt once through his excesses – [12]

and,

I shall vote for Lands with Locks
Granted I can pick 'em –
Transport's doubtful Dividend
Patented by Adam.[13]

Emily Dickinson also gives a brief account of Eve's departure from the garden in "Better – than Music! For I – who heard it," but her version bears closer resemblance to *Paradise Lost* [14] than to the primary source. She was nonetheless aware of the details in Genesis for she noted elsewhere that "there is no account of [Eve's] death in the Bible." [15]

"And why am not I Eve?," she asked, "If you find any statements which you think likely to prove the truth of the case, I wish you would send them to me without delay." [16] She relished identification with personalities of the Old Testament. Of the individuals both mentioned in the Scriptures and cited in her poems, Gabriel appears most frequently. As the extraordinarily articulate archangel bearing great tidings, he was especially appealing. "Get Gabriel – to tell – the royal syllable –," [17] she wrote; and no doubt in the writing had in mind the holy charge in Daniel 8:16, "Gabriel, make this man to understand the vision." She associates herself more closely with Gabriel in "I envy Seas, whereon He rides," as she presumes to envy omnipotence, and, having done so, fears that some intercession must take place, "Lest Noon in Everlasting Night –/Drop Gabriel – and Me –."

Although the opening line of the following poem recalls Ruth 1:16 ("whither thou goest, I will go; and where thou lodgest, I will lodge") and the remainder of the poem is filled with other religious imagery, the most meaningful of the allusions is to Gabriel.

> Where Thou art – that – is Home –
> Cashmere – or Calvary – the same –
> Degree – or Shame –
> I scarce esteem Location's Name –
> So I may Come –
>
> What Thou dost – is Delight –
> Bondage as Play – be sweet –
> Imprisonment – Content –
> And Sentence – Sacrament –
> Just We two – meet –

Where Thou art not – is Wo –
Tho' Bands of Spices – row –
What Thou dost not – Despair –
Tho' Gabriel – praise me – Sir –

The allusion in the final line refers to Gabriel's singular praise
of Mary: "Blessed art thou among women" (Luke 1:28). By
hyperbolic implication Emily Dickinson is able to convey the
extent of the devotion that she proclaimed in the first two stanzas.
On another occasion, recalling Gabriel's words to Mary, she wrote
Higginson, "– Gabriel's Oration would adorn his Child –." [18]
This phrase is part of a late letter in which the praise accorded
the "Child" was an oblique expression of Emily's great admiration for Helen Hunt Jackson, who had passed away a few months
before.

By Emily Dickinson's standards, association with Gabriel was
tantamount to distinction. In one poem, she introduced the robin
as "a Gabriel/In humble circumstances," [19] and announced elsewhere:

Forever honored be the Tree
Whose Apple Winterworn
Enticed to Breakfast from the Sky
Two Gabriels Yestermorn.

They registered in Nature's Book
As Robins – Sire and Son –
But Angels have that modest way
To screen them from Renown.

Although Gabriel may have seemed the most exciting of all
the individuals in the Bible, Moses was the one that Emily
found most sympathetic. She comprehended not only the responsibilities and the dangers he endured as the leader in the
wilderness but also the poignant disappointment of his being
denied the worldly fulfillment of entrance into the promised

land. She firmly protests that "Moses was'nt fairly used –," [20] and voices an even stronger complaint in these lines:

> It always felt to me – a wrong
> To that Old Moses – done –
> To let him see – the Canaan –
> Without the entering –
>
> *   *   *   *   *   *
>
> Old Man on Nebo! Late as this –
> My justice bleeds – for Thee!

To her Moses was the wise old man of courage and vision; and she points out to pedantic scholars that much might be gained,

> Could we stand with that Old "Moses" –
> "Canaan" denied –
> Scan like him, the stately landscape
> On the other side –
>
> Doubtless, we should deem superfluous
> Many Sciences,
> Not pursued by learned Angels
> In scholastic skies! [21]

Recalling his courage, she paraphrased a part of the thirty-third chapter of Exodus: "'Am not consumed,' old Moses wrote,/'Yet saw him face to face.'" [22] The pertinent verses in Exodus relate Moses' confrontation of God after Moses and the entire "stiff-necked" band of Israelites had been threatened with extinction, and the metaphor of the poem equates his attitude to that of one who would willingly face life's awesome unknowns.

Although he is not mentioned by name in "'Red Sea,' indeed! Talk not to me," the speaker in this late poem is a reconciled Moses viewing his ultimate disappointment with equanimity and sensing fulfillment in having met the demands of the past:

> The Eye inquires with a sigh
> That Earth sh'd be so big –
> What Exultation in the Woe –
> What Wine in the fatigue!

Remembering Emily Dickinson's fondness for Moses helps one to grasp more quickly the basic imagery of the following elegy:

> From Us She wandered now a Year,
> Her tarrying, unknown,
> If Wilderness prevent her feet
> Or that Etherial Zone
>
> No Eye hath seen and lived
> We ignorant must be –
> We only know what time of Year
> We took the Mystery.

The fifth line again recalls God's words to Moses in Exodus 33:20, "for there shall no man see me and live," and complements the image of "wandering in the wilderness" established in lines one and three.

Although Emily Dickinson was more sympathetic toward Moses, the ostensibly unrewarded lawgiver, she showed a considerable interest in Noah and in the persisting hope that survived the flood. Emily and Noah had at least this much in common: the winter's desolation was to her an interruption of life comparable to the Deluge. In early spring 1870, she happily recorded winter's end by remarking in a letter to the Norcross sisters that "Mother went rambling, and came in with a burdock on her shawl, so we know that the snow has perished from the earth. Noah would have liked mother." [23] Noah appears in two poems, the first of which deals with the dove's reconnaissance from the ark and concludes:

> Thrice to the floating casement
> The Patriarch's bird returned,
> Courage! My brave Columba!
> There may yet be *Land*! [24]

"Columba" here suggests Columbus' voyage as well as Noah's, but this is a double image, for Columba is the name of the constellation that is also known as "Noah's Dove." The second poem that mentions Noah presents another analogy of winter and the Flood, and its last stanza notes that the memory of such cataclysms is short-lived:

> And so there was a Deluge –
> And swept the World away –
> But Ararat's a Legend – now –
> And no one credits Noah – [25]

Several Dickinson poems are redactions of fragments of Old Testament stories. Elijah's ascent into heaven on the whirlwind, described in II Kings 2:11, is the basis of "Elijah's Wagon knew no thill." "A first Mute Coming –" is a variation upon the theme of Lot's demonstration of faith in entertaining the strangers, a story told in the nineteenth chapter of Genesis. "Abraham to kill him" presents a summary of the story of Abraham and Isaac (Genesis 22:1–20), with an epigrammatic moral appended in the last two lines; and "A little East of Jordan," as has been noted, is Emily Dickinson's version of Jacob's wrestling with the angel. In two letters written a number of years after the poem on Jacob, she inverted the climax of Jacob's match by writing: "I will not let thee go, except *I bless thee*." [26] This type of deliberate inversion occurs occasionally in Dickinson, usually for emphasis or specific effect. In the two letters with the reference to Jacob, she apparently was seeking to express her affection fully and chose to do so by using an ironic paraphrase of the well-known verse from the twenty-third chapter of Genesis. She uses the story of David and Goliath to warn against ill-considered aspirations, and, in the role of David, Emily loses. Having lost, she wonders, "Was it Goliah – was too large –/Or was myself – too small?" [27] These examinations of man's spiritual trials fit neatly into the patterns of American religious poetry. The conflict symbolized by Jacob's wrestling with the angel is one of the archetypal images by which R. P. Blackmur establishes connection between American verse and the whole corpus of Christian religious poetry. Although he omits Emily Dickinson from the Jacob tradition, the poems cited fit exactly into that portion of his essay "Religious Poetry in the United States," [28] which does include Anne Bradstreet's "The Flesh and the Spirit," Herman Melville's "Art," and Henry Adams' "A Prayer to the Virgin and the Dynamo."

Two other Dickinson poems concerned with Old Testament personages deal with Daniel and Enoch. In "Belshazzar had a Letter –" the subject is the handwriting which appeared on Belshazzar's wall and which Daniel interpreted. There is prophecy in the Bible that anyone may read with the facility of Daniel; it is intelligence, she says, that

> The Conscience of us all
> Can read without it's Glasses
> On Revelation's Wall –

She treats the assumption of Enoch in a poem that expands half of Genesis 5:24 ("and he was not; for God took him") into an eight-line explanation of Enoch's sudden absence. [29] Although Belshazzar and Enoch can be used to identify by chapter and verse her point of departure in the two poems just mentioned, the poems are more concerned with the implications of the Scripture than with the personalities involved. The themes are prophecy and immortality, and the poems, in this respect, are more typical of those related to the New Testament: her references to the Old Testament generally focus upon narratives and individuals while her New Testament allusions are more likely to reflect explorations of the faith and prophecy in the Gospels and Revelation.

Emily Dickinson found verses from the Psalms and from Isaiah useful in letters, even though she rarely employed them in poems. The poetic qualities of certain of the Psalms probably increased her interest in them, and there was the additional advantage that excerpts from the Psalms would be more generally comprehensible to her correspondents. Her interest in Isaiah was no doubt heightened by the close relation of that book's prophecy to the Gospels. She makes scattered references to the remaining books of the Old Testament, but they might just as easily have been derived from conversation or sermons as from her own reading. No other Old Testament books in their entirety seem to have had special significance for her. The twenty-eighth chapter of Job, however, contains an unusual collection of favorite Dickinson images: a variety of jewels, gold and silver, floods and storms, and secret paths to wisdom. She does not quote this chapter directly in extant poems or letters, but she must have found its contents attractive.

Verses from the Old Testament appear less than half as often in Emily Dickinson's writings as do verses from the New Testament. No doubt the New Testament was a more rewarding reference for her inquisitive analysis of the elements of life, faith, death, and immortality. Matthew, Luke, and John account for half her New Testament references; and, although she may have heard or read many of the verses in sermons and hymns, her predilection for these three books indicates that she knew them with a thoroughness that could only have come with repeated reading. The passages she took from Matthew, for example, come from nineteen of the twenty-eight chapters and are twice as numerous as those taken from any other book of the Bible, even when verses appearing identically in Mark, Luke, and John are omitted. When one remembers that these data are drawn from only the letters and poems that have survived, it becomes apparent that her knowledge of certain sections of the Bible, especially the Gospels, was extraordinary. In this conclusion, however, references to the Gospel according to St. Mark should be excepted, for if one deducts from them all allusions to verses that are duplicated in Matthew, only a single reference to Mark remains.

In Matthew, Emily Dickinson's attention was focused upon the repeated expressions of gentleness and hope. Her remarks to Emily Fowler in a letter written about 1853 give some indication of what she read in the Bible when she picked it up with no specific purpose in mind:

Vinnie left her Testament on a little stand in our room, and it made me think of her, so I thought I w'd open it, and the first words I read were in those sweetest verses — [Matthew 5:3-4]. "Blessed are the poor – Blessed are they that mourn – Blessed are they that weep, for they shall be comforted." [30]

Considered as a group, her references to Matthew indicate that she looked to that book for the promise of mercy manifest in the love of children, birds, and flowers, and for confirmation of the paradox of ultimate triumph and reward for the least of beings. This accounts in great measure for the ingenuous innocence reflected in the poems related to passages from Matthew.

She found assurance in the promise of God's concern for the fall of a sparrow, and offers it as a partial compensation in "Victory comes late –," by concluding, "God keep His Oath to Sparrows –/Who of little Love – know how to starve –." The same Bible verses are the basis of a poem that she sent to the Norcross sisters shortly after the death of their mother:

> Mama never forgets her birds,
> Though in another tree –
>
> *   *   *   *   *   *
>
> If either of her "sparrows fall,"
> She "notices," above.

At about the same time, she used the sparrow allusions to sharpen a reflection on the burial of children:

> Some, too fragile for winter winds
> The thoughtful grave encloses –
>
> *　　*　　*　　*　　*　　*
>
> This covert – have all children
> Early aged, and often cold,
> Sparrows, unnoticed by the Father –
> Lambs for whom time had not a fold.[31]

In still another poem, as she contemplates death and judgment, she seeks the promise assured the sparrow:

> I think just how my shape will rise –
> When I shall be *"forgiven"* –
> Till Hair – and Eyes – and timid Head –
> Are *out of sight* – in Heaven –
>
> I think just how my lips will weigh –
> With shapeless – quivering – prayer –
> That you – *so late* – *"Consider"* me –
> The *"Sparrow"* of your Care –

It was not Emily Dickinson's habit to use a phrase or an image repeatedly; the "sparrow" was an exception. And, as a gardener, she found Matthew 6:28, "Consider the lilies of the field," appropriate to at least half a dozen letters. This "lily" passage from the Sermon on the Mount occurs in both Matthew and Luke, but Matthew is the more probable source because Dickinson usually included the "of the field" phrase that is not part of the verse in Luke. "Consider the lilies" was appropriate in her enclosures with flowers given and in her thanks for flowers received, but the "lilies that neither toil nor spin" appear in the poems only in this paraphrase of the entire verse: "Not any House the Flowers keep –/The Birds enamor Care." [32] On two occasions she used Matthew 7:16, another "gardener's verse," in notes of thanks. In the first, she combined Aesop with Matthew as she wrote to thank Mrs. Edward Tuckerman for some unspecified gift, "Do 'Men gather Grapes of Thorns?' No—but they do of *Roses*—and even the classic Fox hushed his innuendo, as we unclasped the little Box—." [33] In the second note, she returned Mrs. Todd's favor of a brass plaque painted with thistles by sending her a hyacinth with a slip of paper bearing the other half of the sentence from Matthew 7:16, "Or Figs of Thistles?" [34] Nor did she overlook the parable of the grain of mustard seed (Matthew 13:32), for she wrote a cheering letter to the ailing Mrs. Higginson, reminding her that "the Heart is the 'seed' of which we read that 'the Birds of Heaven lodge in it's Branches.'" [35]

Emily Dickinson extended to few individuals the warmhearted concern apparent in her letter to Mrs. Higginson. Her heart, however, held an undying love for children, a natural affection heightened by her awareness of the child's privilege of access in the Christian hierarchy. "Suffer little children, and forbid them not . . . : for of such is the kingdom of heaven" (Matthew 19:14) was a passage especially meaningful for her. She recalls the verse in two poems, both of which indicate a desire to maintain the unspoiled freshness of childhood. One of these poems is the well-known "Arcturus is his other name—," which concludes:

> Perhaps the "Kingdom of Heaven's" changed—
> I hope the "Children" there
> Wont be "new fashioned" when I come—
> And laugh at me—and stare—
>
> I hope the Father in the skies
> Will lift his little girl—
> Old fashioned—naughty—everything—
> Over the stile of "Pearl."

The second poem, which reflects much the same attitude, was

sent to Mrs. Samuel Bowles soon after the birth of her son
Charles.

> Teach Him – when He makes the *names* –
> Such an one – to say –
>
> *   *   *   *
>
> "Forbid us not" –
> Some like "Emily."

The petition with which she concludes the second poem seeks
in her behalf the divine acceptance that the Scripture guaran-
tees innocent children. Again she requires her reader to call to
mind the context of her source in order to complete the thought.
Such elliptical expression indicates a studied familiarity with
the source itself and strongly suggests her acceptance of it. She
assumes a similar acceptance on the part of her correspondent
and takes for granted that he will not only be aware of her
reference but also will be able to interpret the reference accurately. Because her estimate of her reader's power of imagination and recall was often an exaggerated one, many of her carefully constructed poems and letters were received as clever
eccentricities. Those who received her letters must frequently
have had to satisfy themselves with something less than the full
meaning of what she had written. Helen Hunt Jackson, for
instance, was puzzled by three lines from "Upon a Lilac Sea"
because the last line, "To Dooms of Balm," seemed out of place
in a letter congratulating her on her marriage to William S.
Jackson.[36] Another complex reference is Emily's quotation from
Matthew 18:3 in a note acknowledging a friend's placing a
Christmas wreath on her father's grave: "I am sure you must
have remembered that Father had 'Become as Little Children,'
or you would never have dared send him a Christmas gift, for
you know how he frowned upon Santa Claus – and all such
prowling gentlemen." [37] The basic import of this note is clear,
but its somewhat jovial mood is not at all consistent with her

THE KING JAMES VERSION

usually doleful utterances regarding the death of her father—
unless one takes into account more of the Scripture, which reads,
"Except ye be converted, and become as little children, ye shall
not enter into the kingdom of heaven." By stating flatly that
"Father had 'Become as Little Children,'" Emily reaffirms her
conviction that Edward Dickinson with his "pure and terrible"
heart was securely established in "the kingdom of heaven."

Emily Dickinson expressed her Wordsworthian regard for the
acute sensibilities of youth in a letter to Maria Whitney in
which she wrote, "The ravenousness of fondness is best disclosed
by children. . . . The angel begins in the morning in every
human life." [38] Included at the end was this poem:

> No ladder needs the bird but skies
> To situate its wings,
> Nor any leader's grim baton
> Arraigns it as it sings
> The implements of bliss are few —
> As Jesus says of *Him*,
> "Come unto me" the moiety
> That wafts the cherubim.

The last four lines in slightly variant form appear in a second
poem, "To her derided Home." And "Come unto me," Jesus'
comforting words from Matthew 11:28, she repeated elsewhere,
usually in letters of consolation at the death of a child. Her
belief that the innocents had unchallenged access to the deity
is reflected in the note she wrote to Mrs. Henry Hills on the
death of an infant son: "'Come unto me.' Beloved Commandment. The Darling obeyed." [39]

The importance she attached to becoming "as little children"
was related to her high regard for the innocent candor of child-
like expression. She could address a prayer:

> Papa above!
> Regard a Mouse,

and, when a prayer seemed unanswered, she could complain:

> Of Course – I prayed –
> And did God Care?
> He cared as much as on the Air
> A Bird – had stamped her foot –
> And cried "Give Me" –

Because of such unabashed directness and honesty in spiritual matters, she did not find the Lord's Prayer exactly satisfactory either, and recorded her sentiments in "I have a King, who does not speak –":

> And I omit to pray
> 'Father, thy will be done' today
> For my will goes the other way,
> And it were perjury!

And yet, in later years when life seemed warm and full, as it did in the autumn of 1884, she could survey the natural beauty of her Amherst world and write: "– Each Tree a Scene from India, and Everglades of Rugs. Is not 'Lead us not into Temptation' an involuntary plea under circumstances so gorgeous?" [40]

What Emily Dickinson termed differences between her will and God's will resulted, at least in part, from the fact that her religious convictions and the promises of the Scriptures did not always coincide. In a letter to Dr. and Mrs. Holland, she speculates, "If prayers had any answers to them, you were all here to-night, but I seek and I don't find, and knock and it is not opened. Wonder if God is just — presume he is, however, and t'was only a blunder of Matthew's." [41] Although she accepted Matthew's assurance that prayers are answered, she carefully restrained her own requests. In a letter to Mrs. Holland, for example, she writes, "But you must go to Sleep. I, who sleep always, need no Bed. Foxes have Tenements, and remember, the Speaker was a Carpenter –." [42] And in "For every Bird a

Nest," the wren, a bird with which she occasionally identified herself, makes only a "timid quest . . . of twig so fine." Both the poem and the letter recall the simple providence mentioned in Matthew 8:20: "The foxes have holes, and the birds of the air have nests; but the Son of man hath not where to lay his head." "I meant to have but modest needs –," she writes in the opening line of a poem that recounts a prayer for "A Heaven not so large as Your's,/But large enough – for me –." She goes on to describe the obvious amusement of the heavenly hierarchy at their finding a supplicant naive enough to "take the Tale for true –/That 'Whatsoever Ye shall ask –/Itself be given You' –" (Matthew 7:7–8). She would not smile, as did they, at such ingenuousness. In "Why – do they shut Me out of Heaven?" she supposes what she might do if given the power and confronted with the petition of one so meek:

> Oh, if I – were the Gentleman
> In the "White Robe" –
> And they – were the little Hand – that knocked –
> Could – I – forbid?

At times such as this, she seems convinced that she was as close to God's sentiments as Matthew had been.

Whether the promises in Matthew appear to her to have been kept or not, she was intrigued by them, especially the paradoxical ones. She could accept "To him that hath shall be given," [43] but of the converse she said, "No Verse from the Bible frightened me so much from a Child as 'from him that hath not, shall be taken even that he hath.'" [44] She also made use of the two versions of "the first shall be last, and the last shall be first" that appear in the nineteenth and twentieth chapters of Matthew. This inversion she found to her liking. She begins one poem "Had I known the first was the last/I should have kept it longer." In "'Unto me?' I do not know you –," she used a paraphrase of the passage to complete a dialogue with Christ:

> I am spotted – "I am Pardon" –
> I am small – "The Least
> Is esteemed in Heaven the Chiefest –
> Occupy my House" –

If her context presented the opportunity, Emily Dickinson's wit could trim or alter the Scripture for the occasion. When Dr. Stearns died unexpectedly, she adapted Matthew 24:44 ("Therefore be ye also ready: for in such an hour as ye think not the Son of man cometh") in order to comment on the event to the Norcross sisters: " 'In such an hour as ye think not' means something when you try it." [45] Or, when she drafted an affectionate letter to Judge Lord, she could paraphrase a part of the Sermon on the Mount to make it read: "Lay up Treasures immediately – that's the best Anodyne for moth and Rust and the thief whom the Bible knew enough of Banking to suspect would break in and steal." [46]

Among her numerous references to Matthew, there are additional allusions and quotations that fall outside the patterns of gentle nature, hope and promise, or wit and paradox. A return to Matthew 7:13–14 confirms a reader's understanding of the poem that begins:

> You're right – "the way *is* narrow" –
> And "difficult the Gate" –
> And "few there be" – Correct again –
> That "enter in – thereat" –

And "I bring an unaccustomed wine" is a poem of altruism that ends:

> And so I always bear the cup
> If, haply, mine may be the drop
> Some pilgrim thirst to slake –
>
> If, haply, and say to me
> "Unto the little, unto me,"
> When I at last awake.

The analogue of the quoted line is in Matthew 25:40: "Inasmuch as ye have done it unto one the least of these my brethren, ye have done it unto me." When the Scripture is called to mind, the poem as a whole becomes a statement of one of the basic tenets of Christian stewardship.

Her treatment of the agony and the triumph of Passion Week in "I should have been too glad, I see—" contains these lines:

> That I could spell the Prayer
> I knew so perfect—yesterday—
> That Scalding One—Sabacthini—
>
> *   *   *   *   *   *
>
> The Reefs in Old Gethsemane
> Endear the Shore beyond—

Although the details of the subject were clear enough in her mind that she did not have to return to her Bible for reference, the source recalled from memory was probably Matthew 26 and 27, for the words "Gethsemane" and "Sabacthani" appear only in Matthew and Mark, and her preference was for the former. The description of Christ's cry from the cross as "scalding" brings to mind an earlier poem drawn from the same two chapters of Matthew, a poem in which she is troubled by "the drop of Anguish/That scalds."

> I shall know why—when Time is over—
> And I have ceased to wonder why—
> Christ will explain each separate anguish
> In the fair schoolroom of the sky—
>
> He will tell me what "Peter" promised—
> And I—for wonder at his woe—
> I shall forget the drop of Anguish
> That scalds me now—that scalds me now!

The scalding anguish is the doubt voiced in "Sabacthani, why has thou forsaken me?" She senses in Christ's cry a disturbing echo of Peter's denial after his impassioned promises of fidelity. The anguish raises a similar agonizing doubt for the poet, even though faith offers hope that she "shall know why—when Time is over." It is this same faith that she reiterates in the last two stanzas of "Do People moulder equally,/ They bury, in the Grave?"

> I say to you, said Jesus —
> That there be standing here —
> A Sort, that shall not taste of Death —
> If Jesus was sincere —
>
> I need no further Argue —
> The statement of the Lord
> Is not a controvertible —
> He told me, Death was dead —

Her reference to Christ's declaration that "there be some standing here, which shall not taste of death" is recorded identically in Matthew, Mark, and Luke.

It would be difficult to deny that the Gospel according to St. Matthew enhanced Emily Dickinson's innately gentle nature. Her fondness for the book and her affinity for the beatific simplicity it extols are clearly reflected in her poems and letters. Though she contemplates religious dogma and spiritual trial, she is capable of obviating both by direct approach to the Deity; and, when she assumes the ingenuous role of a child or articulates the truth embodied in the natural beauty of a bird or flower, she gives her uninhibited appeal the sanction implicit in Christ's "Suffer the little children" or "Consider the lilies." This was for her a natural and satisfying relationship with God, with truth, and with poetry, a relationship reinforced by Matthew's assurances of its validity.

Emily Dickinson's allusions to Luke, like her infrequent references to Mark, are usually to verses duplicated in Matthew or elsewhere in the Bible. Her favorite benediction, "I give his

Angels charge," can be found in both the fourth chapter of Luke and the ninety-first Psalm. But there are some scattered quotations in the letters, and at least one poem, certainly derived from Luke. The theme of the poem is unexpected friendship and its opening stanza is based on Christ's promise to the condemned man in Luke 23:42–43.

> "Remember me" implored the Thief!
> Oh Hospitality!
> My Guest "Today in Paradise"
> I give thee guaranty.[47]

Luke, however, was a relatively unimportant Dickinson reference compared to Matthew or John.

To the same slight degree that her reading of Matthew appears to have been primarily concerned with hope, her reading of John seems to have been an exploration of the subject of faith. In the letters there is a variety of reference and quotation required by the occasional nature of correspondence; but in the poems allusion to the Gospel according to St. John is for the most part associated with faith and regeneration.

Taking a text from the first chapter of John, she probes the implications of Christ's divinity:

> A Word made Flesh is seldom
> And tremblingly partook
> Nor then perhaps reported
> But have I not mistook
> Each one of us has tasted
> With ecstasies of stealth
> The very food debated
> To our specific strength –
>
> A Word that breathes distinctly
> Has not the power to die
> Cohesive as the Spirit
> It may expire if He –

"Made Flesh and dwelt among us
Could condescension be
Like this consent of Language
This loved Philology

Both the opening line and the unclosed quotation come from John 1:14. The verse, "And the Word was made flesh, and dwelt among us," must have excited her poet's mind, for she was extremely aware of vitality's contribution to effective expression and here imputes a sacramental nature to the process of communication. While the second stanza does not resolve the question of faith that the poem raises, it does reiterate Emily Dickinson's belief in the strength and dignity of the well-chosen word.

The third chapter of John begins with the dialogue of Christ and Nicodemus concerning entry into the kingdom of heaven and the consequent immortality. After Nicodemus has been told that "except a man be born again, he cannot see the kingdom of God," he inquires, "How can these things be?" To this, Christ replies, "If I have told you earthly things, and ye believe not, how shall ye believe, if I tell you of heavenly things?" Emily Dickinson alludes to these verses in two poems. The first, "An altered look about the hills –," views the renascence of spring, then concludes,

> And Nicodemus' Mystery
> Receives it's annual reply.

The second "Nicodemus poem," which deals with human regeneration, asks,

> The Bone that has no Marrow,
> What Ultimate for that?

*   *   *   *   *   *

But how shall finished Creatures
A function fresh obtain?
Old Nicodemus' Phantom
Confronting us again!

This was a mystery she investigated often, but with mixed success. In "The Frost was never seen—" she remembers from John 14 the insistence of Philip the disciple that he be "shown the Father," and finally she decides that the difficulties of analyzing the unknowns of faith are too much to be undertaken:

Unproved is much we know —
Unknown the worst we fear —
Of Strangers is the Earth the Inn
Of Secrets is the Air

To analyze perhaps
A Philip would prefer
But Labor vaster than myself
I find it to infer.

In addition to the "Labor" involved, there was another reason for her reluctance to perform clinical analysis of mystical matters: she was firmly of the opinion that heavy-handed investigation of such things very often destroys the subject. This is the theme of "Split the Lark—and you'll find the Music—," a poem in which she supports her argument by allusion to "Sceptic Thomas," the disciple whose doubt is described in John 20:24–25.

The long and mysterious route to heaven and immortality sometimes caused Emily Dickinson to pause and question seriously the existence of both. St. John was reassuring, for the mansions described in John 14:2 were for her real and enticing:

'Mansions'! Mansions must be warm!
Mansions cannot let the tears in,
Mansions must exclude the storm!

'Many Mansions', by 'his Father',
I dont know him; snugly built!
Could the Children find the way there –
Some, would even trudge tonight! [48]

And, after she archly prayed to "Papa above," she added, "Reserve within thy kingdom/A 'Mansion' for the Rat!"

At least two additional poems derived from the Gospels appear ultimately to have come from John. "He forgot – and I – remembered –," a version of Peter's denial of Christ, contains details that are closer to John 18:18–27 than to any of the three accounts given elsewhere. Because of the details of Christ's trial related in John 18 and 19, the same inference can be drawn regarding "One crown that no one seeks," a speculation on Pontius Pilate's contemplation of the crown of thorns.

An excellent bit of evidence of her detailed knowledge of the book of John is contained in this opening paragraph of a letter to Abiah Root:

"Yet a little while I am with you, and again a little while and I am *not* with you" because you go to your mother! Did she not tell me saying, "yet a little while ye shall see me and again a little while and ye shall *not* see me, and I would that where I am, there *ye* may be also" – but the virtue of the text consists in *this* my dear – that "if I *go*, I *come* again, and ye shall be with me where I *am*;" that is to say, that if you come in *November* you shall be mine . . .[49]

The quotations, which come from John 14:3 and 16:16–19, vary enough from the text to show that she was writing from memory, yet are sufficiently accurate to indicate that she was aware of the existence of the three slightly differing verses in the source.

She makes references to the New Testament books between the Gospels and Revelation, but most of these are simply topical quotations appropriate to the letters in which they appear. In the poems allusions to these books are few; most come from

Paul's First Epistle to the Corinthians. The opening line of "And with what body do they come?" is taken directly from I Corinthians 15:35. The poem envisions the joy of the resurrection foretold in the scripture, and it footnotes the prophecy by adding, "Paul knew the Man that knew the News—/He passed through Bethlehem—." Two other poems mention Paul; both contain inaccuracies. One sets Paul and Silas free when, according to the Scripture (Acts 16:23–40), they remain prisoners; the second credits Paul with a martyr's death comparable to Stephen's,[50] although Paul's death is not reported anywhere in the Bible. This error is probably due to her exposure to apocryphal church tradition rather than to a lack of familiarity with the Bible.

I Corinthians 2:9 was a verse that stirred her imagination. Its challenge to a poet is apparent: "Eye hath not seen, nor ear heard, neither have entered into the heart of man, the things which God hath prepared for them that love him." Time and again she accepted the challenge to give expression to emotions and experience that ordinarily pass unnoticed. In a poem that begins "Just lost, when I was saved!/Just felt the world go by!" she paraphrases part of the verse:

> Next time, to stay!
> Next time, the things to see
> By Ear unheard,
> Unscrutinized by Eye—

Elsewhere she advises that anticipation of the unknown should not dull appreciation of the sensible present:

> "Eye hath not seen" may possibly
> Be current with the Blind
> But let not Revelation
> By theses be detained—[51]

Emotions perceived, however, do not always necessitate overt announcement; calculated reticence may on occasion be the best means of expression.

Speech is one symptom of Affection
And Silence one –
The perfectest communication
Is heard of none

Exists and it's indorsement
Is had within –
Behold said the Apostle
Yet had not seen!

The final lines of this poem are closely related to the sense of the "Eye hath not seen" passage. Their source, however, is I Peter 1:7–8 ("Jesus Christ: Whom having not seen, ye love"). Emily did not always reserve her favorite verse from I Corinthians for serious thought; she once recalled it in a comic sense to describe one of her father's horses: "the horse looked round at me, as if to say 'eye hath not seen nor ear heard the things that' I would do to you if I weren't tied!" [52]

In one poem she obligingly identifies both the book and the chapter of her reference; this is a unique instance. The exact verse is I Corinthians 15:42–43, and the text reads: "So also is the resurrection of the dead. It is sown in corruption; it is raised in incorruption: It is sown in dishonor; it is raised in glory." Her ten lines of poetry based on this Scripture include only half the antitheses, "Sown in dishonor" and "Sown in corruption," and after asking, "May *this* 'dishonor' be?," she sends her reader scurrying for his Bible by saying, "Not so fast!/Apostle is askew!/Corinthians 1. 15. narrates/A Circumstance or two!" [53]

Had Emily Dickinson been asked to name the book of the Bible most interesting to her, she would without question have replied that it was Revelation. When she listed her reading interests for Higginson, this was the only book of the Bible included and the only item that might not have been suggested by his "Letter to a Young Contributor." [54] It is true that she makes fewer substantial references to Revelation than to Mat-

thew or John, but the vision and prophecy of Revelation were
for her a return to the images of Eden that brought her Bible-
reading full circle. She anticipates a verdant Eden-Paradise with
its "Droughtless Wells," where people "thirst no more." [55] She
brings the images from Genesis and Revelation together in the
second stanza of "What is—'Paradise'—":

> Do they wear "new shoes"—in "Eden"—
> Is it always pleasant—there—
> Wont they scold us—when we're hungry—
> Or tell God—how cross we are—
>
> You are sure there's such a person
> As "a Father"—in the sky—

She might question others about their certainty of belief; but
for her there *was* "such a person/As 'a Father,'" and she knew
him well enough to expect his helping hand "over the stile of
'Pearl'" when she reached the gates of heaven. This was part of
her belief, and individual interpretation and opinion were readers'
prerogatives that she stubbornly upheld. The Book of Revelation
was not an exception to be interpreted by others for her acceptance without comment or reservation:

> Those who read the "Revelations"
> Must not criticize
> Those who read the same Edition—
> With beclouded Eyes! [56]

When she read "Be thou faithful unto death, and I will give
thee a crown of life," the conclusion of Revelation 2:10, she
found it too businesslike to accept. True faith serves without the
incentive of reward, and she criticizes the verse from Revelation
on that basis:

> "Faithful to the end" Amended
> From the Heavenly Clause—
> Constancy with a Proviso
> Constancy abhors—

> "Crowns of Life" are servile Prizes
> To the stately Heart,
> Given for the Giving, solely,
> No Emolument.

Another reference to Revelation demonstrates that Emily was not always insensitive to the bewilderment that her paraphrases might cause her reader. When she concluded a poem with "'All' Rogues 'shall have their part in' what—/The Phosphorus of God—,"[57] she noted for Sue's benefit the quotation's source, Revelation 21:8, which reads: "But the fearful, and unbelieving, and the abominable . . . and all liars, shall have their part in the lake which burneth with fire and brimstone." She was seldom so helpful, for her easy familiarity with the King James version made such documentation artificial and, to her, superfluous. More significantly, her affinity for the Scripture is reflected in her choice of words and metaphors as well as in her aphoristic style. Some of these characteristics doubtlessly were the result of her New England upbringing, but they are far less pronounced in the letters written by other members of her own family.[58] Perhaps the other Dickinsons read their Bible just as assiduously as did Emily, but it was she who assimilated what she read in a way that caused her own writing to reflect the tone and flavor of the reference. She succeeded in embodying not only the Bible's style but also its universality. This she achieved without design; she made no conscious attempt to emulate her source, but used it as a point of departure and a source of oblique, yet pointed allusion. Her summary view of the Bible is contained in these sixteen lines that she sent to her nephew Ned late in 1882:

> The Bible is an antique Volume—
> Written by faded Men
> At the suggestion of Holy Spectres—
> Subjects—Bethlehem—

Eden – the ancient Homestead –
Satan – the Brigadier –
Judas – the Great Defaulter –
David – the Troubadour –
Sin – a distinguished Precipice
Others must resist –
Boys that "believe" are very lonesome –
Other Boys are "lost" –
Had but the Tale a warbling Teller –
All the Boys would come –
Orpheus' Sermon captivated –
It did not condemn –

Emily Dickinson is very often the Bible's "warbling Teller" when she uses a biblical word or phrase as foundation or keystone for her own expression. She declared as much when she wrote to Mrs. Holland, "All grows strangely emphatic, and I think if I should see you again, I sh'd begin every sentence with 'I say unto you –' The Bible dealt with the Centre, not with the Circumference." And she had much earlier informed Higginson: "My Business is Circumference." [59]

British Literature:
Renaissance and Eighteenth Century

"Stratford on Avon" – accept us all.
— *Emily Dickinson to Mrs. J. G. Holland, 1877*

Shakespeare and the King James version of the Bible are sufficient to establish the prose and poetry of Renaissance England as the most important body of literature in Emily Dickinson's reading.[1] Her assimilation of these Renaissance classics, which she knew thoroughly, plus her schooling, which was in the eighteenth-century tradition, made her receptive to Augustan literary standards. Although these standards heightened her regard for accepted masters, she did not allow them to intimidate her sensibilities. They were standards that had progressed beyond the seventeenth century yet did not indulge in the philistinism decried by her father and her tutors. In school it was proper to memorize Pope and to parse Goldsmith and Johnson; at home it was proper to read the English classics and contemplate Watts's hymns; and from these prescribed fundamentals Emily derived a number of her own critical values.

Shakespeare was the earliest literature in which Emily Dickinson showed any considerable interest. There was little that antedated Shakespeare in the family library, and selections reprinted in the magazines and newspapers of the time were seldom from works written before 1700. The Chaucer volumes in the Dickinson Collection at Harvard were acquired by the family about 1880 and belonged to Austin Dickinson's household. There were also translations of Homer and Horace, but Emily makes no reference to them, and they bear no marks that she might have made. She seems to have been familiar with the edition of *Don Quixote* among her father's books. At Christmas 1876, Sue gave her a copy of a new edition of the fifteenth-century devotional work *Of the Imitation of Christ* by Thomas à Kempis.[2] This copy, now in the Yale University library, is inscribed "Emily wi[th] love." It bears in the margin a number of the light pencil lines of the type that can be found in several volumes identifiable as her own. The content of these marked passages increases the probability that they were marked by Emily: "In temptations and afflictions a man is proved"; "Sorrow always accompanieth the glory of the world"; "[Christ] findeth many companions of His table, but few of His abstinence." The last passage seems to have been combined with Matthew 26:42 in "Proud of my broken heart, since thou didst break it," a poem that contains these lines:

> Proud of my night, since thou with moons dost slake it,
> *Not* to partake thy passion, *my* humility.

> Thou can'st not boast, like Jesus, drunken without companion
> Was the strong cup of anguish brewed for the Nazarene.

In the same copy of *Of the Imitation of Christ*, the chapter bearing the most marks is one entitled "Of the Love of Solitude and Silence." Such a thesis could hardly have come to more sympathetic eyes than Emily Dickinson's. "The greatest Saints avoided the society of men when they could conveniently; and did rather choose to live to God in secret," wrote Thomas à Kempis. This sentence is marked and invites comparison with these Dickinson lines: "The Soul selects her own Society –/ Then – shuts the Door –."

61

These peculiar markings in the books of the Dickinson library are common to those volumes most probably handled by Emily. They occur frequently in books that were certainly hers. They are not "marginalia" such as Coleridge left in his volumes; comments of that sort rarely occur in any of her books, and when they do, they appear not to have been made by her. The markings are neither notes nor underlinings, but are instead very light, vertical lines in pencil, paralleling the outer margin of the page. Because the marked passages often coincide with references and allusions that appear in Emily Dickinson's poems and letters, it would be convenient to assume that she made all such marks. But there remains the possibility that they were put in by Sue or Lavinia to indicate passages they felt would interest Emily. It is doubtful, however, that either of them would have made the marks in books presented to Emily by someone else or in books that she had already read. Emily's copy of the Thomas à Kempis volume provides a good example. Sue owned an edition of the book (1857), which they shared before she presented Emily with a copy. Sue's copy bears a number of the characteristic marks, though they are not always adjacent to the same passages that have been marked in Emily's. Emily may have marked the copy borrowed from Sue and then marked her own at a later reading. In any event, it appears that Emily was aware of these markings; and they can, if cautiously considered, be helpful in correlating certain passages from her reading with specific references in her writing. Her Shakespeare references, for example, are almost always straightforward and easily identifiable, yet the markings are still significant. Volume V of her father's Shakespeare contains her three favorite plays, *Macbeth*, *Othello*, and *Hamlet*; and in *Othello* almost a dozen speeches have been marked, three of which she quotes in letters.

Emily Dickinson was convinced that "he has had his Future who has found Shakespeare," and that "the most beautiful stigma of Bacon's Life" was his being suspected as the author of Shakespeare's works.[3] These were works that she accepted unconditionally, as the following report by Emily Fowler Ford indicates:

We had a Shakespeare Club — a rare thing in those days, — and one of the tutors [at the academy] proposed to take all the copies of all the members and mark out the objectionable passages. This plan was negatived at the first meeting, as far as "the girls" spoke, who said they did not want their books spoiled with marks. . . . I remember the lofty air with which Emily took her departure, saying, "There's nothing wicked in Shakespeare, and if there is I don't want to know it." The men read for perhaps three meetings from their expurgated editions, and then gave up their plan and the whole text was read out boldly.[4]

She insisted upon reading Shakespeare complete and unabridged, yet did not find him as suitable for incorporation into her writing as other sources. His works failed to provide the vast quantity of usable commonplaces she found in the Bible; furthermore, her favorite passages, though they served admirably as quotations in letters, could not be easily tailored to fit into poems.

There were no phrases from Shakespeare that she quoted repeatedly. On the rare occasions when she did use a Shakespeare quotation a second time, the wide separation of the two citations, often as much as ten years, can be construed as either a compliment to her memory, an indication that she had reread the play, or evidence that she had retained the expression by using it in conversation or in letters now lost. These possibilities are not mutually exclusive. She did reread favorite works; a retentive memory was a part of her poet's stock in trade; and no doubt there were at least as many Shakespeare quotations in letters destroyed as appear in those that have survived. The brevity of the allusions in letters to Sue and Austin suggests that oblique references to Shakespeare were probably common in family conversation and were meant to be immediately understood.

In the poems, direct references to Shakespeare are few. The

lines "Twas a Divine Insanity"[5] and "Much Madness is divinest Sense" are reminiscent of Polonius' appraisal of Hamlet. Polonius' advice to his son and Laertes' answers to Ophelia's question concerning the permanence of Hamlet's affection[6] are recalled by the following Dickinson letter and the poem included in it:

To ask of each that gathered Life, Oh, where did it grow, is intuitive.
That you have answered this Prince Question to your own delight, is joy to us all.

> Lad of Athens, faithful be
> To Thyself,
> And Mystery –
> All the rest is Perjury –[7]

In a poem that begins "Drama's Vitallest Expression is the Common Day," Emily Dickinson uses two of Shakespeare's plays to point out the tragedy common to ordinary lives and to comment on the dramatist's task in portraying such tragedy.

> "Hamlet" to Himself were Hamlet –
> Had not Shakespeare wrote –
> Though the "Romeo" left no Record
> Of his Juliet,
>
> It were infinite enacted
> In the Human Heart –
> Only Theatre recorded
> Owner cannot shut –

A number of lines and images in the poems contain a persistent echo of Shakespeare. "Great Caesar! Condescend" is a poem that recalls the Portia of *Julius Caesar*, and "I fear a Man of frugal Speech" may have been suggested by Cassius, but in each case the connection is tenuous at best. The concluding stanza of

"What would I give to see his face?," however, is a certain reference to *The Merchant of Venice* as Emily Dickinson writes:

> *Now* – Have I bought it –
> "Shylock"? Say!
> Sign me the Bond!
> "I vow to pay
> To Her – who pledges *this* –
> *One hour* – of her Sovreign's face"!
> *Extatic* Contract!
> *Niggard* Grace!
> My *Kingdom's worth* of Bliss!

"*One hour* – of her Sovreign's face!" curiously resembles a line from *Richard II*, "Or bend one wrinkle on my sovereign's face." [8] Whicher saw a possible connection between Desdemona's dying words "Nobody, I myself," and "I'm Nobody! Who are you?" He also suggested that the metaphor of "As if no soul the solstice passed/That maketh all things new" [9] was derived from the opening lines of *Richard III*, "Now is the winter of our discontent/Made summer by this sun of York." Henry Wells declared "her twelve-line poem, 'When I see not, I better see,' to be a deliberate and almost line for line translation of the forty-third sonnet that begins, 'When most I wink, then do mine eyes best see.'" Frank Davidson presents a reasonable argument that the metaphor of speech and distance in the concluding lines of "A Route of Evanescence," the "hummingbird poem," is based upon a speech by Antonio in the second act of *The Tempest*. Antonio avers that the "Queen of Tunis" can have no note from Naples "unless the sun were post"; Emily writes "The mail from Tunis, probably,/An easy Morning's Ride –." [10] This last example and Wells's contention regarding the forty-third sonnet notwithstanding, it appears that Emily Dickinson considered Shakespeare as material to be admired, quoted, and absorbed, but not presumed upon. Although she could be impudent with the diety, she displayed remarkable reverence for mortal Shakespeare. She might rap on God's door any day, but she was not so forward with authors whom she considered to be her literary masters. She read their biographies eagerly and sought some vicarious contact with them. She once wistfully wrote Higginson, who was traveling in Europe, "perhaps you have spoken with George Eliot. Will you 'tell me about it'?" Earlier she had asked Mrs. Todd to be her medium who might "touch Shakespeare" for her. This liaison had enchanting potential, for Emily could attach a meaning to the vaguest association with Shakespeare: she once wrote a note to Louise Norcross on a scrap of paper that had "lain for years" in her Shakespeare, and in the note remarked that the stationery "though it is blotted and antiquated is endeared by its resting-place."[11] Shakespeare's influence on Emily Dickinson was very much like his impression upon the letter paper: an absorption that took place over a long period, leaving marks that can be best discerned by careful scrutiny in bright light. Their writing may show some similarities of syntax, and lines out of context may be compared with some success, but Shakespeare's dramatic blank verse and sonnets and Dickinson's compact lyrics are in different provinces of the realm of great poetry.

Although few other Renaissance writers affected Emily Dickinson, she proved highly susceptible to the imagery of the metaphysical poets and to the vocabulary of Sir Thomas Browne. Browne was introduced in Newman's *Practical System of Rhetoric*, one of Emily's Mount Holyoke textbooks, as a "literary curiosity," an "eccentric genius" whose writings are characterized by his "original and striking thoughts. . . , the extravagance of his style . . . [and] strange and unheard of combinations."[12] Thus, Emily was aware of the freshness of Browne's style long before his "vital vigor" was recommended in Higginson's "Letter to a Young Contributor,"[13] even though that recommendation may have reminded her to place Browne on the list of familiar authors she sent to Higginson. A detailed study by Herbert E. Childs,[14] which compares the vocabularies and religious attitudes of Emily Dickinson and Sir Thomas Browne, discusses their peculiar, common use of certain words: "hermetic" meaning "occult, magical, stimulating"; "circumference" used in the sense of a "kind of transcendental spacetime"; and "Peru" as a symbol of wealth. Whicher called attention to the similarity of Browne's "we are ignorant of the back-parts or lower side of His Divinity" and Dickinson's "parts of his far plan/That baffled me –/The underside/Of his Divinity." [15] Childs cites Browne's phrase "this speckled Face of Honesty in the World" [16] because of its apparent relationship to the phrase "freckled human nature" in "What Soft – Cherubic Creatures –." But he does not mention that this is a recurring Dickinson image that appears variously as "This dirty – little – Heart/ . . . /A Freckled shrine," "I am spotted – 'I am Pardon' –," "When they dislocate my Brain!/ Amputate my freckled Bosom!," and "The Stars dare shine occasionally/Upon a spotted World." [17] The single passage cited by Whicher and all those cited by Childs, with the exception of two disputable ones from *Hydriotaphia*, come from *Religio Medici* and *Christian Morals*. This gives some indication of the extent of Emily Dickinson's reading in Browne's works, particularly with added evidence from the family library, which contains a three-volume *Works of Sir Thomas Browne* that belonged to Sue. The pages of volume I in this set remain uncut, and the only cut pages in the others are "Religio Medici" in volume II and "Christian Morals" in volume III. A number of passages in "Christian Morals," have been marked, again with thin, light pencil lines in the outer margins.

Surely Emily Dickinson would have been receptive to Browne's expression of this bit of seventeenth-century philosophy: "There is no man alone, because every man is a Microcosm, and carries the whole World about him." [18] Her well-known poem beginning "The Soul selects her own Society –/Then – shuts the Door –" represents a distillate of opinions from Thomas à Kempis and the following additional discourse from Browne regarding

the virtues of solitude: "Unthinking Heads, who have not learn'd
to be alone, are in a Prison to themselves. . . . Be able to be
alone. Loose not the advantage of Solitude, and the Society of
thy self . . . but delight to be alone and single with Omni-
presency."[19] While some critics merely suggest that between
Emily Dickinson and the metaphysicals there exists "a kinship
of spirit rather than anything specific [and that] a painstaking
study might yield more," others conclude after investigating
similarities of style and imagery that "from the poets of this tradition [she] doubtless sought imaginative stimulus and an occasional technical lesson."[20]

For such lessons there was a considerable amount of seventeenth-century verse available in the family library, although
most of it was in anthologies. Both Edward Dickinson and Sue
had copies of Chambers' ponderous two-volume *Cyclopaedia of
English Literature*. These, along with Dana's *Household Book
of Poetry* and Griswold's *Sacred Poets of England and America*,
are now in the Dickinson Collection at Harvard. Volume I of
Chambers includes selections from Cowley, Waller, Vaughan,
Thomas Stanley, and Crashaw, and in each case the poetry is
preceded by a biographical sketch of the author and a short
critical appraisal of his work. The page devoted to Crashaw has
been creased from right to left and, though there are no marks,
Emily probably found this portion of Crashaw's biography interesting:

A religious poet, whose devotional strains and lyric raptures evince
the highest genius. . . . But amidst all his abstractions, metaphors,
and apostrophes, Crashaw is never tedious. . . . No poet of his day
is so rich in "barbaric pearl and gold," the genuine ore of poetry.

She also could sympathize with George Herbert when she read
in the same anthology this criticism of *The Temple*:

The lines on Virtue . . . are the best in the collection; but even in
them we find, what mars all the poetry of Herbert, ridiculous con-

ceits of coarse unpleasant similes. . . . The most sacred subject could not repress his love of fantastic imagery, or keep him for half a dozen verses in a serious and natural strain.[21]

In a separate edition of *The Temple* owned by Sue several lines of "The Church-Porch" have been marked. Two of the marked lines express one of Emily Dickinson's characteristic attitudes: "Dare to look in thy chest; for 'tis thine own; And tumble up and down what thou find'st there." And from among Herbert's poems she transcribed the second two stanzas of his "Matin Hymn" to keep among her own papers. The poem was published in *The Springfield Republican* for October 28, 1876 with the title "Mattens," and is included in the Chambers anthology. She chose to copy the following lines:

> My God, what is a heart,
> Silver, or gold, or precious stone,
> Or star, or rainbow, or a part
> Of all these things – or all of them in one?

> My God, what is a heart,
> That thou shouldst it so eye and woo,
> Pouring upon it all thy art
> As if that thou hadst nothing else to do?

These stanzas bore enough resemblance to Dickinson poems for Millicent Todd Bingham to publish them as Emily's own in the first edition of *Bolts of Melody*.[22] The conceit in the first stanza and the wit in the final line might be found in either poet; but they were discovered to be Herbert's, and this last poem of a section entitled "The Mob within the Heart" was deleted from the second printing of the Bingham collection.

In the same volume of Chambers' *Cyclopaedia* containing the folded Crashaw page and Herbert's "Matin Hymn," these lines from Henry Vaughan's "Early Rising and Prayer" are carefully marked on a page that is also folded so that the marked passage is inside the fold:

> And heaven's gate opens when the world's is shut.
>
> *   *   *   *   *   *   *   *   *
>
> Serve God before the world, let him not go
> Until thou hast a blessing; then resign
> The whole unto him, and remember who
> Prevail'd by wrestling ere the sun did shine;
> Pour oil upon the stones and weep for thy sin,
> Then journey on, and have an eye to heaven.[23]

Vaughan's attitude toward God as put forward here would coincide with Emily Dickinson's. And, in her writing of Jacob's wrestling with the angel,[24] her Jacob, like Vaughan's, infers that his antagonist was surely God. With another line from Vaughan she described to Higginson her emotions on recalling a particularly moving pastoral scene: "'Twas noting some such Scene made Vaughn humbly say 'My Days are at best but dim and hoary'—I think it was Vaughn—."[25] She was obviously writing from memory, for the line is slightly misquoted and the poet's name is misspelled. This and the detailed descriptions of the letter's opening paragraph indicate that she knew Vaughan's poem, "They are All Gone into the World of Light," quite well. She may have read that and other poems of his either in the anthologies or in *The Springfield Republican*, which occasionally published such verse in a Saturday column entitled "Books, Authors, and Art." On Valentine's Day, 1863, the column presented five selections from Vaughan with an introduction that included this estimate:

Here and there you find thoughts simply, strongly and tenderly expressed; a volume in a line; a nineteenth century essay in three words. And over all shines the hallowing lustre of a truly Christian spirit. As he himself says: "He that desires to excel in this kind of . . . holy writing, must strive by all means for perfection and true holiness . . . and then he will be able to write with Hierotheus and holy Herbert, 'a true hymn.'"

In closing, the article described "They are All Gone into the World of Light" as "tender and mournful . . . better known than most,"[26] but did not reprint it. Whether all this moved her to further reading of Vaughan and "holy Herbert" we do not know, but it is safe to say that the works were available and that the similarities between her poems and theirs are not entirely coincidental. She twice quotes one other poet of this period, Edmund Waller, but she never mentions him by name. Both references are in letters to the Hollands,[27] and both refer to the "Soul's poor cottage," an image taken from Waller's poem "The Last Prospect."

Neither the Puritan writers of the Commonwealth nor the worldly poets of the Restoration interested Emily Dickinson. She once recommended to Austin that he read "Pilgrim's Progress" and "Baxter upon the will," but that seems to be the extent of her enthusiasm for either of these authors. And her only quotation from Dryden is one vaguely attributed to "The Stranger"[28] and drawn indirectly from an essay by James Russell Lowell. There was at least one copy of Milton's *Paradise Lost* in the family library, and Emily was familiar enough with the work to quote it in a number of letters. She seems to have had Book I in mind when she closed a letter to the Norcross sisters: "We read in a tremendous Book about 'an enemy,' and armed a confidential fort to scatter him away. The time has passed, and years have come, and yet not any 'Satan.' I think he must be making war upon some other nation."[29] On two separate occasions[30] she refers to Eve's reluctant departure from Eden, and both instances seem closer to Milton's description of the expulsion[31] than the concluding verses of the third chapter of Genesis.

Her interest in Milton was a continuing one that included more than *Paradise Lost*. It extended as far as Ann Manning's biography of Milton's first wife, *The Maiden and Married Life of Mary Powell*; and in the family copy of Dana's *Household Book of Poetry*, the last twenty lines of "Il Penseroso" are marked as are two separate ten-line passages of "L'Allegro." Milton's sonnet, "To the Lord General Cromwell," which Emily quoted in a letter to Mrs. Sweetser in the spring of 1884, also appears in the Dana anthology but is unmarked. "If the Spirits are fair as the Faces 'Nothing is here for Tears —,' " [32] is a line from *Samson Agonistes* [33] that she may have picked up from George Eliot, who used it to close the final chapter of *Daniel Deronda*, a novel of which Emily was especially fond. Dickinson references to Milton appear both early and late, and the nature of the later quotations makes it appear that she reread *Paradise Lost* sometime after 1880. Although she probably enjoyed Milton thoroughly, she found no place in her own writing for the involved apparatus of classical and Christian mythology characteristic of his grand style.

Although the major eighteenth-century influence on Emily Dickinson was exerted by the hymn writers, she knew a number of other authors from the period. She was familiar enough with Addison to apply his standards to a friend whose argument she considered "the apex of human impudence": "If Joseph Addison were alive, I should present [George Allen] to him as the highest degree of absurdity." [34] Selections from Addison were available both in anthologies and in current periodicals, and there was a twelve-volume edition of his works in her father's library. She was aware of Defoe's *Robinson Crusoe* and Goldsmith's *Vicar of Wakefield*. [35] She read more Goldsmith while at Mount Holyoke: her textbooks there included no less than three of his histories. And chapter VI of Johnson's *Rasselas* came to mind when the winter of 1859 trapped her in the "Happy Valley" of the homestead: "I cannot walk to distant friends on nights piercing as these, so I put both hands on the window-pane, and try to think how birds fly, and imitate, and fail, like Mr 'Rasselas.' " [36] It has been suggested that she read *Tristram Shandy*,[37] but there is no concrete evidence of this; and even though Sterne's well-known phrase "God tempers the wind to the shorn lamb" turns up in some form in two letters and a poem,[38] the chances are that Emily acquired it from conversation rather than from reading his *Sentimental Journey*.

She showed little voluntary interest in Augustan poetry, and her only mention of Pope is in a letter from Mount Holyoke in which she reported, "At. 11. I recite a lesson in 'Pope's Essay on Man' which is merely transposition." She may have derived the following two lines from Pope's "The Dying Christian to His Soul": "Death has mislaid his sting — the grave forgot his victory," and "Oh, Death, where is thy Chancellor?" [39] She knew the Pope poem as Hymn 448 in Watts's *Psalms, Hymns, and Spiritual Songs*, but her lines could just as easily have come from I Corinthians 15:55 or any one of several other hymns that mention the "sting of death" and the dubious "victory of the grave."

Though many of the hymns with which Emily Dickinson was familiar were not products of the eighteenth century, they were of the same general tradition. Three important collections of hymns were readily accessible to her: Watts's *Christian Psalmody*, his *The Psalms, Hymns, and Spiritual Songs*, and a tiny volume entitled *Village Hymns*. All three were available to the family at home; the last two were recommended in the Seminary Catalogue for the personal libraries of young ladies attending Mount Holyoke. It is not particularly important to determine whether it was the singing of the hymns at church and school or the reading of them at home that made the more lasting impression. No doubt the singing did much to establish in Emily's mind the rhythm of hymn meter; the relation of her prosody to the various types of hymn meter is an established fact.[40] The reading of the hymns contributed to her store of ideas and metaphors and must have emphasized much of the biblical imagery that she preferred. In her day, reflection upon the hymns was recommended as an edifying tonic for the devout. For this reason she could make scraps of hymns part of letters and conversation in much the same manner that she used passages from other familiar family reading. This is reflected in a lighthearted letter to Austin, written while he was in Cambridge attending Harvard Law School. After recommending that he read Bunyan and Baxter, Emily inquired about his physical and moral comforts:

> Trust you enjoy your closet, and meditate profoundly upon the Daily Food! I shall send you Village Hymns, by earliest opportunity.
> I was just this moment thinking of a favorite stanza of your's, "where congregations ne'er break up and Sabbaths have no end." [41]

The quotation is from a hymn by William Burkitt and was one Emily had paraphrased in an earlier letter to Austin, saying, "Mother . . . consoles herself by thinking of several future places 'where congregations ne'er break up,' and Austins have no end!" [42] In her letters the quotations from hymns were variously used: many of the references were as gay as the one just cited; and others were sentimental, as was the enclosure of a stanza from James Montgomery in a letter to the newly married Emily Fowler Ford. Still others were somber indeed, as was her writing to the Norcross sisters of her father's death, "I cannot write anymore, dears. . . . Thank you each for the love though I could not notice it. Almost the last tune that he heard was, 'Rest from thy loved employ.'" [43]

In one poem she turned to a Watts hymn, "There is a land of pure delight," for two suitable lines that she incorporated easily and smoothly into the third stanza of "Where bells no more affright the morn –." When she quoted from "Light Shining out of Darkness," [44] she probably remembered it as the hymn that included "God moves in a mysterious way, his wonders to perform" rather than remembering a poem read from William Cowper. She did read some of Cowper's poetry, however, "John Gilpin's Ride" at least, for she refers to it in two letters [45] and could have found it in the Chambers anthology or in a collection of Cowper poetry that belonged to her mother.

In the variety of her reading, Emily Dickinson found some of the early voices of the Romantic Movement worth remembering. When she came to write of autumn, she alluded to part IV of Thomson's *The Seasons*. In two early letters to Abiah Root she included quotations from a new volume in the family library, an 1845 edition of Edward Young's *Night Thoughts*. In a later letter to Abiah (1850) she incorporated a line from Gray's "Elegy." [46] One line from this latter work, "The paths of glory lead but to the Grave," is paraphrased in "Our salary the longest Day/Is nothing but a Bier" from "The Notice that is called the Spring."

Of the eighteenth-century Romantics, Emily most frequently quoted Robert Burns. A Burns source can be fixed exactly for at least six passages, and several more that appear to be his dialect phrases are adapted to Dickinson letters. [47] The earliest appearance of Burns in the letters antedates Sue's 1853 edition of his complete works that is in the Harvard Collection, but his poetry was readily available in other volumes that Emily read. She took phrases from Burns for two lines of "I had a guinea golden–": her first stanza concludes, "I sat me down to sigh"; Burns's "Despondency" reads "I set me down and sigh"; the last line of her second stanza is "I kept the 'house at hame'"; Burns's "We're a' Noddin" reads "At our house at hame!" There are several indications that she had in mind his song "Here's to Thy Health" when she wrote "Poor little Heart!" His song begins:

> Here's to thy health, my bonnie lass!
> Guid night and joy be wi' thee!
> I'll come nae mair to thy bower – door
> To tell thee that I lo'e thee.
> O, dinna think, my pretty pink,
> But I can live without thee:
> I vow and swear I dinna care
> How lang ye look about ye!

Her first stanza reads:

> Poor little Heart!
> Did they forget thee?
> Then dinna care! Then dinna care!

As different as Burns and Dickinson are in some respects, they had a number of qualities in common. Each relished the independence that pride in provincialism afforded. Burns considered his mind as well as his heart to be "in the Highlands," and Emily Dickinson declared "Because I see – New Englandly –/The Queen, discerns like me –/Provincially." [48] Both were masters of the technique of presenting effective images drawn from simple scenes of nature and ordinary domestic activity. The natural, untutored Burns would have understood Emily's explaining to critic Higginson, "I went to school – but in your manner of the phrase –had no education." [49] She, in turn, sensed the lyric freedom Burns gained by calculated departure from standard verse forms and by uninhibited choice of words and phrases.

Emily Dickinson was sufficiently aware of the writers of the Renaissance and eighteenth century to be an informed and enthusiastic observer of the contemporary literary scene. She had absorbed basic materials from the two great Renaissance works, the King James Bible and Shakespeare's plays; to these she added the subtle wit and concrete imagery of the metaphysical poets and the control characteristic of the neoclassical era. Although her reading was not the orderly process that this implies, she was well qualified as a potential disciple of Coleridge, Wordsworth, and the Romantic Movement.

British Literature: Romantic and Victorian

He questioned softly "Why I failed"?
"For Beauty", I replied –
"And I – for Truth – Themself are One –
We Brethren, are", He said
                              — *Emily Dickinson, c. 1862*

To Emily Dickinson, nineteenth-century British literature was new and imported; it was especially attractive even though she found its authors too recent to be taken seriously as "masters." She maintained an active, and in some cases detailed, interest in the principal figures of the Romantic Movement. She did not, however, anticipate their works with the same enthusiasm that was aroused by the fresh publications of her English contemporaries. Having grown up with the Victorian era, Emily came to feel an intimate kinship with such writers as George Eliot, Elizabeth Barrett Browning, and the Brontë sisters. She eagerly read much that they wrote, along with a large amount of Robert Browning and Charles Dickens. In spite of the considerable bulk of this reading and the specific relationship that exists between some of her poems and certain works of the period, nineteenth-century British authors affected her poetry neither so often nor so deeply as did the Bible and the verse of the Metaphysicals and the hymn writers. Nevertheless, Emily Dickinson's reading from nineteenth-century British literature is significant because of the analogues to her poems that it does contain and because her allusions and comments reveal how much a part of the Victorian world she considered herself to be.

Although she seldom uses quotations from the Romantic poets, her own writing shows a love of natural beauty, a belief in man's innate goodness, and a faith in human intuition typical of the Romantic attitude. There is, for instance, no concrete evidence of her having read Blake, still she realized as completely as he how

> To see a World in a grain of sand,
> And a Heaven in a wild flower;
> Hold infinity in the palm of your hand,
> And eternity in an hour.[1]

She undoubtedly knew a variety of selections from the Romantic poets, but her romantic tendencies were only intensified by and not derived from the Romantic Movement. Nowhere in her poems or letters does she mention Southey or Coleridge, although she was aware of the poets of the Lake District for she wrote the Norcross sisters, "I think of your little parlor as the poets once thought of Windermere, – peace, sunshine, and books." [2] Quotations from Wordsworth appear in three of her letters; two of these quotations are lines from "Elegiac Stanzas" which she credits to "the Stranger," and the third is taken from "We are Seven." She presents only these slight recollections of Wordsworth's works, yet the relation of the following Dickinson stanzas to his "I Wandered Lonely as a Cloud" seems unmistakable:

> Absent Place – an April Day –
> Daffodils a-blow
> Homesick curiosity
> To the Souls that snow –
>
> Drift may block within it
> Deeper than without –
> Daffodil delight but
> Him it duplicate –

From the roll of major Romantic poets only the names of Byron and Keats appear in Emily Dickinson's letters. She included Keats in her list of preferred poets, and later repeated to Higginson a quotation from *Endymion* that he had cited in an *Atlantic* essay.[3] In a late letter (1885) she asked Forrest Emerson to seek out for her some details of Helen Hunt Jackson's death and lamented, "Oh had that Keats a Severn!"[4] These brief references may be the extent of the direct evidence of her attachment to Keats; but, like the relation of the "daffodil" poems, her equating of truth and beauty in "I died for Beauty" seems a restatement of "beauty is truth, truth beauty," from his "Ode on a Grecian Urn." From Byron, she recalled "Maid of Athens, ere we part" as she wrote "Lad of Athens, faithful be," the first line of her fourteen-word version of Polonius' speech on integrity. In addition to the few, scattered examples of Byron's poetry that she remembered, she knew something of his life, for when the Holland's young son required surgery to correct a malformed foot, she asked, "How is your little Byron? Hope he gains his foot without losing his genius. Have heard it ably argued that the poet's genius lay in his foot."[5]

Byron's hapless "Prisoner of Chillon" deeply impressed her. She had an understandable fondness for the unfortunate captive and more than once identified herself with him. In a period of improvement during her last illness, she included the poem's last line in this brief note to Sue: "How lovely every solace! This long, short, penance 'Even I regain my freedom with a Sigh.'"[6] Byron's prisoner had recounted:

> My very chains and I grew friends,
> So much a long communion tends
> To make us what we are — even I
> Regained my freedom with a sigh.

Taking these lines as a theme, Emily Dickinson in an earlier poem had explored the subject of unaccustomed liberty even further:

A Prison gets to be a friend –
Between it's Ponderous face
And Our's – a Kinsmanship express –
And in it's narrow Eyes –

We come to look with gratitude
For the appointed Beam
It deal us – stated as our food –
And hungered for – the same –

We learn to know the Planks –
That answer to Our feet –
So miserable a sound – at first –
Nor even now – so sweet –

As plashing in the Pools –
When Memory was a Boy –
But a Demurer Circuit –
A Geometric Joy –

The Posture of the Key
That interrupt the Day
To Our Endeavor – Not so real
The Cheek of Liberty –

As this Phantasm Steel –
Whose features – Day and Night –
Are present to us – as Our Own –
And as escapeless – quite –

The narrow Round – the Stint –
The slow exchange of Hope –
For something passiver – Content
Too steep for looking up –

The Liberty we knew
Avoided – like a Dream –
Too wide for any Night but Heaven –
If That – indeed – redeem –

Her "Talk with prudence to a Beggar," a shorter poem that is a variation on this same theme, concludes:

> Cautious, hint to any Captive
> You have passed enfranchized feet!
> Anecdotes of air in Dungeons
> Have sometimes proved deadly sweet!

Of the other poets of the Romantic Period, Thomas Moore is the only one Emily Dickinson mentions. His "Last Rose of Summer" she knew as both a poem and as a musical arrangement.[7] She may also have read her brother's copy of *Lalla Rookh*,[8] and she noted in a letter to Abiah Root that Moore's *The Epicurean* was part of her reading in the spring of 1848. Her source of some additional detail concerning the Romantic authors is suggested by a remark to the Norcross sisters that she would like to pay them "as long a call as De Quincey made North." This allusion is to Mary Gordon's biography of her gossipy savant father, John Wilson (Christopher North), in which she relates that an overnight visit by De Quincey eventually lasted "the greater part of *a year*."[9]

Emily was curious about De Quincey, and in the summer of 1858 she actively sought copies of his *Klosterheim* and *Confessions of an Opium Eater*. When she could not get them from the Northampton Library, she asked Mrs. Havens, wife of an Amherst professor, to help her locate them. Whether she succeeded in borrowing the books we do not know; there are, however, ten volumes of a twelve-volume set of De Quincey's works in the Harvard Collection.[10] If the evidence of her interest is used to date the acquisition of these books, perhaps it was portions of "The Avenger" (volume XII) that Edward Dickinson was reading in the winter of 1859 when Emily recorded his unusual amusement concerning the "letters of suspected gentlemen," a new book in the family library.[11] There are further indications that Emily used this set of books. In chapter I of *Auto-*

biographical Sketches the following passages are marked by the typical light pencil lines:

For I was the shyest of children; and at all stages of life, a natural sense of personal dignity held me back from exposing the least ray of feeling which I was not encouraged *wholly* to reveal.

*   *   *   *   *   *   *   *   *   *   *   *

Rightly it is said of utter, utter misery, that it "cannot be *remembered*."

*   *   *   *   *   *   *   *   *   *   *   *

Grief! Thou art classed amongst the depressing passions. And true it is that thou humblest to the dust but also thou exaltest to the clouds. Thou shakest as with ague, but also thou steadiest like frost.

There is also a note on page 155 of De Quincey's *Essays on the Poets* that reads "View Mrs. Browning's Essays on the Greek Poets." Whether these marks and this handwriting are Emily's is uncertain, but both are related to matters that particularly interested her.

Perhaps the writers of the Romantic Movement affected Emily Dickinson only slightly because she found their basic attitudes so much in consonance with her own that they seemed commonplace and uninspiring. Louise Bogan feels that because of Emily Dickinson's "chief spiritual preoccupations we see how closely she relates to the English Romantic poets who . . . fought a difficult and unpopular battle against the eighteenth century's cold logic and mechanical point of view." [12] The part about spiritual preoccupations is true enough, but the conflict in which the Romantics were engaged never really troubled Emily Dickinson because she was able to maintain equilibrium between "cold logic" and the imagination and to bring the two forces together successfully within the limits of a single poem in much the same manner that seventeenth-century writers unified the "new science" with the traditional tenets of their society. Emily

Dickinson might admire intuition, but she was not ready to abandon entirely the "mechanical point of view":

> "Faith" is a fine invention
> When Gentlemen can *see* –
> But *Microscopes* are prudent
> In an Emergency.

Nonetheless, when Higginson inquired about her reading, she replied, "For Poets – I have Keats – and Mr and Mrs Browning." [13] Of the three, she was most fond of Elizabeth Barrett Browning, and references to her begin to appear in the poems and letters of late 1861, probably prompted by the eulogy of Mrs. Browning that appeared in *The Atlantic Monthly* in September of that year. [14] In the opening paragraph of the article is this triplet, quoted from Mrs. Browning's "A Vision of Poets,"

> poet true
> Who died for Beauty, as martyrs do
> For Truth, – the ends being scarcely two. [15]

These lines bring poems by Keats, Mrs. Browning, and Emily Dickinson close together indeed. The apparent relation of Keats's "Ode on a Grecian Urn" and Dickinson's "I died for Beauty" has already been mentioned, but she is more indebted to Mrs. Browning for the images of brotherhood and martyrdom used in these stanzas:

> I died for Beauty – but was scarce
> Adjusted in the Tomb
> When One who died for Truth, was lain
> In an adjoining Room –
>
> He questioned softly "Why I failed"?
> "For Beauty", I replied –
> "And I – for Truth – Themself are One –
> We Bretheren, are", He said –

Even though Emily Dickinson first mentions Elizabeth Browning in 1861, she implies that she had read some of her poetry considerably earlier.

> I think I was enchanted
> When first a sombre Girl –
> I read that Foreign lady
> The Dark – felt beautiful –

Whenever it was that she read "Catarina to Camoens," she was impressed by the "sweetest eyes" described in the refrain, and she refers to that line in two letters to Mrs. Holland. And when she wrote, "But if 'Little Margaret's love' is so vivid, is it quite safe to ignite it?," [16] she probably had in mind the ill-starred damsel, in the concluding stanzas of Mrs. Browning's "The Romaunt of Margret," who discovered love too late and drowned herself.

Of all Elizabeth Barrett's poems, Emily preferred *Aurora Leigh*, the 11,000-line blank verse romance. She frequently refers to it in letters and seems to have found its metaphors to her liking. But when Emily read of Chimborazo and Teneriffe in book I of *Aurora Leigh*, she was not introduced to new names but was only re-encountering ones she had learned years before in studying Professor Hitchcock's *Elementary Geology*. Other images in Dickinson poems, though a remarkably diverse group, certainly must have originated in *Aurora Leigh*. Mrs. Browning's Aurora, for example, expresses her distaste for the good neighbor who

> Is fatal sometimes, — cuts your morning up
> To mincemeat of the smallest talk,
> Then helps to sugar her bohea at night
> With your reputation . . . (IV, 489–492)

Emily Dickinson, reflecting upon the uncertainty in the lonely grave, observes that the tomb admits "No Chatter – here – no

tea/So Babbler, and Bohea—stay there." [17] Elsewhere, Aurora
reported that her cousin, Romney, in saying farewell "touched,
just touched/My hatstrings tied for going (at the door/the carriage stood to take me)"; and Emily Dickinson, in anticipating a
departure of her own, writes, "I sing to use the Waiting/My
Bonnet but to tie/And shut the Door unto my House." More
significantly she comments in another poem:

> Tie the Strings to my Life, My Lord,
> Then, I am ready to go!
> Just a look to the Horses —
> Rapid! That will do!

To Aurora, hope is a balloon "Which, whether caught by blos-
soming tree or bare,/Is torn alike" (V, 425–426), while to
Emily it is a balloon that

> . . . strains — and spins —
> Trips frantic in a Tree
> Tears open her imperial Veins —
> And tumbles in the Sea —[18]

Marian Erle's speech in book VI of *Aurora Leigh* suggests a
number of the details of "I heard a Fly Buzz—when I died—":

> "She told me tenderly (as when men come
> To a bedside to tell people they must die),
>
> *   *   *   *   *   *   *   *
>
> That Romney Leigh had loved *her* formerly.
> And *she* loved *him*, she might say, now the chance
> Was past, — but that, of course, he never guessed, —
> For something came between them, something thin
> As a cobweb, catching every fly of doubt
> To hold it buzzing at the window-pane
> And help to dim the daylight. . . ." (VI, 1079–1087)

The final stanzas of the Dickinson poem are similarly concerned
with fading light and the doubt raised by the buzzing fly:

I willed my Keepsakes – Signed away
What portion of me be
Assignable – and then it was
There interposed a Fly –

With Blue – uncertain stumbling Buzz –
Between the light – and me –
And then the Windows failed – and then
I could not see to see –

In her own copy of *Aurora Leigh*, Emily marked ten lines that italicize the kinship she felt for the renowned Mrs. Browning:

By the way,
The works of women are symbolical.
We sew, sew, prick our fingers, dull our sight,
Producing what? A pair of slippers, sir,
To put on when you're weary — or a stool
To stumble over and vex you . . . 'curse that stool!'
Or else at best, a cushion, where you lean
And sleep, and dream of something we are not
But would be for your sake. Alas, alas!
This hurts most, this — that, after all, we are paid
The worth of our work, perhaps. (I, 455–465)

Emily's intimate friends seem to have been well aware of her interest in Elizabeth Barrett, for in August 1862 she asked Higginson, "Have you the portrait of Mrs Browning? Persons sent me three – If you have none, will you have mine?" Mme. Bianchi recalls a picture of Mrs. Browning hanging in her Aunt Emily's room, along with one of George Eliot and one of Thomas Carlyle. When Samuel Bowles was in Europe in 1862 Emily requested, "Should anybody where you go, talk of Mrs. Browning, you must hear for us – and if you touch her Grave, put one hand on the Head, for me – her unmentioned Mourner." [19] This request, and possibly the answer to it, can be related to "I went to thank Her–/But She Slept–," one of three poems Dickinson

wrote in Mrs. Browning's memory. "I think I was enchanted,"
is another, and the third is a burial piece that begins:

> Her – 'last Poems' –
> Poets – ended –
> Silver – perished – with her Tongue –
> Not on Record – bubbled other,
> Flute – or Woman –
> So divine –

It was by the standard of Mrs. Browning's verse that Emily
Dickinson judged other women's poetry. And it was Robert
Browning's ability to sustain the loss of such a poetess-wife that
made Emily regard him as "the bravest man alive." [20] In her letters, she mentions Robert Browning almost as frequently as she
does his wife, and one would like to think that his effect on
Dickinson the poet was the greater of the two. The first indication of her having read Robert Browning occurs in the letter to
Higginson that mentions both Keats and the Brownings. His
name then disappears from her letters until she reports to the
Norcross sisters that she "noticed that Robert Browning had made
another poem." [21] She apparently had learned of his recently
published *Dramatis Personae* [22] from the following notice that
appeared in *The Springfield Republican* on September 14, 1864.

There is no denying the genius of Browning. He is a man of vigorous thought in poetic form. But his forms of expression are so angu-
lar and obscure that his thoughts are inaccessible to by far the greater
part of his perplexed and mystified readers. He does not coin his
gold for general circulation . . . , but he gives you the quartz of
rock, rich indeed in the precious metal . . . Dramatis Personae, the
new collection of his poems . . . will be admired understandingly
by an appreciative few

Emily Dickinson was one of the appreciative few; when she
speaks of Robert Browning, she never suggests that his obscurities have troubled her in any way. In fact, the obscurity probably

heightened her reading pleasure, and when she declared, "Tell all the Truth but tell it slant–," she echoed his explanation that "Art may tell a truth/obliquely."[23] This Browning passage is one of several marked by light pencil lines parallel to the outer margins in Sue's copy of *The Ring and the Book*, a copy more than likely shared with Emily.

The table of contents of Emily's own copy of Browning's *Men and Women* shows the titles of three poems marked in the same manner — "Evelyn Hope," "In Three Days," and "One Way of Love." The first two of these are the source of quotations that she used in at least three letters; and of all Browning's books, *Men and Women* was probably the one she knew best. She speaks of it as "a broad Book" and of the author as "the consummate Browning." The poem from this collection that is of most importance so far as Dickinson is concerned is "The Last Ride Together." She included its twenty-first line in a late letter (1885) but omitted her usual quotation marks and made no mention of the author.[24] This alone indicates her familiarity with a poem that has surprising similarities to her "Because I could not stop for Death."[25] The basic metaphor in both poems is that of a chivalrous gentleman riding in the company of a congenial feminine companion. In each case the ride is an unending one. The contemplative speaker in the Dickinson poem is the lady; in Browning's it is the gentleman; but the reflections on life, death, and immortality are very much the same. Browning wrote:

> We rode; it seemed my spirit flew,
> Saw other regions, cities new,
>   As the world rushed by on either side.
>
> I thought, — All labor, yet no less
> Bear up beneath their unsuccess

and Dickinson writes:

We slowly drove – He knew no haste
And I had put away
My labor and my leisure too,
For His Civility –

We passed the School, where Children strove
At Recess – in the Ring –
We passed the Fields of Gazing Grain –
We passed the Setting Sun –

Both speakers look back upon life and view its apparent end in the grave: Browning questions a poet, a sculptor, and a composer about lives that end under "Abbey-stones"; Dickinson reflects calmly on life's experiences ending in that "House" with "The Cornice – in the Ground –." And in each of the poems the final lines look hopefully toward immortality.

Browning asks:

What if we still ride on, we two,
With life forever old yet new,
Changed not in kind but in degree,
The instant made eternity, –
And heaven just prove that I and she
    Ride, ride together, forever ride?

Dickinson observes:

Since then – 'tis Centuries – and yet
Feels shorter than the Day
I first surmised the Horses Heads
Were toward Eternity –

While the chances are good that Emily Dickinson read Browning's *Paracelsus*, her letters contain neither the title nor any quotations from it. Assuming that she did read this verse drama, Theodora Ward points out that the following lines suggest the full significance of the pearl imagery in two Dickinson poems:

> Are there not, Festus, are there not, dear Michal,
> Two points in the adventure of the diver,
> One — when a beggar, he prepares to plunge,
> One — when, a prince, he rises with his pearl?
> Festus, I plunge! [26]

This is Paracelsus' declaration as he sets out to discover the secrets of the world, and Emily Dickinson seems closest to the Browning lines in these stanzas:

> The Malay – took the Pearl –
> Not – I – the Earl –
> I – feared the Sea – too much
> Unsanctified – to touch –
>
> Praying that I might be
> Worthy – the Destiny –
> The Swarthy fellow swam –
> And bore my Jewel – Home –

She used another version of the same image to point out the risks inherent in any aspiration to live life fully. The poem begins *"One Life* of so much Consequence!" and the second stanza reads:

> *One Pearl* – to me – so signal –
> That I would instant dive –
> Although – I *knew* – to *take* it –
> Would *cost* me – *just a life*!

A third poem, "Removed from Accident of Loss," can be related to the Browning lines because of its similarity to the two poems mentioned. Dickinson writes of the "Brown Malay" who is unconscious of "Pearls in Eastern Waters," and the reader who is aware of Browning's metaphor of the pearl diver turned prince can appreciate more fully the potential opulence implied in the concluding lines of the Dickinson poem:

. . . – What Holiday

> Would stir his slow conception –
> Had he the power to dream
> That but the Dower's fraction –
> Awaited even – Him –

Robert Browning seems to have been one who could give acceptable words to Emily Dickinson's thoughts, and in one instance she credits him by saying "Browning told me so" and in another declares that his statement would be true "even were there no Browning." [27] In addition to the Browning poems already mentioned, her letters contain quotations from "Love Among the Ruins" and *Sordello*. Her letter references to Browning are unusual in that more often than not she in some way includes his name. This may indicate either enthusiasm or respect; but the fact remains that Emily Dickinson rarely mentions Shakespeare, Dickens, or Longfellow by name, as she does Browning.

While Emily Dickinson's fondness for the Brownings was self-sustaining, her knowledge of Sir Henry Taylor's *Philip van Artevelde* is an example of an interest that she merely shared with the remainder of the family. There are two copies of Sir Henry's verse drama in the Harvard Collection: an 1835 edition that belonged to Austin and an 1863 edition of Emily's. Although there is little doubt that Emily must have read this play at least once, the only indication that she may have returned to it is a poem that includes these lines:

> If those I loved were lost
> The Crier's voice w'd tell me –
> If those I loved were found
> The bells of Ghent w'd ring –
>
> *   *   *   *   *   *
>
> Philip – when bewildered
> Bore his riddle in!

Philip's "riddle," the final allusion of her poem, has its probable source in the last act of the Taylor play, in which the ill-fated hero at Ghent, mortally wounded and cursed by his comrades, asks, "What have I done? — Why such a death? — Why thus?" [28]

Also among Victorian poetry available in the family libraries were at least eight assorted volumes of Tennyson. [29] Emily Dickinson's letters indicate that she read his *Idylls of the King*, *The Princess*, and *Harold*, the verse-tragedy; and in one letter she quotes lines from both *In Memoriam* and *Love and Duty*. [30] Thomas Johnson senses an echo of *Locksley Hall* in the second stanza of "This — is the land — the Sunset washes —," but that appears to be the extent of Tennyson's influence on her poetry. In Sue's household there were also editions of the works of Arthur Hugh Clough and Coventry Patmore. Emerson, visiting the Austin Dickinsons in December 1857, complimented Sue for her taste in having Patmore's *Angel in the House* in evidence on her library table and recommended it highly. [31] Emily surely heard the recommendation, either from Sue or from Emerson himself. She may have read Patmore, and Clough as well, but if she did, she has left no clear indication of having done so.

Emily Dickinson did, however, read George Eliot's poetry. Her father gave her a volume of Eliot's poems in early 1874; but, because he died shortly afterward, she "felt unwilling to open [it]" and offered the book to Higginson. She was, nevertheless, already familiar with George Eliot's verse, for she had reported two years earlier that it was better than Helen Hunt's and almost as good as Mrs. Browning's. [32] Emily does not sustain this relatively high opinion elsewhere: the only other traces of George Eliot's poetry in all her writings are two minor allusions to "The Choir Invisible." Emily's regard for this poetry was merely an extension of her interest in George Eliot the novelist and Mary Ann Evans the person. She found a number of Eliot characters sufficiently real to identify them with certain friends and members of her family: Louise Norcross with Mrs. Ladislaw of

Middlemarch and her aunt, Mrs. Elizabeth Dickinson Currier, with Maggie Tulliver's sympathetic Aunt Glegg of *The Mill on the Floss*.[33] Eliot's "Aunt Glegg" was the owner of "a brocaded gown that would stand up empty like a suit of armor, and a silver-headed walking-stick," two heirlooms that belonged to a family that "had been respectable for many generations."[34] The peculiar strength of the brocade gown and the distinction it symbolized struck Emily Dickinson's fancy; and she recalled the image on one occasion to explain that "truth like Ancestor's Brocades can stand alone," and on another to tell Samuel Bowles that her memory of him could "stand alone, like the best Brocade."[35] Many of the earnest virtues extolled in Eliot's novels coincided with values professed in Amherst. It was easy for Emily to regard *Middlemarch* as "glorious" and to consider *Daniel Deronda* "the Lane to the Indes, Columbus was looking for." This latter judgment of *Daniel Deronda* was expressed when she read it for the first time, serialized in *Harper's Magazine* beginning in March 1876; nine years later she still regarded it as a "wise and tender Book . . . full of sad (high) nourishment."[36]

She was just as fascinated by George Eliot's private life as she was by her novels, and in letters variously refers to her as Marian Evans, Mrs. Lewes, and Walter Cross's wife. She followed "Mrs. Lewes's" activities as they were reported in the literary columns of *The Springfield Republican*, and she probably took more than passing notice of this item which appeared November 28, 1866:

The common explanation or rather excuse of Miss Evans's (George Eliot) anomalous social relations with Mr. Lewes . . . has been that Mr. Lewes's original or real wife was hopelessly insane. . . . But Louise N. Alcott of Boston [reports]: Mr. Lewes having forgiven and received back an unfaithful wife, cannot, according to English law obtain a divorce . . . Miss Evans is considered his wife, and is called Mrs. Lewes by their friends, in spite of the gossip and scandal. Owing to her peculiar position, Mrs. Lewes seldom goes into general society or sees strangers.

In any event, Emily must have been in sympathy with George Eliot's self-imposed seclusion, and when Mathilde Blind's *Life of George Eliot* appeared she read it closely and reported to Thomas Niles, who had given her the book, that it contained "much I never knew." When publication of Walter Cross's biography of Eliot was announced, she began "watching like a vulture for" its appearance.[37] In 1886 the first volume was published, and she sent a gift copy to Higginson with a memorial poem and this comment: "Biography first convinces us of the fleeing of the Biographied —."[38] After reading that George Eliot was dead, she had written,

> . . . The look of the words as they lay in print I shall never forget. Not their face in the casket could have had the eternity to me. Now, *my* George Eliot. The gift of belief which her greatness denied her, I trust she receives in the childhood of the kingdom of heaven.[39]

Marian Evans' morality did not meet the inflexible standards of New England; what one poet could do in London another might not attempt in Amherst. Perhaps this accounts for Emily's reservations when she wrote of George Eliot: "except that in a few instances this 'mortal has already put on immortality.'"[40]

Emily Dickinson was considerably drawn to the Brontë sisters. Though her enthusiasm for them was far less intense than that which she manifested for George Eliot, it lasted throughout her lifetime. She liked their poems well enough to send a volume of them to Samuel Bowles in 1864. Emily Brontë's "No Coward Soul is Mine" was a favorite: lines from it appear in three late letters, and it was this poem that Colonel Higginson read at her funeral in May 1886. During the last ten years of her life, Emily Dickinson read Elizabeth Gaskell's *Life of Charlotte Brontë* and Mary Robinson's *Life of Emily Brontë*; but the five memorial stanzas of "All overgrown by cunning moss," a rather perfunctory memorial to Charlotte, constitute the only mention of the Brontë

sisters in her poems. Her interest in the Brontës, like her interest
in George Eliot, seems not to have been in their poetry but in
their lives and in their novels. In 1849, when Emily Dickinson
was nineteen, she had read Elbridge Bowdoin's copy of *Jane
Eyre*,[41] and in 1865 she was given a later edition by Mrs. Charlotte Eastman. When Emily wrote of her dog Carlo, the perceptive qualities that she attributed to him showed a curious similarity to those characteristic of St. John Rivers' dog, also named
Carlo and described in chapter 31 of *Jane Eyre*. Mrs. Eastman's
gift copy of *Jane Eyre* is in the Harvard Collection along with
copies of Charlotte Brontë's *The Professor* and *Villette*, Anne's
The Tenant of Wildfell Hall, and Emily's *Wuthering Heights*.

Of all the Victorian novelists, however, Charles Dickens was
the family favorite, and Emily knew his novels just as well or
perhaps better than did the rest of her family. Edward Dickinson
may have classified him among the worthless "modern Literati," [42]
but shortly after this declaration he presented a copy of Dickens'
Sunshine on Daily Paths to Sue, and much later Mme. Bianchi
reported that Dickens was actually one of the authors that Edward Dickinson preferred.[43] There was a wide selection of Dickens in the family library, and it is likely that Emily read it all,
even though she does not mention five of the nine titles that still
remain in the collection.[44] She makes single references, all in
early letters, to the *Pickwick Papers, The Haunted Man and the
Ghost's Bargain,* and *Bleak House*. Allusions to *David Copperfield, Dombey and Son,* and *The Old Curiosity Shop* appear over
a number of years, and the references to these three novels recur
sufficiently often to substantiate Mme. Bianchi's statement "that
many of the expressions used in [Dickens'] stories became household words." [45] Such expressions rarely occur in the poems; and
in the letters they are addressed only to those close friends and
members of the family who would be certain to grasp their implications. Mrs. Holland, the most frequent recipient of letters
which included Dickensian phrases, was expected to remember

Dombey and Son when Emily described her father's horse as "the 'Cap'n Cuttle' of Amherst" and *David Copperfield* when she wrote that "[Cupid's] affecting toils are not what Mrs Micawber would call 'remunerative.' "[46] Although most such references are transparent, two letters to Samuel Bowles that contain allusions to *The Old Curiosity Shop* are significant. Both were written following calls which Bowles had made at the Dickinson home. He was a frequent visitor, but he was never sure whether or not Emily would appear during his stay. After one visit, when she had preferred not to see Bowles, she wrote:

> Perhaps you thought I did'nt care — because I stayed out, yesterday, I *did* care Mr Bowles. I pray for your sweet health – to "Alla" – every morning – but something troubled me – and I knew you needed light – and air – so I did'nt come.
>
> *   *   *   *   *   *   *   *   *   *   *
>
> This is all that I have to say – Kinsmen need say nothing – but "Swiveller" may be sure of the
>
> "Marchioness." [47]

Dickinson apparently hoped that Bowles's recollection of the faithfulness of the "Marchioness" would be an adequate explanation of her attitude. The second letter followed a similar series of events except that Bowles reportedly responded to Emily's absence by shouting upstairs: "Emily, you damned rascal! No more of this nonsense! I've traveled all the way from Springfield to see you. Come down at once." [48] She came down and was brilliant. She signed her next letter to him "Your 'Rascal' " and included a postscript, "I washed the Adjective." In this case she had in mind Dickens' Mr. Brass, who, we are told in chapter 33 of *The Old Curiosity Shop*, would "Often call Miss Brass a rascal, or even put an adjective before the rascal."

Because Charles Dickens' works were often recalled for Emily in reading, in letters, and in conversation, it was almost inevitable that some of his characters and a few of his phrases should turn up in her poems: Her line "The Bustle in a House" appears as "a bustle in the house" in chapter XIV of *Dombey and Son*, and there the activity is excited by a party at Dr. Blimber's Brighton school where Paul Dombey is a student. Her lines "For whom I robbed the Dingle –/For whom betrayed the Dell –" [49] recall the free supper that Mr. Jingle had at the expense of Mr. Wardle and the Dingley Dell club following their unsuccessful cricket match with Muggleton in chapter VII of *The Pickwick Papers*. The "robbed and betrayed" in the Dickinson context refer to her picking a wild flower as a gift for a friend whose name she will not reveal. In another instance, a Dickens character identifies her poem's subject:

> Trudging to Eden, looking backward,
> I met Somebody's little Boy
> Asked him his name – He lisped me "Trotwood" –
> Lady, did He belong to thee?
>
> Would it comfort – to know I met him –
> And that He did'nt look afraid?
> I could'nt weep – for so many smiling
> New Acquaintance – this Baby made –

Betsey Trotwood was, of course, David Copperfield's aunt, a character from one of the three Dickens novels most often recalled. If, in reading this poem, one takes into account Emily's occasional inversions, the child of the poem can be recognized as her nephew Ned, whom she referred to as "Little Uncle." [50] He was not a robust boy, and the poem's theme and reassuring tone may have been suggested by one of Ned's not infrequent illnesses that had disturbed the family.

Emily herself associated her poem "A poor – torn heart – a tattered heart" with *The Old Curiosity Shop*. She attached to one of the two existing manuscripts of the poem two illustrations clipped from her father's copy of the Dickens novel, and the sense of the poem leads to the conclusion that it was inspired by the image of Little Nell's mourning grandfather, who dies on her grave at the end of chapter LXXI of the book.[51]

One poem interestingly related to Dickens, is the widely anthologized "I like to see it lap the Miles," Emily Dickinson's social satire concerned with the railway train. Various sources have been suggested for the first line of the final stanza in which the locomotive is said to "neigh like Boanerges –." One of those suggested is Cotton Mather's "Boanerges, A Short Essay to strengthen the impressions Produced by Earthquakes," but only the title offers any connection with the poem, and there is no evidence that Emily was aware of even that. The usual annotation of the poem refers the reader to Mark 3:17, a verse in which Christ surnames two of his disciples Boanerges, the sons of thunder. This analogue, while it may be the ultimate source, is still not entirely suitable. Dickens' *The Uncommercial Traveller* (1861) offers a more credible allusion. In chapter IX, "City of London Churches," the author describes his reluctance to attend a sermon to be delivered by a ranting preacher named Boanerges Boiler:

I have in my day been . . . carried off highly charged with saponaceous electricity, to be steamed like a potato in the unventilated breath of the powerful Boanerges Boiler . . . at this present writing I hear his lumbering jocularity . . . , and I behold his big round face, and I look up the inside of his outstretched coat-sleeve as if it were a telescope with the stopper on, and I hate him with an unwholesome hatred for two hours.

The Dickinson poem is not unwholesome hatred, but the character of Boanerges Boiler nicely complements a description, which she read earlier in *The Springfield Republican*, of the individuality of locomotives. These two sources seemed to have combined in Dickinson's imagination to give her the images necessary to express effectively her feelings regarding the impositions of mechanization and modern technology.

Charles Dickens, the Brontës, and George Eliot were not the only nineteenth-century British novelists that Emily Dickinson read. Her letters indicate that there were a number of others. The earliest was Jane Porter. Emily's father owned a copy of Miss Porter's *Thaddeus of Warsaw*, a book that he had autographed "E. Dickinson 1827." Sometime later "& Miss E. Dickinson" was added in pencil to his inscription. Two passages in the book were marked in the margin, again with pencil. One reads, "I feel as if love sat upon my heart, and flapped it with his wings"; the other, "Frightened love, like a wild beast shakes the wood in which it hides." [52] The extravagant nature of these passages suggests that she may have read this book about the same time she read Ik Marvel's *Dream Life*, for the Marvel book repeatedly recommends *Thaddeus of Warsaw* as a novel that every well-read young lady ought to know. Emily also read a translation of Saintine's *Picciola* during the winter of 1848; and, while she was still a student at Mount Holyoke, she read two short novels by Martin Tupper, *The Twins* and *The Heart*. Her copy of Tupper's *Proverbial Philosophy*, signed "E. Dickinson, 1846," is in the Harvard Collection. The volume is filled with platitudinous epigrams; and, in the chapters enumerating the virtues of "Writing" and "Solitude," these lines have been marked:

> And shouldst thou ask my judgment of
>   that which hath most profit in the world,
> For answer take thou this, the prudent
>   penning of a letter
>
> *   *   *   *   *   *   *   *
>
> Reading is an unremembered pastime;
>   but a writing is eternal;
>
> For mind hath its influence on mind;
>   and no man is free but when alone,
>
> *   *   *   *   *   *   *

99

He that dwelleth mainly by himself,
  heedeth most of others
But they that live in crowds, think
  chiefly of themselves.

Such thoughts would have appealed to her, and she first read them in her formative years. If she was the person who marked these passages, the date of the marking is not so important as the fact that the ideas were impressive enough for her to mark them at the first reading or for her to reread the book and mark them at a later date. Beyond Tupper, other minor nineteenth-century British novelists whom she read further confirm her preference for women writers. In the spring of 1852 she read Mathilde Mackarness' *Only* and *A House upon a Rock*, Dinah Maria Craik's *Olive* and *Head of a Family*, and Georgiana Fullerton's *Ellen Middleton*. She read Charles Kingsley's *Hypatia*, and *Yeast*, and made a passing reference to *Vanity Fair's* Captain Dobbin in an 1858 letter to Sue; but, in general, from about 1850 to 1880 there is little evidence of her interest in any English novelists other than Eliot, the Brontës, and Dickens. At Christmas 1880, Sue presented her with a copy of Disraeli's *Endymion*, and in 1883 both Emily and Lavinia read the melodramatic *The Story of Ida*,[53] a short novel by Francesca Alexander with a preface and notes by John Ruskin.

One of the last novels she comments upon, and perhaps one of the last she read, was Hugh Conway's (Frederick John Fargus) *Called Back*. In January 1885, she wrote to the Norcross sisters, "A friend sent me *Called Back*. It is a haunting story, and as loved Mr. Bowles used to say, 'greatly impressive to me.'" Fifteen months later what was probably her last letter was sent to the same address; it contained only these words: "Little Cousins, Called Back." [54] And in the Dickinson family plot in the Amherst cemetery, repeated on the headstone which Emily's niece erected at her grave, is the inscription: "Called Back."

❧ V ❧

American Reading:
Colonial and Contemporary

Hawthorne appalls, entices – . . . but of Howells
and James, one hesitates –
— *Emily Dickinson to T. W. Higginson, 1879*

Like any other reader of nineteenth-century American literature, Emily Dickinson was confronted with a flood of works of
varying quality and found her situation aggravated by criticism
that was often misleading or unacceptable. But, far more than
the ordinary reader, she was aware of the currents in the literary
waters. Amherst was near enough to Boston and Cambridge for
her to feel the influence of the major writers of the time. Emerson lectured in Amherst and visited in Austin Dickinson's home;
both Samuel Bowles and Dr. Holland, two of her closest friends,
were writers and critics; and in later years Colonel Higginson
and Mrs. Jackson provided additional, active contacts with the
literary world. Although she belonged to no coterie, she was
nonetheless an interested observer of the activities of the other
writers of her era. Some of the best periodicals of the time came
to the homestead, and their pages were filled with contemporary
pieces that she carefully read. For these reasons, Emily Dickinson was not, as has often been implied, isolated from the main-
stream of nineteenth-century American letters. A consideration
of the two categories of American works that she read in her

formative years contributes to a clearer picture of the background of her mature reading. The first is that limited amount of writing of the colonial period that she knew, and the second is the series of textbooks that she used at Amherst Academy and Mount Holyoke.

When one considers the devout, conservative atmosphere of Amherst, it is surprising that the religious writings of colonial America formed such a small part of Emily Dickinson's reading. She did have the benefit of Watts's *Psalms and Hymns* that had been standard fare in churches for nearly a century, but there is no evidence of her having been exposed to the writings of such authors as Nathaniel Ward, Cotton Mather, or Jonathan Edwards, even though she was aware of Edwards, as this note to Gilbert Dickinson implies:

"All Liars shall have their part" –
Jonathan Edwards –
"And let him who is athirst come" –
Jesus –[1]

In Amherst she could hear sermons delivered in the Edwards tradition almost any Sunday. T. H. Johnson notes that

she would probably have been surprised to know that the quatrain she wrote in the late seventies [P 1474] is a twenty-word summary of Edwards' thoughts on the subject [of beauty and immortality], expressed one hundred and twenty years before in his greatest essay, *The Nature of True Virtue.*[2]

There were a few selections from other colonial writers available in the family library in Griswold's anthology, *Gems from the American Poets*; in addition, Edward Dickinson owned a two-volume set of Benjamin Franklin's essays and letters. But if Emily read these she was not sufficiently impressed either to note having done so or to quote from them. One traditional book, *The New England Primer*, did maintain its place, however. She knew it as a child and occasionally referred to it as an adult: in 1850 she clipped the illustration for the letter "X" ("Xerxes did die/And so must I") from a copy that belonged to her father and fastened it to a verse she sent to William Cowper Dickinson; almost ten years later she used the illustration for "T" ("Young Timothy/Learnt sin to fly") to decorate a short note she had written to Sue.[3] The copy of the primer from which these were taken and from which "C" ("Christ crucified") has also been removed is in the Harvard Collection.

The textbooks that Emily Dickinson used in Amherst and South Hadley are the earliest significant group of American works that she read. They can hardly be classified as "vigorous American prose" because most of them were merely British books reworked by editors in Boston, Philadelphia, and New York; and the texts that Emily studied had been in print for a number of years before she first encountered them in the 1840's. There is no record of the books she used in her early years at Amherst Academy; and, aside from *The New England Primer*, none of the juvenile books that remain in the family library are ones that she might have read as a small child. There are in the collection, however, two books that she studied while preparing to enter Mount Holyoke. One of these is an algebra text that belonged to Austin, and the other is a Latin book, later used by Lavinia. Because the Mount Holyoke catalogue was very specific in prescribing subjects to be mastered by prospective students and because of Emily's eagerness "to be upon the safe side of things"[4] when she arrived in South Hadley, she probably studied the recommended books very carefully. The catalogue listed these "Studies Required for Admission to the Seminary":

A good knowledge of Wells' English Grammar, with an ability to apply the principles in analyzing and parsing, and of Modern Geography, and a readiness in Mental Arithmetic. . . . Adams' New Arithmetic and Greenleaf's are particularly recommended. A good knowledge of Mitchell's Ancient Geography, of Andrews' and

Stoddard's Latin Grammar, and Andrews' Latin Reader, of the History of the United States, and of Watts on the Mind is also required.[5]

The last of the required books, Watts's *Improvement of the Mind* was a small volume designed

to unfold and invigorate the faculties; to store the mind with the most useful knowledge . . . ; to subject every power, thought and pursuit, to the empire of reason; . . . in short, to prepare the mortal and immortal part of our nature, for the greatest possible usefulness and enjoyment both here and forever.[6]

The portion of this all-encompassing and worthy goal most relevant to the study of Emily Dickinson's reading is the stated intention of attempting "to store the mind with the most useful knowledge." The book's longest chapters are devoted to "enlarging the capacity of mind" and "improving the memory." The "Hints for the Teaching of Watts on the Mind" printed on the back of the title page recommend that students read the text three times, commit to memory the answers to the scores of detailed questions, and "after two or three years . . . go through the course again." One would like to think that Emily Dickinson conformed at least partially to this procedure and that, in the process, she learned Watts's advice to aspiring poets, which was included in the same volume:

If the question were offered me, "Shall a bright genius never divert himself with writing poesy?" I would answer, "Yes, when he cannot possibly help it.". . . But there may be seasons, when it is hardly possible for a poetic soul to . . . prevent the imagination from this sort of style or language. That is the only season, I think, wherein this inclination should be indulged.[7]

Whether she studied Watts's treatise or not, Emily Dickinson was subject in her formal schooling to an educational philosophy that placed great emphasis on repeated readings and the memorizing of vast quantities of detail, a fact that accounts in some measure for her extensive vocabulary and for her unusual variety of metaphor.

Her academic preparation for Mount Holyoke seems to have been adequate. During her stay she did not find her studies easy, but there never seems to have been any indication that she could not meet the seminary's standards. She had recited Latin and German [8] at Amherst Academy, and her Latin was good enough when she entered Mount Holyoke to excuse her from courses in the "Philosophy of Natural History" and "Ecclesiastical History." Her letters contain references to all Junior Class studies except these, which were "not strictly required of those who have a good knowledge of Latin." [9] Although one or two of her early poems contain some Latin words and phrases, she soon neglected the language; and in the spring of 1852 after calling herself a "Femina Insania" in a letter to Sue, she confessed, "I made up the Latin—Susie, for I could'nt think how it went, according to Stoddard and Andrew!" [10] Some other basic subjects were more enduring than her Latin. She seems to recall terms from geometry and botany with ease, and they are fairly common in her poems; but algebra, like the Latin and German, was abandoned for more compatible interests.

> Life set me larger—problems—
> Some I shall keep—to solve
> Till Algebra is easier—
> Or simpler proved—above—[11]

Parts of a few of her textbooks at Mount Holyoke can be related more directly to her poetry. In considering these sources one should remember that she probably never reread her texts and that a period of several years intervened between the study in South Hadley and the writing of the poems in Amherst. Her astronomy text [12] was filled with information credited to Herschel (both father and son), whom she recalls in "Nature and God – I neither knew"; and the same textbook is also the possible source of a number of technical terms that occur in such stanzas as:

> Enchantment's Perihelion
> Mistaken oft has been
> For the Authentic orbit
> Of it's Anterior Sun.[13]

Some of Emily Dickinson's favorite place names appear in groups in Professor Hitchcock's *Elementary Geology*, another of her Mount Holyoke texts. One table lists "the height of a few of the most elevated mountains of the globe . . . Himmalayah, E. Indies; Chimborazo, Andes; Ararat"; another shows the world's important volcanoes: "Vesuvius, Etna, Popocatapetl, Teneriffe"; and in a third, "The *Diamond* [is] associated with . . . Golconda, India, and . . . Brazil." If she applied Watts's methods of study, she committed these items to memory. Each chapter had a new series of terms to be learned; and among other details, she found that "when pure, [marl] is white and as light as the carbonate of magnesia," a definition that may account for her association of "marl" with frost, in the poem that begins, "A Visitor in Marl –/Who influences Flowers."

Newman's *Practical System of Rhetoric*, which introduced her to Sir Thomas Browne, was filled with short examples of English masters, ranging from Sir Thomas Malory to John Dryden. Some of the selections that she studied in this text appear to have supplied, at a much later date, bits of material for a few of her poems. The opening lines of "I started Early – Took my Dog –/And visited the Sea –" introduce a seaside setting which Emily Dickinson never knew, one which reflects this passage that Newman quoted from Gray's letters:

I set out one morning before five o'clock, the moon shining through the dark and misty autumnal air, and got to the seacoast, in time to be at the sun's levee. I saw the clouds and dark vapors open gradually to the right and left, rolling over one another in great smoke wreaths, and the tide (as it glowed in on the sands) first whitening, and then slightly tinged with gold and blue, and all at once a little line of insufferable brightness, that before I can write these five words is grown to half an orb, and now a whole one, too glorious to be distinctly seen.[14]

The description of the obscuring vapors and Gray's concluding phrase also bring to mind these Dickinson lines:

> The thought beneath so slight a film –
> Is more distinctly seen –
> As laces just reveal the surge –
> Or Mists – the Appenine –

And, in discussing proper transitions in composition, Newman offered this analysis of an example from Goldsmith's *Traveller*:

His [Goldsmith's] description of Italy closes with the mention of its inhabitants, feeble and degraded, pleased with low delights and the sports of children. The transition to the Swiss is thus made:
  My soul, turn from them; turn we to survey
  Where rougher climes a nobler race display.
The principle on which the transition is here made, is that of contrast. And since the mind is often wont to look at objects as opposed to each other, it naturally in this way passes from the Italians to the Swiss.[15]

About 1859, before her good friends Dr. Holland and Samuel Bowles had gone to Europe and reported their travels, and before she had demonstrated active interest in Mrs. Browning's Italy, Emily Dickinson wrote:

> Our lives are Swiss –
> So still – so Cool –
> Till some odd afternoon
> The Alps neglect their Curtains
> And we look farther on!

> *Italy* stands the other side!
> While like a guard between –
> The solemn Alps –
> The siren Alps
> Forever intervene!

The Mount Holyoke textbook most directly related to specific poems and references is one of Emily's Junior Class histories, Worcester's *Elements of History, Ancient and Modern*. Recalling the Greek heroism against the Persians, she begins a letter, "How martial the Apology of Nature! We die, said the Deathless of Thermopylae, in obedience to Law." [16] One of her poems begins with an oblique allusion to the same battle: "Too scanty 'twas to die for you/The merest Greek could that." This latter reference could have come from either Worcester's *Elements* or Goldsmith's *Grecian History*, which she also studied, but the detail of death in obedience to law, omitted by Goldsmith, is included in Worcester's account, which concludes with these two sentences: "Two only of the Spartans . . . survived the battle. A monument was erected on the spot, bearing this inscription, written by Simonides: 'O stranger! tell it at Lacedaemon, that we died here in obedience to her laws.'" [17] Emily Dickinson had that epitaph in mind when she wrote:

> "Go tell it" – What a Message –
> To whom – is specified –
> Not murmur – not endearment –
> But simply – we – obeyed –
> Obeyed – a Lure – a Longing?
> Oh Nature – none of this –
> To Law – said sweet Thermopylae
> I give my dying Kiss –

She recalled the battle again in these lines:

It feels a shame to be Alive –
When Men so brave – are dead –
One envies the Distinguished Dust –
Permitted – such a Head –

The Stone – that tells defending Whom
The Spartan put away
What little of Him we – possessed
In Pawn for Liberty –

The source of this last stanza is more certainly Worcester, in that
she mentions specifically not only the epitaph but the monument
as well.

Worcester also provided at least one bit of English history
that Emily Dickinson used in the poems. She relied on her
memory for his account of the death of the Earl of Essex in
writing:

Elizabeth told Essex
That she could not forgive
The clemency of Deity
However – might survive –
That secondary succor
We trust that she partook
When suing – like her Essex
For a reprieving Look –

This is the Worcester version:

The earl was at last convicted of high treason, and beheaded. While
under sentence of death, he sent, by the countess of Nottingham,
to Elizabeth, a ring, which she had given him, with an assurance
that the sight of it, in any momentous crisis, would recall her ten-
derness. The countess neglected to deliver it; and when on her death-
bed, sent for the queen to inform her of the fact. Elizabeth in a
frenzy of passion, shook the dying countess, exclaiming; "God may
forgive you, but I never can." [18]

At first reading, it appears that Emily has confused some histori-
cal details by addressing Elizabeth's speech to Essex rather than
to the culpable Countess of Nottingham. The final lines, however, make it seem more likely that the Elizabeth of the poem
is speaking to Essex's shade and that in Emily Dickinson's judgment the unforgiving Elizabeth, when she came to die, could
rely only on the clemency of God.

Emily seems to have remembered the account of the Battle of
Quebec from Worcester's chapter on United States history, and
to have had it in mind when she ended a letter to Higginson:
"Abroad is close tonight and I have but to lift my Hands to
touch the 'Hights of Abraham.'" [19] In this same account of the
battle she found the basis of a poem on the deaths of Wolfe and
Montcalm.

Wolfe, having received a fatal wound, was carried to the rear. . . .
Faint with the loss of blood, and his eyes dimmed by the approach
of death, he was roused at the words, "They fly, they fly." "Who
fly?" he exclaimed. He was told, "The enemy." "Then," said the
hero, "I die contented;" and having said this, he expired in the moment of victory. . . . The same military enthusiasm animated *Montcalm*. Being told that he could not continue more than a few hours,
he said, "It is so much better; I shall not then live to see the surrender of Quebec." [20]

In the three extant manuscript versions of her poem, there are
enough variations in the wording of the dialogue to indicate
that she was not attempting to recall the words of the source; but
in all three, the details agree with the passage from Worcester's
Elements. Her poem reads:

> Wolfe demanded during dying
> "Which obtain the Day"?
> "General, the British" — "Easy"
> Answered Wolfe "to die"

Montcalm his opposing Spirit
Rendered with a smile
"Sweet" said he "my own Surrender
Liberty's beguile"

Textbooks and eighteenth-century works were but a small percentage of the total volume of American literature that Emily Dickinson knew. Most of the American works that she read were written during her lifetime, and she read them soon after they appeared. Her general reading in newspapers and periodicals is discussed in Chapter VI, but those nineteenth-century authors who merit individual attention are considered here in related groups of poets and prose writers.

The family library contained collections of poems by Bryant, Emerson, Longfellow, Whittier, and others, along with Rufus Griswold's ponderous anthology, *Gems from the American Poets*.[21] The earliest American poems to appear in her letters are Fitz-Greene Halleck's "Marco Bozzaris" and "On the Death of Joseph Rodman Drake." From the first of these she takes two elegiac passages: one to describe the cemetery at Mount Auburn as a spot where "wearied & disappointed [Nature's children may] stretch themselves . . . & close their eyes 'calmly as to a nights repose of flowers at set of sun'"; and the other to comment on the death of Frazar Stearns, "brave Frazer . . . 'We conquered, but Bozzaris fell.'"[22] Lines from the first stanza of the elegy on Drake, "None knew thee but to love thee,/Nor named thee but to praise," are recalled in a letter in which Emily describes Mrs. Carmichael as one "whom 'to name is to praise.'" These two poems were apparently the only ones from Halleck that she knew well. She seems, however, to have been familiar with a more considerable number from William Cullen Bryant. In adding her voice to the tune which "Autumn poets sing,"[23] she cites the harvest sheaves of James Thomson's *The Seasons* and the goldenrod that Bryant describes in "My Autumn Walk" and "The Death of the Flowers." Elsewhere she quotes from "Thanatopsis" and "June"; and the inspired certainty that Bryant offers in "To a Waterfowl" seems to be restated in these Dickinson lines:

> These tested Our Horizon –
> Then disappeared
> As Birds before achieving
> A Latitude.
>
> Our Retrospection of Them
> A fixed Delight,
> But our Anticipation
> A Dice – a Doubt –

In Sue's volume of Bryant's poems, a copy that Emily may very well have shared, pages folded from left to right mark "Thanatopsis," "To Cole, the Painter, Departing for Europe," and "The Death of the Flowers." In the last of these three poems, the margin of the "goldenrod" stanza is, in addition, lined in pencil. A short note signed "Cole" and sent by Emily to Sue suggests that Bryant's poem on Cole's departure may have had some passing significance between the two, particularly in light of this explanation added by Mme. Bianchi: "Sent over the morning after a revel — when my Grandfather with his lantern appeared suddenly to take Emily home the hour nearing indecent midnight." [24]

Emily Dickinson never completely abandoned the conservative Puritan ethic under which she was reared, but the proximity of Concord and the contagious nature of Transcendental thought exposed her to liberal, Romantic doctrines. She liked Bryant, but some of the later poetry of New England seems to have affected her more deeply. She was moved by Emerson and Thoreau, yet never lost her grip on reality. When she took a line from Channing and incorporated it into a poem of her own, she added a qualification. She was, according to Henry Wells, "the only person in America who really made Transcendentalism practical." [25] The poem with the line from Channing reads,

If my Bark sink
'Tis to another sea –
Mortality's Ground Floor
Is Immortality –

Its first two lines may not have come directly from Channing, for she may have picked them up from Emerson, who used "If my bark sink, 'tis to another sea," to conclude his essay on Montaigne. This is quite possible because, of all American authors whom she read, Emily Dickinson can be most closely associated with Ralph Waldo Emerson.

There is no indication that she heard any of the lectures that Emerson delivered in Amherst or that she met him in December 1857 when he was entertained in the house next door by Sue and Austin. Ben Newton, whom she called her "gentle, yet grave Preceptor," gave her a copy of the 1847 edition of Emerson's *Poems*, in which he had marked those poems he considered best. This volume is among the Dickinson books at Harvard, and opposite five titles in the "Table of Contents" are dark "X's" found in no other book in the collection. Newton marked these poems: "Each and All," "The Problem," "Goodbye," "Woodnotes I," and "Dirge." It should not be surprising that Emily regarded this volume highly, for it was recommended by the tutor who, according to her own estimate, had taught her "what to read, [and] what authors to admire." [26] She was only nineteen when she received this parting gift from Newton, and there is every indication that the early impressions made by Emerson's poetry were lasting ones which she renewed in her reading and which reappear frequently in her writing. In fact, "Success," the only one of her poems published widely enough in her lifetime to attract the attention of critics, was generally attributed to Emerson. [27] Whicher concludes a chapter-long comparison of Emerson and Dickinson by first conceding, "It is easy to find passages that might belong to either writer," and then deciding that "the resemblance in style, like that in substance, is not due to imitation, but to the fact that both poets were sprung from the same soil and never lost their kinship with the earth." [28]

Richard Chase suggests that "the term 'scholar' may have been made resonant for her by the essays of Emerson," [29] and in the Emersonian sense of the word she was indeed the scholar of the "Sage of Concord." In the gift copy of *Poems*, there are, in addition to the "X's" left by Newton, marks that appear to have been made by another hand, probably Emily's. They are the familiar light pencil lines, like those found in other books she used. There are seven poems with these marginal markings: "The Sphinx," "Each and All," "The Problem," "To Rhea," "The Visit," "The Rhodora," and "Woodnotes I." She read these and Emerson's other works attentively but did not accept his philosophy without question. From his essay on "Nature" she recalled that "the power to produce [Transcendental] delight does not reside in nature, but in man," and wrote:

> The "Tune is the Tree –"
> The Skeptic – showeth me –
> "No Sir! In Thee!" [30]

But, when she was tempted to flights of Transcendental ecstasy, her orthodox mores raised such a question as "With the Kingdom of Heaven on his knee, could Mr Emerson hesitate?" and a faith more traditional than Transcendental gave the restraining answer of the Christian believer: "Suffer little Children." [31] She could investigate the imagination with Emerson, but her traditional faith and ties enabled her to discipline the explorations. This slight restriction in no way prevented her assimilation of potentially useful ideas and imagery from Emerson's writings. His phrases appear in her poems and letters just as do Burns's and Browning's. A case in point is the unmistakable resemblance which "I taste a liquor never brewed" bears to Emerson's "Bacchus." "Bacchus" begins "Bring me wine, but wine which never grew/In the belly of the grape." Dickinson's poem reads:

I taste a liquor never brewed –
From Tankards scooped in Pearl –
Not all the Frankfort Berries
Yield such an Alcohol!

Inebriate of Air – am I –
And Debauchee of Dew –
Reeling – thro endless summer days –
From inns of Molten Blue –

When "Landlords" turn the drunken Bee
Out of the Foxglove's door –
When Butterflies – renounce their "drams" –
I shall but drink the more!

Till Seraphs swing their snowy Hats –
And Saints – to windows run –
To see the little Tippler
From Manzanilla come!

There are other minor similarities beyond the two poems' first lines, but the Emerson sources of this Dickinson poem are not quite so simple. It is equally related to "The Poet," the first of Emerson's *Essays: Second Series*.[32] These are the pertinent paragraphs from the essay:

The poet knows that he speaks adequately then only when he speaks somewhat wildly . . . not with the intellect alone but with the intellect inebriated by nectar. . . .

This is the reason why bards love wine, . . . or . . . other procurers of animal exhilaration. . . . These are auxiliaries to the centrifugal tendency of a man, to his passage out into free space, and they help him to escape the custody of that body in which he is pent up . . . The sublime vision comes to the pure and simple soul in a clean and chaste body. . . . the lyric poet may drink wine and live generously . . . for poetry is not "Devil's wine," but God's wine.

If the imagination intoxicates the poet, it is not inactive in other men . . . The use of symbols has a certain power of emancipation . . . We seem to be touched by a want which makes us dance and run about happily, like children.

Here Emerson has characterized the poet as a liberating god whose principal weapon is symbolism. And in the Dickinson family's copy of *Essays: Second Series*, this portion of the discussion of symbolism in "The Poet" has been marked:

Day and night, house and garden, a few books, a few actions, serve us well as would all trades and all spectacles. We are far from having exhausted the significance of the few symbols we use. We can use them yet with a terrible simplicity. It does not need that a poem be long. Every word was once a poem. Every new relation is a new word.

Ben Newton would have been proud of the degree to which Emily applied these and other teachings from the author whom he had recommended for study, for Emily remembered them well. Her "Beauty – be not caused – It Is –" recalls "Then Beauty is its own excuse for being," from Emerson's "Rhodora," one of the poems he marked. Another of her poems is filled with distinct echoes of part I of his essay "Nature."

> "Nature" is what we see –
> The Hill – the Afternoon –
> Squirrel – Eclipse – the Bumble bee –
> Nay – Nature is Heaven –
> Nature is what we hear –
> The Bobolink – the Sea –
> Thunder – the Cricket –
> Nay – Nature is Harmony –
> Nature is what we know –
> Yet have no art to say –
> So omnipotent Our Wisdom is
> To her Simplicity

The metaphors of this poem are a list of favorite Emerson subjects, and the elusiveness of natural beauty that Emily Dickinson points out in the final lines suggests another of her poems related to the same essay.

> Go not too near a House of Rose –
> The depredation of a Breeze
> Or inundation of a Dew
> Alarm it's walls away –
> Nor try to tie the Butterfly,
> Nor climb the Bars of Ecstasy,
> In security to lie
> Is Joy's insuring quality.

In "Nature," Emerson had written:

But this beauty of Nature which is seen and felt as beauty, is the least part. The shows of day, the dewy morning, the rainbow, mountains, orchards in blossom . . . if too eagerly hunted, become shows merely, and mock us with their unreality. . . . The beauty that shimmers in the yellow afternoons of October, who ever could clutch it? Go forth to find it, and it is gone.

Essays: First and Second Series were not the only prose works by Emerson that Emily Dickinson knew well. She thought highly enough of his *Representative Men* to recommend it to Mrs. Higginson as a "little Granite Book you can lean upon," [33] and certain of Emerson's other works had special appeal. Bees fascinated her, and she quoted from Emerson's "The Humble-Bee" three times; but "she connected the bee with processes a good deal more darkly fated than did Emerson." [34]

She sent her love to Mrs. Holland's household with this allusion to Emerson's "Fable": "Remember me to your Possessions, in whom I have a tender claim, and take care of the small Life, fervor has made great — deathless as Emerson's 'Squirrel.'" [35] The following poem recalls the same account of the argument between the mountain and the squirrel, which ends with the squirrel's rejoinder, "If I cannot carry forests on my back,/ Neither can you crack a nut." In addition, in her second stanza, "compensation" is used in the favorite Emersonian sense of the word.

> Light is sufficient to itself –
> If Others want to see
> It can be had on Window Panes
> Some Hours in the Day.
>
> But not for Compensation –
> It holds as large a Glow
> To Squirrel in the Himmaleh
> Precisely, as to you.

In mid-winter 1884 Emily transcribed the phrase "Tumultuous privacy of storm" from Emerson's "The Snow-Storm," and enclosed it in a letter that Lavinia was sending to Mrs. Todd.[36] Earlier, she had recalled his snow that seemed "nowhere to alight" in writing this winter piece of her own:

> Peace is a fiction of our Faith –
> The Bells a Winter Night
> Bearing the Neighbor out of Sound
> That never did alight.

She was conscious of her fondness for Emerson's writings and of her frequent use of Emerson quotations in letters, yet she seems to have been unaware of the way in which the poetic materials that she gleaned from him reappeared in her own verse. Propinquity and environment did cause Dickinson to be susceptible to Emerson's attitudes; but her reading provides a sounder basis for the explanation of their relationship than does Massachusetts soil and New England atmosphere.

Emily Dickinson's readings from Emerson probably included the biographical sketch of Thoreau that he wrote for *The Atlantic Monthly* for August 1862, two months after Thoreau died. She makes no reference to it nor does she ever mention any specific writings of Thoreau; yet she gives evidence of more than passing familiarity with Thoreau in this comment in a letter to the Norcross sisters: "The fire bells are oftener now, almost, than the church-bells. Thoreau would wonder which did the most harm." [37] This is one of the two occasions that she mentions Thoreau, but perhaps her feeling for him was stronger than her letters indicate. After Emily died, Mrs. Ellen E. Dickinson published a short recollection of her cousin in several newspapers. It included this comment:

Thoreau was naturally one of [Emily's] favorite authors from his love of nature and power of description in that direction. On one occasion when a lady recently introduced in the family by marriage quoted some sentences from Thoreau's writings, Miss Dickinson recognizing it hastened to press her visitor's hand as she said, "From this time we are acquainted"; and this was the beginning of a friendship that lasted till the death of the poetess. [38]

Of other Transcendentalists, Emily Dickinson read very little. She may have read Margaret Fuller's translation of *Gunderode* not long after it appeared in 1842, and in 1859 she was introduced to the writing of Theodore Parker. Her comment on the latter was "I never read before what Mr Parker wrote. I heard he was 'poison.' Then I like poison very well." [39] If she liked it well enough to seek more, she did not comment on what she found. Her principal interest in Emerson seems not to have been Transcendentalism but unencumbered ideas that she could detach from his essays and poetry.

Although Emerson provides the strongest and most direct connection between Emily Dickinson's verse and nineteenth-century American literature, Longfellow is the poet whom she quoted most frequently. The variety of his lines which she found conveniently suited to her letters indicates that she read *Kavanagh*, *The Courtship of Miles Standish*, *Evangeline*, and an assortment of shorter pieces. But in only one of her poems is there a clear relation to any of Longfellow's work. In it she took irreverent delight in an analogy that compared Christ and John Alden; and when this poem was published in 1891, it was condemned by some as a "contemptuous bit of Unitarianism." [40]

> God is a distant – stately Lover –
> Woos, as He states us – by His Son –
> Verily, a Vicarious Courtship –
> "Miles", and "Priscilla", were such an One –
>
> But, lest the Soul – like fair "Priscilla"
> Choose the Envoy – and spurn the Groom –
> Vouches, with hyperbolic archness –
> "Miles", and "John Alden" were Synonyme –

Emily Dickinson could find little use for Lowell or Holmes, though she read selections from each. She remembered the "sweet despair" of Lowell's "After the Burial," and decided after reading his "A Good Word for Winter" that "one does not often meet anything so perfect." She read his *Among My Books*, gave a copy of *My Study Windows* to Sue,[41] and doubtlessly encountered a number of Lowell poems and articles in magazines and newspapers, but she does not comment on them. The case of Holmes is very similar. James Kimball gave her a volume of Holmes's poems in 1849, but they failed to impress her, and she appears to have given Holmes little attention other than her reading of his biography of Emerson, published the year before she died. Insofar as contributing imagery or ideas to her poetry, Lowell and Holmes seem to have been read and rejected.

There were some poets whom she refused to read. Whitman she considered "disgraceful." In a letter to Higginson she dismissed Joaquin Miller with "I did not read Mr Miller because I could not care about him." Poe is a bit different; of him, she wrote, "I know too little to think." [42] She may have read one volume of Poe in the 1850's, for in August of that year she wrote to Henry

Emmons to thank him for the gift of an unidentified book, and her note reads in part: "I find it Friend – I read it . . . I thank you for them all – the pearl, and then the onyx, and then the emerald stone." Mrs. Aurelia Scott suspects a cryptic message in the first letters of the three gems: they spell "Poe." [43] This is the nearest one comes to concrete evidence that Emily Dickinson read Edgar Allan Poe.

Some odd bits of contemporary American poetry struck Emily's fancy. She read George P. Lathrop's "The Child's Wish Granted" and called it "piteously sweet," copied all ten six-line stanzas of John Pierpont's "My Child" in a letter to Mary Warner, and told Austin that, while Alexander Smith's poems pleased her very much, she would not judge them until she read them a second time. Occasionally she acquired lines that later proved to be useful raw materials. In an early letter to Abiah Root, she asked, "Have you seen a beautiful piece of poetry which has been going through the papers lately? *Are we almost there?* is the title of it." [44] These five lines from the poem, which was written by Florence Vane, recall the same slow approach of death that Dickinson describes in "I heard a Fly buzz – when I died –"

> "Are we almost there? are we almost there?"
> Said a dying girl, as she drew near home . . .
>
> *   *   *   *   *   *   *   *
>
> For when the light of that eye was gone,
> And the quick pulse stopped
> She was almost there.[45]

On the whole, Emily Dickinson found the poetry and prose of American authors less attractive than that of the British writers of the Romantic and Victorian periods. Aside from her interest in Emerson and Higginson, she showed none of the sustained enthusiasm for American prose writers that she showed for the Brontës, Dickens, and Eliot. Perhaps she was surfeited by the volume and exuberance of the American prose. This problem was made more perplexing by her awareness of her own critical ineptitude and by the fact that the critical standards set by her friends were confusing at best. Higginson, for example, had recommended Whitman, yet Dr. Holland called him "scandalous." [46] The reputed quality of other emerging writers was equally uncertain; as a consequence, Emily Dickinson's reading of nineteenth-century American prose, like her reading of nineteenth-century American poetry, was wide and, for the most part, unselective.

There is slight evidence in her letters of her having read Washington Irving: a single reference to "Rip Van Winkle." [47] But it is safe to assume that she read his biography of Christopher Columbus, for neither she nor Lavinia would neglect a book recommended by Austin. Writing from Harvard, he advised: "I don't think of anything I know that would interest you like Irving's 'Life of Columbus.' I'll bring that and anything else I fancy you would like." [48] Her awareness of Columbus' life in the Indies offers a plausible explanation of the word "Bobadilo" in the following poem:

> I could bring You Jewels – had I a mind to –
> But You have enough – of those –
> I could bring You Odors from St Domingo –
> Colors – from Vera Cruz –
>
> Berries of the Bahamas – have I –
> But this little Blaze
> Flickering to itself – in the Meadow –
> Suits Me – more than those –
>
> Never a Fellow matched this Topaz –
> And his Emerald Swing –
> Dower itself – for Bobadilo –
> Better – Could I bring?

The Johnson edition lists "Bobadilo" among the place names, but the only place with such a name is Bobadilla, an obscure hamlet in Andalusia. The name in the poem seems rather to be an allusion to Francisco Bobadilla, the tyrannical Spaniard who replaced Columbus as governor of the Indies and returned him to Spain in irons. Irving's account states that, after Columbus was imprisoned, Bobadilla appropriated a vast amount of treasure, only part of which was sent back to Spain. Thus, wealth equal to a dower for Bobadilla would be extensive indeed. This explanation of "Bobadilo" is complementary to the other references to wealth and the Indies and to the fact that the poem was written to accompany a bouquet of jewelweed.

Evidence of Emily Dickinson's having read Nathaniel Hawthorne is only slightly more substantial than the evidence of her having read Washington Irving. There is only one reference to a specific Hawthorne work, an allusion to *The House of Seven Gables*. Yet, when Hawthorne died she took specific notice of the fact, a recognition she reserved for favorite authors such as Elizabeth Barrett Browning, Charlotte Brontë, and George Eliot. She was familiar enough with Hawthorne as a writer that, in reacting to Higginson's critical sketch in *Short Studies of American Authors*, she could sum up her own opinion with characteristic brevity: "—Hawthorne appalls, entices—." [49]

In the early 1850's Susan, Lavinia, and Emily were agog over the sentimental fantasies of Ik Marvel (Donald Grant Mitchell). His *Reveries of a Bachelor* was filled with romantic musings that fascinated young feminine readers. In October 1851, Emily wrote Sue: "Perhaps we would have a 'Reverie' after the form of 'Ik Marvel,' . . . Do you know that charming man is dreaming *again*, and will wake pretty soon — so the papers say, with *another* Reverie — more beautiful than the first?" [50] But when *Dream Life*, the next of Mitchell's books appeared, the enchantment was gone. It was filled with chatty, confidential references to the familiar Peter Parley books, *Thaddeus of Warsaw*, and the verse of Dr. Watts and Mrs. Hemans; and, though Emily found in it "the very sweetest fancies," she concluded it was "not near so great a book as 'Reveries of a Bachelor.'"[51] Her reading of the second revery, one entitled "By the City Grate," may account for her use of the word "anthracite" in a poem which begins:

> More Life – went out – when He went
> Than Ordinary Breath –
> Lit with a finer Phosphor –
> Requiring in the Quench –
>
> A Power of Renowned Cold,
> The Climate of the Grave
> A Temperature just adequate
> So Anthracite, to live –

Mitchell differentiates between "sea-coal" and "anthracite" people, a distinction in which the ideal woman is declared to be "anthracite" with "an angel face, that no matter what its angles or its proportions . . . you clasp the image to your heart."[52] Understanding this contributes very little to the Dickinson poem; and, all things considered, Mitchell's books seem to have been a fad, the most enduring effect of which was the possible suggestion of the name Carlo for Emily's dog. Even here, Ik Marvel's dog Carlo may only have reminded her of St. John Rivers' old Carlo in *Jane Eyre*.

In addition to Mitchell, Emily Dickinson sampled other minor American writers. She read Elizabeth Stuart Phelps's *The Last Leaf from Sunnyside*, a collection of sketches and stories presented to her and Lavinia during their Washington visit. Like nearly everyone else, Emily read Mrs. Stowe's *Uncle Tom's Cabin*. It appears that she borrowed Sue's 1871 edition of Bret Harte's short stories, for she makes meaningful allusions to both "Miggles" and "The Outcasts of Poker Flat" in a letter to the

Norcross sisters.[53] The American novelist whom she followed most carefully, however, was Helen Hunt Jackson. Mrs. Jackson was born Helen Fiske in Amherst, and she and Emily were schoolmates for a time. They came to know each other again in the 1870's, and their friendship was heightened by the renewal of their childhood acquaintance and the high opinion that each had of the other's poetry. Mrs. Jackson occasionally sent copies of her poetry and novels to Dickinson, who read them enthusiastically. "Pity me," Emily wrote, "I have finished Ramona." [54] Although Mrs. Jackson's works appeared too late to affect the majority of Dickinson's poetry, her manifest confidence in Emily's strength as a poet and her friendly insistence on publication became a significant influence in later years.[55]

Mrs. Jackson provided one of Emily Dickinson's direct contacts with the active literary world. Her correspondence with Colonel Higginson, which she initiated in April 1862, was another. She cultivated his friendship over the years,[56] and Higginson, with gentlemanly indulgence, never rebuffed her, even though his efforts to understand her invariably failed. His shortcomings as a critic and editor of her poems have more often than not been allowed to overshadow his function as a stimulating correspondent who patiently endured Dickinson's eccentricities, including her rhetorical questions in regard to her verse. By the time she began sending poems to him, the patterns of her prosody were well enough established that his suggestions produced no perceptible changes. Commenting on his criticism, she wrote in her second letter, "Thank you for the surgery – it was not so painful as I supposed. I bring you others – as you ask – though they might not differ –." [57] She ignored his advice concerning her poems but was sensitive to any intimation that he might become inaccessible. Higginson, who urged her not to publish, became a private audience — secure, receptive, and adequate. She never introduced his name in letters to other correspondents, even though they had a number of friends in common;

and her allusions to his essays usually occur in her letters to him.

In Higginson's essays and in his letters, she looked for his opinions of other writers: "I have read nothing of Tourguenéff's, but thank you for telling me — and will seek him immediately." But she did not always accept his opinions — "Mrs Jackson soars to your estimate . . . but of Howells and James, one hesitates." Higginson served as a sounding board for her literary judgments; and, because he was a friend, she read carefully everything he wrote even though her interest in some of the essays must have been limited. There is little doubt that hers was an enduring loyalty. She told Higginson that her opening of his first book was "still as distinct as Paradise . . . It was Mansions — Nations — Kinsmen — too —";[58] and, in the last weeks of her life, she sent him her favorable remarks on his sonnet to Helen Hunt Jackson that had just been published in *Century Magazine*. His elegy, "Decoration," had special appeal in that it was published the month that Emily's father died; and parts of his *Oldport Days* and *Outdoor Papers* she reread with pleasure. Some evidence of her abiding interest appears in the poems. "Decoration" became the source for "Lay this Laurel on the One," and "Water Lilies," one of the essays reprinted in *Outdoor Papers*, provided the theme for these stanzas:

> At Half past Three, a single Bird
> Unto a silent Sky
> Propounded but a single term
> Of cautious melody.
>
> At Half past Four, Experiment
> Had subjugated test
> And lo, Her silver Principle
> Supplanted all the rest.

The Higginson essay reads: "Precisely at half-past three, a song-sparrow above our heads gave one liquid trill that seemed to set to music every atom of freshness and fragrance that Nature held; then the spell was broken and the whole shore and lake were vocal with song."

It would be difficult to appraise exactly the effect that Emily Dickinson's reading from American sources had on her poetry. This is true primarily because her reading was not done in the artificial chronological order which I have discussed. It is apparent, however, that the portions of her American reading most significantly related to her poems are her Mount Holyoke texts, Emerson's essays and poems, and the various writings of Colonel Higginson: her studies at Mount Holyoke contributed to her vocabulary and her wealth of miscellaneous facts; Emerson she took as an antidote to the stultifying effects that latter-day Calvinism had on her imagination; Higginson stimulated her interest in contemporary American literature, particularly her interest in current magazines.

❧ VI ❧

Readings in Newspapers and Periodicals

The Republican seems to us a letter from you, and we
break the seal and read it eagerly.
— *Emily Dickinson to Dr. and Mrs. J. G. Holland, 1853*

In mid-nineteenth-century America, local newspapers provided
information, recreation, and gossip — a function long since generally usurped by more modern communications media. In the
Dickinson household, *The Springfield Republican*, *The Hampshire and Franklin Express*, and *The Amherst Record* were addi-
tionally important because they kept Edward Dickinson informed
of the activities of what was to be, for one term at least, his
Congressional constituency. Along with these newspapers, the
Dickinsons subscribed to *Harper's New Monthly Magazine*,
Scribner's Monthly, and *The Atlantic Monthly*. Because the
entire family was well-educated and because all, with the possible
exception of Emily's mother, were avid readers, both the newspapers and the magazines were thoroughly reviewed. Even
though books were the principal means by which Emily extended
her horizons, most of her knowledge of the detail and action in
a world thus discovered came through her habitual reading of
periodicals.

Of the magazines coming into the homestead, *Harper's New
Monthly* was apparently addressed to Lavinia, for in her diary she
regularly refers to its delivery as the arrival of "my usual magazine."[1] The first such diary entry appeared in January 1851,

and there is no indication that the subscription was ever allowed to lapse. During the period that Lavinia and Emily knew *Harper's*, it was a magazine filled largely with reprints from British publications such as the *London Times* and *Chambers's Edinburgh Journal*. Each issue contained a "Monthly Record of Current Events," an illustrated article on ladies' fashions, and several pages of humor and satire, including reprints from *Punch*. The *Punch* cartoons stimulated Emily's quick wit, and one in particular that stuck in her mind appeared in the June 1851 issue. It depicted a dejected little girl being consoled by her grandmother, and carried this caption:

Grandmamma: "Why, what's the matter with my pet?"
Child: "Why, Grandma, after giving the subject every consideration, I have come to the conclusion that – the world is hollow, and my doll is stuffed with sawdust, so – I – should – like – if you please, to be a nun?"

In writing to Austin, whom she later congratulated for being "much funnier" than *Punch*, Emily jokingly confessed, "I had written a *sincere* letter, but since the 'world is hollow, and Dollie is stuffed with sawdust,' I really do not think we had better expose our feelings."[2]

Beyond the humor, fashion, and current events, *Harper's* offered a variety of subject matter ranging from literary criticism to Arctic exploration and zoology. Selections from well-known English authors like Coleridge, Hunt, Dickens, and Thackeray appeared often, but items from Americans were less frequent. There were articles on the poisonous qualities of toads, on the life of Napoleon, and on the symptoms of hydrophobia. The first twenty pages of the April 1851 issue, for example, included biographical sketches of Washington Irving and William Cullen Bryant, an article on London's Crystal Palace, and an account of the "Voyage in Search of Sir John Franklin." This last item discussed Lady Franklin's efforts to find her husband, who had

vanished along with his party while on an Arctic expedition in
1847. Dickinson, as she wrote the first of these two stanzas,
recalled Lady Franklin's persistent hope:

> When the Astronomer stops seeking
> For his Pleiad's Face –
> When the lone British Lady
> Forsakes the Arctic Race
>
> When to his Covenant Needle
> The Sailor doubting turns –
> It will be amply early
> To ask what treason means.

Six months later in the October 1851 issue, *Harper's* offered a
more definite discussion of treason: "The Treason of Benedict
Arnold." While subjects like Arnold's treason and Lady Franklin's perseverance were recurring topics, some of the details that
Emily Dickinson introduces help to establish her sources more
certainly. When she writes of the death of Major André, Benedict Arnold's accomplice, the poem begins:

> The Manner of it's Death
> When Certain it must die –
> 'Tis deemed a privilege to choose –
> 'Twas Major Andre's Way –

A paragraph near the conclusion of the *Harper's* article gives
this version of his request:

Andre exhibited no fear of death . . . but the *manner* of his
death disturbed his spirit. He pleaded earnestly to be *shot* as a soldier,
not *hung* as a spy. But even this poor boon could not be allowed,
for the rules of war demanded death by a cord and not by a bullet.[3]

Benedict Arnold and Major André are included in Worcester's
Elements of History, Emily's Mount Holyoke textbook, and they
are also the subject of a later article in *Harper's*, but neither of

these sources presents André's plea for a soldier's execution, and the recurrence of the word "manner" brings the poem closest to the 1851 *Harper's* essay.

Like most of her reading, *Harper's* was for Emily Dickinson an adventure. Although the twentieth-century reader finds its issues a model of restraint, the subscribers of a hundred years ago were regarded as liberal indeed, and *Harper's* was not so openly received throughout Amherst as it was at the homestead. Emily gives this account of an inhibited young visitor's enjoying her family's subscription: "D—— fed greedily upon *Harper's Magazine* while here. Suppose he is restricted to Martin Luther's works at home. It is a criminal thing to be a boy in a godly village, but maybe he will be forgiven." [4] This is the reaction one should expect from the young lady who nodded to her father's literary conservatism, who resented the seminary's restriction of her reading, and who preferred her Shakespeare unabridged. After all, her good friend Dr. Josiah Holland edited a publication similar to *Harper's*, and she trusted his judgment fully.

Emily had read with pleasure Dr. Holland's earlier columns in *The Springfield Republican*; and, even though some considered his *Scribner's Monthly* just as worldly as *Harper's*, she did not question his taste. In addition to editing the magazine, Josiah Holland was also one of its major contributors. When his *Nicholas Minturn* appeared serially in *Scribner's*, Emily informed Mrs. Holland, "Would you believe that our sacred Neighbors, the Mr and Mrs Sweetser, were so enamored of 'Nicholas Minturn' that they borrow our Number before it is cold?" [5] Emily missed none of it, to be sure; she makes it clear that she read everything of Dr. Holland's she could obtain, yet her interest seems to have come more from loyalty to the person than from enthusiasm for the work. She writes of having read his poem, "My Dog Blanco," in the August 1881 issue, but this is the only piece of his verse that she ever mentions. [6] There were other authors in *Scribner's* to catch her eye, however. Unlike *Harper's*, it was somewhat more devoted to literature, particularly works by American writers, and Emily's letters to the Hollands frequently comment on the offering in current issues. When William Dean Howells' *A Fearful Responsibility* appeared in *Scribner's*, she asked, "Doctor — How did you snare Howells?" and he replied, "Emily — Case of Bribery — Money did it —." And after the Howells serial was completed, Emily asked skeptically, "Who wrote Mr Howells' story? Certainly he did not." She seems to have been mildly surprised to see installments of one Howells novel in *Scribner's* while she was reading another Howells novel serialized in the *Atlantic*.[7] But more significant in this exchange is the fact that she was sufficiently aware of the American literary scene to raise the question of how Dr. Holland happened to publish in *Scribner's* a novel by Howells, the editor-in-chief of the *Atlantic*.

She knew *The Atlantic Monthly* well; the family's copies that remain in the Harvard Collection begin with the magazine's first issue, November 1857. Like *Harper's* and *Scribner's*, the *Atlantic* professed to be primarily literary in tone, but it differed from the others in that it was, as advertised, "a magazine of literature, art, and politics." As such, it became a major contributor to the broadened point of view that Emily's reading fostered. A sampling of the January 1861 issue gives an indication of the magazine's scope: an essay on the political and social atmosphere of "Washington City," "Recollections of Keats," Longfellow's "Paul Revere's Ride," a commentary on "The European Crisis" precipitated by Napoleon III, and a review of Dr. Holland's new novel, *Miss Gilbert's Career*. The next month's copy opened with a lengthy article on "Our Artists in Italy." All these were items of interest to Emily Dickinson. A number of contemporary novels were first published serially in the *Atlantic*; and she probably read most of them, although the only ones she mentions specifically are Henry James's *The Europeans* and Howells' *The Undiscovered Country*.[8] It was in the *Atlantic* that she learned more about "The Lights of the English Lake District," the life of Mrs. Browning, and Darwin's *The Origin of Species*. She was exposed to a variety of didactic and occasional pieces; and once, when her copy was misplaced, she asked for Sue's so that she could read a Rebecca Harding Davis social protest entitled "Life in the Iron Mills." [9] She read the articles carefully, always alert for the familiar style of Holland or Higginson in the untitled items and retaining an accumulation of thoughts and phrases from what she read. As Theodora Ward has pointed out,

> . . . in one instance [she] sent back to [Higginson] a thought of his she had read fifteen years before. . . . In an article called "My Outdoor Study," published in the *Atlantic Monthly* for September 1861, he had said, "One can find summer in January by poring over the Latin catalogues of Massachusetts plants and animals in Hitchcock's reports." In a letter written in the winter of 1877, Emily wrote, "When Flowers annually died and I was a child, I used to read Dr. Hitchcock's Book on the Flowers of North America. This comforted their Absence — assuring me they lived." [10]

The Higginson essays are by far the most significant group of items that Emily Dickinson read in the *Atlantic*. But she remembered odd scraps from other articles as well. In April 1863, Joseph Severn's essay "On the Viscissitudes of Keats's Fame," appeared; and among the details that Severn included was his statement that "[Keats] tranquilly rehearsed to me what would be the process of his dying, what I was to do, and how I was to *bear it*." [11] This problem of bearing the death of another is one that Emily Dickinson continually raises in her letters, and she recalled the quotation above as she lamented, after Helen Hunt Jackson's death, "Oh had that Keats a Severn!" [12] — a wistful suggestion that Mrs. Jackson's "Severn" might instruct her how to bear the grief of Mrs. Jackson's passing.

By providing such specific references for both letters and poems, the magazines that Emily Dickinson read did much to enliven the world that her imagination encompassed. The newspapers, particularly the *Springfield Republican*, contributed to the same stock of information, but her newspaper reading performed a slightly different function by reporting, in addition, the details of happenings in Amherst, Springfield, and Boston. Thus, through the newspapers, she was able to gain intelligence of the society of her correspondents without having to venture into it physically.

The Amherst newspaper that Emily Dickinson read was known first as *The Hampshire and Franklin Express*, then for a short period (July 1866 to May 1868) it was simply *The Hampshire Express*, and finally it became *The Amherst Record*. Whicher called it "one of the best country newspapers in New England." [13] Its weekly pages were crowded with items of both local and general interest. Inserted among the advertisements for Greeley's Bourbon Bitters, Great Indian Female Remedy, and Allen's Dry Goods were Mr. Adams' announcements of new books for sale. The front page usually carried a selection or two of poetry, though it was mostly of the Adelaide Procter – Kate Cameron variety and only occasionally rose to the level of Mrs. Stowe or Longfellow.

Two poems that appeared in the *Express* were of special interest. Both were related to the death of Dr. Jacob Holt, a young dentist from Boston who had established himself in Amherst, where he subsequently became a friend of the Dickinson family. Several of Emily's letters from Mount Holyoke contain inquiries about his illness; and on May 14, 1848, while she was still in South Hadley, he died. He was the author of the first of the poems in question, a ten-line conceit entitled "The Bible," which Emily carefully transcribed from the *Express* onto the back flyleaf of her Bible. At the end of the poem she added, "Composed by Dr. J. Holt during his last sickness," and pasted on the same page two lines of his obituary, clipped from a Boston newspaper. On May 25, two weeks before Holt's poem appeared, the *Express* had published a three-stanza elegy in memory of the recently deceased dentist. There is little doubt that Emily read it and that it was something, under the circumstances, that she would remember well. The memorial poem's last stanza reads:

> . . . It was quite near the close of the Sabbath, —
> Just as its sun was setting, — that death came,
> And gave the spirit its long-sought release,
> Not in his terrors did death then appear,
> But came like some kind angel of mercy,
> Whose delightful mission it is to bless.
> Oh how sweet for the Christian thus to die!
> And exchange an earthly Sabbath, for one
> That is heavenly, and never to end.

Years later it appears that Emily Dickinson combined images from this elegy and from Browning's "The Last Ride Together" as basic ingredients for one of the finest of her poems:

> Because I could not stop for Death –
> He kindly stopped for me –
> The Carriage held but just Ourselves –
> And Immortality.
>
> We slowly drove – He knew no haste
> And I had put away
> My labor and my leisure too,
> For His Civility –
>
> We passed the School, where Children strove
> At Recess – in the Ring –
> We passed the Fields of Gazing Grain –
> We passed the Setting Sun –
>
> * * * * * * * *
>
> Since then – 'tis Centuries – and yet
> Feels shorter than the Day
> I first surmised the Horses Heads
> Were toward Eternity –

To Browning's metaphor of the carriage ride has been added the picture of Death, the gentle caller who arrives as the sun is setting to offer the immortality of a Sabbath that is "never to end." While there is no direct evidence of the connection between her stanzas and the memorial to her friend Dr. Holt, the similarity of the imagery in the two poems is too marked to be coincidental. Because she occasionally reread poems that were meaningful to her, it is not too much to conclude that she reread this poem as she did the one copied in the back of her Bible, and that she may have relied upon it very much as she did Higginson's "Decoration" when she was writing "Lay this Laurel on the One."

A year or so before the Holt poems appeared, the *Hampshire Gazette* and the *Northampton Courier* carried another poem that Emily chose to remember. Entitled "The Life Clock," it begins:

> There is a little mystic clock,
> No human eye hath seen,
> That beateth on and beateth on
> From morning until e'en.[14]

She quotes from this stanza in two letters, one to Sue and one to Austin,[15] and repeats the clock-heart metaphor in two poems. In the first poem, "The Rose did caper on her cheek –," two lovers' hearts danced excitedly

> To the immortal tune –
> Till those two troubled – little Clocks
> Ticked softly into one.

And in the second, death is described as a time when

> A Clock stopped –
> Not the Mantel's –
> Geneva's farthest skill
> Cant put the puppet bowing –
> That just now dangled still –

In this poem's remaining stanzas the "Life Clock" is presented as one that "will not stir for Doctor's—" because there are

> Decades of Arrogance between
> The Dial life —
> And Him —

She may have had this same image in mind when she began "T'was comfort in her Dying Room/To hear the living Clock," but the connection in this last case is more remote than in the other two.

Of all the newspapers Emily Dickinson knew, the most important was Samuel Bowles's *Springfield Republican*; Whicher found it "next in importance to the Bible in determining the mental climate of [her] formative years." [16] It was reputedly "the best daily newspaper in the country," [17] and one cannot deny the exceptional variety of its news and editorial commentary. The Dickinsons were attracted to the paper by more than journalistic quality, however. Emily, for one, regarded the paper as something akin to personal communication, as this letter to the Hollands indicates:

One glimpse of *The Republican* makes me break things again — I read in it every night.

Who writes those funny accidents, where railroads meet each other unexpectedly, and gentlemen in factories get their heads cut off quite informally? The author, too, relates them in such a sprightly way, that they are quite attractive. Vinnie was quite disappointed to-night, that there were not more accidents — I read the news aloud, while Vinnie was sewing. *The Republican* seems to us like a letter from you, and we break the seal and read it eagerly.[18]

The accounts of accidents that the Dickinson ladies enjoyed were probably those reported under "Miscellaneous News," a column that contained items such as these:

It is rumored that two artists of New York city have had a duel near Norfolk, Va., and that both are wounded.

The boiler of the tannery at Dunnings near Scranton, Pa., exploded last Thursday night, seriously injuring two persons.

A conductor fell under the engine at Lehigh, Pa., breaking his legs, ribs, etc.; he will not recover.[19]

There were other "sprightly" features in the *Republican*. The front page for December 26, 1850 carried a short discussion of the "Individuality of Locomotives." The possibility of Emily's recollection of paragraphs from that article suggests it as the source of the "horrid, hooting" monster-engine that she brings to a "Stop – docile and omnipotent/At it's own stable door –" in "I like to see it lap the Miles –," for the personality of the Dickinson engine places it in the genus of independent locomotives described by the *Republican* article.

INDIVIDUALITY OF LOCOMOTIVES

It is a remarkable truth . . . that every locomotive engine running on a railway has a distinct individuality of its own.

*　*　*　*　*　*　*　*　*　*　*

It would seem as if some of these "excellent monsters" declared on being brought out of the stable, "If Smith is going to drive me I wont go. If it's my old friend Stockes, I am agreeable to anything." All locomotive engines are low-spirited in damp and foggy weather. They have a great satisfaction in their work when the air is crisp and frosty. At such time they are cheerful and brisk; but they strongly object to haze and Scotch mists.

Along with accidents and locomotives, the girls enjoyed Samuel Fiske's (Mr. Dunne Browne's) travel reports and Frank Sanborn's letters on art and literature.[20] There were book reviews and literary gossip; but most of all, Emily looked forward to Dr. Holland's contributions. On January 2, 1854, in anticipation of his forthcoming *History of Western Massachusetts*, she wrote to him and asked, "*May* it come *today?*"[21] and found her answer when that day's *Republican* arrived with the first weekly installment. She also read Holland's advice to young people, written under the pen name "Timothy Titcomb," and followed his year-long series entitled "Ruminations — A series of Essays on Human Life" that began in the *Republican* in 1861. When he published an editorial "'Leaves of Grass' — Smut in them," Emily read it and accepted his judgment that Whitman's verse was "about as much like poetry as tearing off a rag, or paring one's corns. . . . a scandalous volume." [22] Poetry that appeared in the paper had his implicit approval, and generally the selections were good — poems from Herrick, Vaughan, the Brownings, and Tennyson, to name a few. One of the minor poems Emily saw in the *Republican* was Charles Mackay's "Little Nobody." T. H. Johnson has suggested [23] that Mackay's line "Who would be a Somebody? — Nobody am I" inspired this Dickinson poem:

> I'm Nobody! Who are you?
> Are you – Nobody – too?
> Then there's a pair of us!
> Dont tell! they'd banish us – you know!
>
> How dreary – to be – Somebody!
> How public – like a Frog –
> To tell your name – the livelong June –
> To an admiring Bog!

In addition to printing poetry, essays, and criticism, the *Republican* occasionally offered advice to aspiring writers. In September 1864, a short article on "Literary Women" appeared. In it was this paragraph that would have been particularly meaningful for Emily:

To a woman at least, literature is not an easy profession . . . Any woman who enters the path of literature with no higher aim than that of worldly applause and notoriety, will find herself sorely deceived and disappointed in the end. . . . So if a woman enter the field of authorship let her do it always in the spirit which seeks for other rewards than the world can give; let her feel that the mission of her poem is to elevate and bless humanity, that she always speaks for the right, the true, the good.[24]

It is doubtful that Emily Dickinson kept all such particulars as the "Literary Women" article, the elegy of Dr. Holt, or the report on the "Individuality of Locomotives" in her "hermetic" memory. Albeit, she kept a vast store there, but considerable evidence exists that she habitually clipped and saved many of those items that interested her and sifted through them at later dates in search of materials uniquely suited to her purpose of the moment. It is certain that she clipped pictures from her father's copies of the *New England Primer* and *The Old Curiosity Shop* in order to illustrate letters and poems she had written, for her clippings remain attached to manuscripts. Furthermore, a part of one page of the book of Revelation has been clipped out of her Bible. One side of the clipping included the portion of Revelation 21:1 that she quoted in a letter to Mrs. Holland; the other contained that part of Revelation 22:16 that she included in a letter to Higginson.[25] Also missing from her Bible is the word "Timothy," neatly cut from the center of the title page of I Timothy. This clipping may well have found its way into a letter to Dr. Holland ("Timothy Titcomb"). One of her poems, apparently written in 1877, was illustrated with two clippings,[26] one of which was taken from the *Hampshire and Franklin Express* of December 12, 1856. This leads Johnson to conjecture from "the disparity in the date of the clipping and the poem . . . that she kept a scrapbook or file of items which to her were meaningful." [27] His hypothesis is further borne out in a letter that Emily wrote to Sue after recovering from an illness during the summer of 1884: "I wish I could find the Warrington Words, but during my weeks of faintness, my Treasures were misplaced, and I cannot find them –." [28] "Warrington" (William S. Robinson), a writer for the *Springfield Republican*, died eight years

before this letter was written. When he was the Boston correspondent for the newspaper, he would have received Emily's
special notice because of his outspoken comments on her father's
political activities. "Warrington Words" were apparently some
she had chosen to retain. Her "treasures," both those that she
clipped and saved and others that she had written herself, may
well have been the subject of these stanzas:

> I made slow Riches but my Gain
> Was steady as the Sun
> And every Night, it numbered more
> Than the preceding One
>
> All Days, I did not earn the same
> But my perceiveless Gain
> Inferred the less by Growing than
> The Sum that it had grown.

Considering that Lavinia, after Emily's death, saved only the
poems from her sister's accumulation of letters, manuscripts,
and clippings,[29] one wonders how many sources and analogues
for Dickinson poems were included in the material destroyed.
Had Emily, for instance, kept the *Springfield Republican's* front-
page report on the 1864 social season at Newport? That was her
friend Higginson's first season there; and the satirical article,
subtitled "A Human Menagerie," with its description of prome-
naders in "a concentrated world of scandal, backbiting, display,
ignorance, and vulgarity" would not have passed unnoticed.[30] In
any event, eight years later she wrote:

> The Show is not the Show
> But they that go —
> Menagerie to me
> My Neighbor be —
> Fair Play —
> Both went to see —

And in late 1872 she concluded a letter to Higginson, "Menagerie to me/My Neighbor be." It was her first letter to Higginson following his return from Europe, and its beginning suggests that perhaps she had looked through her scraps and clippings in search of some special reference appropriate to his return to Newport:

I am happy you have the Travel you so long desire and [I am] chastened – that my Master met neither accident nor Death.
    Our own Possessions though our own
    'Tis well to hoard anew
    Remembering the dimensions
    Of Possibility.
I often saw your name in illustrious mention and envied an occasion so abstinent to me.[31]

Perhaps among her "own Possessions" she kept this notice of "the Last of the Brontës":

The father of Charlotte Bronte . . . had long survived the three marvellous daughters that gave him happiness, pride and fame. They were an eccentric family . . . and their history if faithfully written, might prove more intensely interesting than any of the tales they have bequeathed us.[32]

Twenty-two years later Emily wrote to Mrs. Holland: "I wish the dear Eyes would so far relent as to let you read '[The Life of] Emily Bronte'– more electric far than anything since 'Jane Eyre.'"[33] This paraphrase seems to indicate that she had refreshed her knowledge of the Brontë article sometime between its publication in 1861 and the spring of 1883 when she wrote the letter. Thus, the probable content of Emily Dickinson's accumulated correspondence, notes, and clippings permits the association of some of her poems and letters with sources that would otherwise be chronologically too remote for serious consideration.

In evaluating her reading in newspapers and periodicals, it should be remembered that religion and politics were two vital interests in the household and that Edward Dickinson was a respected leader in both fields. Just as the Bible was expected to keep the family spiritually well-informed, so were the pages of *The Springfield Republican* and *The Hampshire and Franklin Express* expected to keep them politically well-informed. Emily found these newspapers as well as the literary magazines constantly before her inquisitive eyes; they exposed her unavoidably to the living language of nineteenth-century America and, in doing so, contributed to the variegated array of subjects and ideas that she could treat knowledgeably in letters and poems.

In Fine

A Word dropped careless on a Page
May stimulate an eye
                        — *Poem 1261, c. 1873*

One of Emily Dickinson's most enticing characteristics is her ability to "tell all the Truth but tell it slant," to relay a "thought beneath so slight a film." Yet a reader whose interest has been aroused by her indirect but concise approach to her subject occasionally is thwarted by a cryptic word or phrase. This seeming impasse is often a part of the poet's design:

> Good to hide, and hear 'em hunt!
> Better, to be found,
> If one care to, that is,
> The Fox fits the Hound –
>
> Good to know, and not tell,
> Best, to know and tell,
> Can one find the rare Ear
> Not too dull –

The opening stanza notwithstanding, Emily Dickinson's intention was not to be deliberately obscure or abstruse but rather to achieve exactness of expression — an exactness that allows her more perspicacious readers to reconstruct in large measure her creative experience as they move toward the full meaning of her

144

poetry. The Dickinson cosmology presented in Jay Leyda's *The Hours and Years of Emily Dickinson* provides detail that is generally helpful in this interpretive process. The correlation of her reading with her letters and poems affords another significant means of focusing the understanding of intellectual and literary influences affecting both the poetry and the poet.

Through her reading, Emily Dickinson gained the vicarious experience and perspective that made possible the perceptive observations and penetrating analyses characteristic of her poetry. Her fondness for books and reading developed long before she sequestered herself in the homestead, and the reading interests that she manifested in her adolescent and young adult life were not inhibited by the seclusion of later years. For that seclusion she carefully chose her closest companions: her Bible, Watts's *Psalms and Hymns*, Shakespeare, the seventeenth-century Metaphysicals, Emerson, Dickens, George Eliot, and the Brownings. To these she added the daily newspaper, a number of periodicals, and the lively letters from Bowles, Higginson, and Holland. By this means she was able to exploit her physical isolation and achieve an intellectual expansion that might otherwise have been impossible. Her reading reveals that she was related to her literary peers by no accident of mystical experience but by her own extensive knowledge of their lives and works. It also indicates that, although Emily Dickinson's poetry was created by imaginative genius and conscious artistry, many of her poems can be meaningfully related to a wide variety of identifiable sources. By reviewing these sources and her reading in general, the inquisitive reader achieves a clearer understanding of the poet and of the varied implications and nuances of her verse.

Appendix A

An Annotated Bibliography of Emily Dickinson's Reading

This listing points out whenever possible the relation of Emily Dickinson's reading to specific poems and letters. Both poems and letters are referred to by the numbers assigned in the Johnson editions. For ease of reference, the Dickinson phrases are repeated. If the exact edition that she read is ascertainable, the title is marked by an asterisk (*) and the pertinent publication data shown. Autographs or inscriptions in books which belonged to her, or which she presented, have been included along with the present location of such volumes.

Abbreviations used:

> LTRS — *The Letters of Emily Dickinson*, Johnson edition, 1958.
>
> Poems — *The Poems of Emily Dickinson*, Johnson edition, 1955.
>
> PF — Prose fragment in *LTRS*.
> HCL — Dickinson Collection, Harvard College Library.
> MHT — Textbook used by Dickinson at Mount Holyoke.
> * — Edition verified as the one used by ED.

Adler, G. J. *Olendorff's New Method of Learning . . . the German Language . . .* New York: D. Appleton and Co., 1846. HCL. Signed, "Emily E. Dickinson, 1845."

Alexander, Francesca. *The Story of Ida*. Boston, 1883. HCL. Ltr 955, *LTRS*, III, 853: "The etherial Volume [identified by Mabel Loomis Todd] is with us."

The *Amherst Record*, May 1868 to May 1886. See Chapter VI.

Arabian Nights. Ltr 19, *LTRS*, I, 57: "You are reading Arabian Nights. . . . presume your powers of imagining will vastly increase thereby." Ltr 22, *LTRS*, I, 63: "But I will no longer imagine, for your brain is full of Arabian Nights fancies." Ltr 335, *LTRS*, II, 465: "The 'Arabian Nights' unfit the heart for it's Arithmetic." Ltr 438, *LTRS*, II, 540: "We who arraign the 'Arabian Nights' for their under statement." Ltr 698, *LTRS*, III, 696: "Thank the 'Arabian Nights.'"

The Atlantic Monthly. HCL. November 1857 through May 1886 (lacks Nov. 58; May, July 60; Mar., May 61; Aug. 63; Feb. 64; Sept. 66; Mar., July 67, Mar., Aug. 68; June 69; Feb., Mar., Apr., June, Aug., Sept. 70; Feb., Mar., May 71; May, July, Aug., Sept., Oct., Dec. 72; all 73 except Mar., Nov., Dec.; Apr. 78).

Badger, Mrs. C. M. *Wild Flowers Drawn and Colored from Nature.* New York, 1859. HCL. Inscribed, "To my daughter Emily from her father Edw. Dickinson January 1, 1859."

Barbauld, Mrs. Anna L. "How blest the righteous when he dies." Ltr 146, *LTRS*, I, 277: "'So fades a summer cloud away/ . . ./ So dies a wave along the shore."

*The Holy Bible. Philadelphia: J. B. Lippincott and Co., 1843. HCL. Inscribed: "Emily E. Dickinson a present from her Father 1844."

GENESIS

Ltr 552, *LTRS*, II, 610: "and with no disrespect to Genesis, Paradise remains." Ltr 690, *LTRS*, III, 691: "– but Genesis is a 'far journey.'" P 1369, *Poems*, III, 945: "In Genesis' new house." P 1569, *Poems*, III, 1081: "A Vagabond from Genesis."

(1–3) Ltr 9, *LTRS*, I, 24: "Eve, alias Mrs. Adam. . . . there is no account of her death in the Bible." P 1119, *Poems*, II, 787: "Adam taught her Thrift/Bankrupt once through his excesses." P 1195, *Poems*, III, 832–833: "Transport's doubtful Dividend/ Patented by Adam."

(3:10) Ltr 946, *LTRS*, III, 847: "those guileless words of Adam and Eve. . . . 'I was afraid and hid Myself.'"

(3:24) Ltr 304, *LTRS*, II, 440: "I shall think of my little Eve going away from Eden." Ltr 628, *LTRS*, III 655: "Had it been a Mastiff that guarded Eden, we should have feared him less than we do the Angel." Ltr 864, *LTRS*, III, 796: "I had feared that the Angel with the Sword would dissuade you from Eden."

(5:24) P 1342, *Poems*, III, 927: "Because 'God took him' mention."

(7–8) P 403, *Poems*, I, 315: "But Ararat's a Legend – now –/ And no one credits Noah."

(8:11) Ltr 399, *LTRS*, II, 470: "Noah would have liked mother." Ltr 864, *LTRS*, III, 796: "There is more than one 'Deluge,' . . . the duplicate of the 'Dove,' hallows your own Heart." P 48, *Poems*, I, 38: "Thrice to the floating casement/ The Patriarch's bird returned."

(19) P 702, *Poems*, II, 541. "For Lot – exhibited to/Faith – alone."

(22:1–20) P 1317, *Poems*, III, 911: "Abraham to kill him/ Was distinctly told –/Isaac was an Urchin –/Abraham was old."

(22:7) Ltr 1006, *LTRS*, III, 883: "Isaac pleads again, 'but where is the Lamb for the Sacrifice?'"

(24:15) Ltr 836, *LTRS*, III, 784: "The Pitcher shall be an emblem – 'Rebecca.'"

(32:26) Ltr 720, *LTRS*, III, 705: "'Let me go for the day breaketh.'" Ltr 1035, *LTRS*, III, 898: "'I will not let thee go, except I bless thee.'" Ltr 1042, *LTRS*, III, 903: "said Jacob, to the Angel 'I will not let thee go except I bless thee.'"

(32:26–30) P 59, *Poems*, I, 44: "A little East of Jordan,/ Evangelists record,/A Gymnast and an Angel/Did wrestle long and hard."

EXODUS

(14) P 1642, *Poems*, III, 1124: "'Red Sea,' indeed! Talk not to me/Of purple Pharaoh."

(20:3) Ltr 1016, *LTRS*, III, 889: "'Thou shalt have no other Gods before Me?'"

(32:9, 33:3) Ltr 9, *LTRS*, I, 24 (also Deuteronomy 9:6): "the prophet calls them a stiff-necked generation."

(33:5–11) P 1733, *Poems*, III, 1167: "'Am not consumed,' old Moses wrote,/Yet saw him face to face.'"

EXODUS (continued)

(33:20) P 890, *Poems*, II, 657: "No Eye hath seen and lived."
P 1247, *Poems*, III, 866: "For None see God and live."

(34:14) Ltr 397, *LTRS*, II, 512: "'God is a jealous God.'"
P 1260, *Poems*, III, 876 (also Deuteronomy 5:9; Joshua 24:19):
"Because he is a 'jealous God.'" P 1719, *Poems*, III, 1159 (also
Deuteronomy 5:9): "God is indeed a jealous God."

DEUTERONOMY

(5:9) P 1260, *Poems*, III, 876 (also Exodus 34:14; Joshua
24:19): "Because he is a 'jealous God.'" P 1719, *Poems*, III,
1159 (also Exodus 34:14; Joshua 24:19): "God is indeed a
jealous God."

(9:6, 13) Ltr 9, *LTRS*, I, 24 (also Exodus 32:9; 33:3): "the
prophet calls them a stiff-necked generation."

(33:25) Ltr 409, *LTRS*, II, 522: "'As thy day is so shall
thy' stem 'be.'" Ltr 683, *LTRS*, III, 686: "'As thy Day so shall
thy Strength be.'"

(34:1–4) P 168, *Poems*, I, 123: "Could we stand with that
Old 'Moses'–/'Canaan' denied." P 1201, *Poems*, III, 835:
"Moses was'nt fairly used."

JOSHUA

(24:15) Ltr 840, *LTRS*, III, 785: "'Choose ye which ye will
serve'!"

(24:19) P 1260, *Poems*, III, 876 (also Exodus 34:14; Deuteronomy 5:9): "Because he is a 'jealous God.'"

JUDGES

(16:29–30) Ltr 154, *LTRS*, I, 284: "Samson – to pull the
whole church down."

RUTH

(1:16) Ltr 732, *LTRS*, III, 714: "'Where thou goest, *we*
will go.'"

I SAMUEL

(4:21–22) Ltr 723, *LTRS*, III, 707: "If the 'Ark of the Lord'
must be 'taken.'"

(17:50) P 540, *Poems*, II, 415: "'Twas not so much as
David – had –/But I – was twice as bold –/ . . . Was it Goliah –
was too large –/Or was myself – too small?"

(28) Ltr 845, *LTRS*, III, 787: "call it Endor's Closet."

II SAMUEL

(1:23) Ltr 987, *LTRS*, III, 874: "'Lovely in their Lives, and in their Death, not divided.'"

(12:23) Ltr 534, *LTRS*, II, 600: "David's route was simple – 'I shall go to him.'"

(13) Ltr 644, *LTRS*, III, 663: "David's grieved decision haunted me. . . . I hope he has found Absalom."

I KINGS

(12:11) Ltr 17, *LTRS*, I, 50: "I will . . . pursue you with a 'whip of scorpions.'" Ltr 57, *LTRS*, I, 147: "'lest with a whip of *scorpions* I overtake your lingering!'"

(17:6) Ltr 326, *LTRS*, II, 458: "My Breakfast surpassed Elijah's."

(19:12) Ltr 35, *LTRS*, I, 94: "the 'still small voice' grows earnest and rings."

II KINGS

(2:11) Ltr 75, *LTRS*, I, 178: "like Enoch of old . . . and the 'chariot of fire, and the horses thereof.'" P 1235, *Poems*, III, 859: "Then like Elijah rode away/Upon a Wheel of Cloud." P 1254, *Poems*, III, 869: "Elijah's Wagon knew no thill/Was innocent of Wheel."

(2:11–12) Ltr 787, *LTRS*, III, 751: "as if I were returning Elisha's Horses."

JOB

(3:17) Ltr 678, *LTRS*, III, 683. "I trust the 'Hand' has 'ceased from troubling.'" Ltr 737, *LTRS*, III, 717: "Emily's heart is the edifice where the 'wicked cease from troubling.'"

(13:15) Ltr 808, *LTRS*, III, 765: "'Though he slay me, yet will I trust him.'"

(14:14) Ltr 727, *LTRS*, III, 711: "–for if a pod 'die, shall he not live again.'"

(28:18) Ltr 461, *LTRS*, II, 555: "the fabrics which the Bible designates as beyond rubies?"

PSALMS

(7:11) Ltr 502, *LTRS*, II, 582: "I suppose he [God] is too busy, getting 'angry with the Wicked – every Day.'"

PSALMS (continued)

(18:28) P 871, *Poems*, II, 648: "The Lord a Candle entertains/Entirely for Thee."

(19:2) Ltr 1000, *LTRS*, III, 880: "'Day unto Day uttereth Speech' if you don't tease him."

(23:4) Ltr 820, *LTRS*, III, 773: "'Though thou walk through the Valley of the Shadow of Death, I will be with thee.'"

(42:7) Ltr 899, *LTRS*, III, 822: "'Deep calls to the Deep' in the old way."

(90:9–10) Ltr 266, *LTRS*, II, 410: "The long life's years are scant, and fly away, . . . like a told story."

(91:11) Ltr 820, *LTRS*, III, 774 (also Luke 4:10): "Tell her . . . 'I give my Angels charge.'" Ltr 975, *LTRS*, III, 865 (also Luke 4:10): "I give his Angels Charge." Ltr 991, *LTRS*, III, 877 (also Luke 4:10): "'I give his angels charge!'" Ltr 1012, *LTRS*, III, 887 (also Luke 4:10): "I give 'his Angels Charge.'"

(103:14) P 1461, *Poems*, III, 1009–1010. "More respectful – 'We are Dust.'"

(116:12) Ltr 439, *LTRS*, II, 541: "The embarrassment of the Psalmist who knew not what to render his friend."

(121:4) Ltr 94, *LTRS*, I, 212: "something faithful which 'never slumbers nor sleeps.'"

(127:2) Ltr 796, *LTRS*, III, 757: "'He giveth *our* Beloved Sleep.'"

(137:5) Ltr 45, *LTRS*, I, 119: "if you forget me now your right hand *shall* it's cunning."

(147:9) Ltr 668, *LTRS*, III, 676: "The 'Ravens' must 'cry,' to be ministered to."

PROVERBS

(14:10) Ltr 750, *LTRS*, III, 728: "but 'the Heart knoweth its own' Whim."

(23:26) Ltr 608, *LTRS*, II, 642: "'Give me thine Heart' is too peremptory a Courtship for Earth."

(27:1) Ltr 708, *LTRS*, III, 700: "'Boast not' myself 'of To-morrow' for I 'knowest not what a' Noon 'may bring forth.'"

APPENDIX A

ECCLESIASTES

(12:5) Ltr 13, *LTRS*, I, 38: "'the mourners go about the streets!'" Ltr 666, *LTRS*, III, 675: "to explain . . . *why* the grasshopper is a burden."

(12:6) Ltr 11, *LTRS*, I, 31: "'when the silver cord is loosed & the golden bowl broken.'" Ltr 948, *LTRS*, III, 848: "The 'golden bowl' breaks soundlessly."

ISAIAH

(6:2) Ltr 883, *LTRS*, III, 812: "If the 'Archangels vail their faces.'" P 65, *Poems*, I, 51: "With our faces vailed –/As they say polite Archangels/Do in meeting God!"

(11:6) Ltr 729, *LTRS*, III, 712: "'A little child shall lead them.'" Ltr 952, *LTRS*, III, 851: "'and a little child shall lead them.'"

(35:8) Ltr 562, *LTRS*, II, 617: "the 'wayfaring Man, though a Fool – need not err therein.'"

(43:2) Ltr 221, *LTRS*, II, 364: "'When thou goest through the Waters, I will go with thee.'"

(53:3) Ltr 932, *LTRS*, III, 837: "he is 'acquainted with Grief.'"

(53:4) Ltr 875, *LTRS*, III, 804: "She has 'borne our grief and carried our sorrow.'"

(53:5) Ltr 564, *LTRS*, II, 619: "'Bruised for our iniquities.'"

(55) Ltr 398, *LTRS*, II, 513: "If you sell your Goods at Isaiah's price, I will take them all."

JEREMIAH

(33:11) Ltr 727, *LTRS*, III, 711: "the mind turns to the myth 'for His mercy endureth forever,' with confiding revulsion."

LAMENTATIONS

(3:23) Ltr 889, *LTRS*, III, 815: "'New every morning and fresh every evening.'"

DANIEL

(5:5) Ltr 603, [P 1459], *LTRS*, II, 640: "Belshazzar had a Letter."

(6:21–22) Ltr 29, *LTRS*, I, 79: "Old fashioned Daniel could'nt take things more coolly."

153

DANIEL (continued)

(8:16) P 195, *Poems*, I, 140: "Get Gabriel – to tell – the royal syllable." Ltr 726, *LTRS*, III, 709: "and Gabriel no more ideal than his swift eclipse."

MATTHEW

(4:3–11) Ltr 36, *LTRS*, I, 98 (also Luke 4:2–13): "I had read of Christ's temptations."

(5:3–4) Ltr 98, *LTRS*, I, 218: "'Blessed are the poor – Blessed are they that mourn – Blessed are they that weep, for they shall be comforted.'"

(5:10) Ltr 152, *LTRS*, I, 280–281: "'Blessed are they that are persecuted for righteousness' sake, for they shall have their reward!'" Ltr 690, *LTRS*, III, 691: "Blessed are they that play, for theirs is the kingdom of heaven."

(6:9) Ltr 776, *LTRS*, III, 745: "till he assists me in another World — 'Hallowed be it's Name'!"

(6:10) P 103, *Poems*, I, 79: "And I omit to pray/'Father, thy will be done' today."

(6:13) Ltr 951, *LTRS*, III, 850: "Is not 'Lead us not into Temptation' an involuntary plea."

(6:19) Ltr 50, *LTRS*, I, 130: "could'nt 'the moth corrupt, and the thief break thro' and steal." Ltr 843, *LTRS*, III, 786: "– Lay up Treasures immediately – that's the best Anodyne for moth and Rust and the thief."

(6:21) Ltr 313, *LTRS*, II, 446 (also Luke 2:34): "'Where the treasure is,' there is the prospective."

(6:28) Ltr 119, *LTRS*, I, 246: "please accept them — the 'Lily of the field.'" Ltr 213, *LTRS*, II, 358: "Even the 'Lilies of the field' have their dignities." Ltr 683, *LTRS*, III, 686 (also Luke 12:27): "Please 'consider' me — An antique request, though in behalf of Lilies." Ltr 824, *LTRS*, III, 776 (also Luke 12:27): "Must it not have enthralled the Bible, . . . 'The lily of the field!'" Ltr 897, *LTRS*, III, 821 (also Luke 12:27): "Thank you for 'considering the Lilies.'" Ltr 904, *LTRS*, III, 825 (also Luke 12:27): "the only Commandment I ever obeyed – 'Consider the Lilies.'" P 1310, *Poems*, III, 909: "Not any House the Flowers keep –/The Birds enamor Care."

(7:7–8) Ltr 133, *LTRS*, I, 263–264 (also Luke 11:9): "but I seek and I don't find and knock and it is not opened." Ltr 830, *LTRS*, III, 780 (also Luke 11:9): "yet 'Seek and ye shall find' is the boon of faith." P 248, *Poems*, I, 179 (also Luke 11:9): "Oh, if I – were the Gentleman/In the 'White Robe' –/And they – were the little Hand – that knocked." P 476, *Poems*, I, 366: "That 'Whatsoever Ye shall ask –/Itself be given You.'"

(7:13–14) P 234, *Poems*, I, 169: "You're right – 'the way *is* narrow' –/And 'difficult the Gate.'"

(7:16) Ltr 883, *LTRS*, III, 811: "Do 'Men gather Grapes of Thorns?'" Ltr 1033, *LTRS*, III, 897: "'Or Figs of Thistles?'"

(8:20) Ltr 979, *LTRS*, III, 871 (also Luke 9:58): "Foxes have Tenements, and remember, the Speaker was a Carpenter." P 143, *Poems*, I, 102 (also Luke 9:58): "For every Bird a Nest."

(10:29–31) Ltr 724, *LTRS*, III, 708 (also Shakespeare, *Hamlet*): "Mr. Samuel's 'sparrow' does not 'fall' without the fervent 'notice.'" Ltr 1044, *LTRS*, 905: "recall the 'Sparrows' and the great Logician." P 141, *Poems*, I, 100 (also Luke 12:6–7): "Sparrows, unnoticed by the Father." P 237, *Poems*, I, 171 (also Luke 12:6–7): "That you – so late – 'Consider' me –/The 'Sparrow' of your Care." P 690, *Poems*, II, 533 (also Luke 12:6–7): "God kept His Oath to Sparrows."

(10:29) P 164, *Poems*, I, 120 (also Luke 12:6–7): "If either of her 'sparrows fall',/She 'notices,' above."

(10:42) Ltr 670, *LTRS*, III, 678: "'A cup of cold water in my name' is a shivering legacy."

(11:11) Ltr 947, *LTRS*, III, 847: "She that is 'least in the kingdom of Heaven.'"

(11:19) Ltr 647, *LTRS*, III, 665: "with the hope that 'Wisdom is justified of her Children.'"

(11:25) Ltr 853, *LTRS*, III, 790: "'We thank thee that thou hast hid these things.'"

(11:26) Ltr 377, *LTRS*, II, 497: "'Even so, Father, for so it seemed faithful in thy Sight.'"

(11:28) Ltr 536, *LTRS*, II, 601. "its low 'Come unto me.'" Ltr 595, *LTRS*, II, 636: "'Come unto me.' Beloved Command-

MATTHEW (continued)

ment." Ltr 620, *LTRS*, II, 648: "'Come unto me' could not alarm those minute feet." Ltr 653, *LTRS*, III, 669: "is 'Come unto me' for Father or Child." Ltr 824, [P 1574], *LTRS*, III, 777: "As Jesus says of *Him*,/'Come unto me' the moiety." P 1586, *Poems*, III, 1093: "As Jesus cites of Him –/'Come unto me' the moiety."

(11:29) Ltr 685, *LTRS*, III, 687: "'a meek and lowly Spirit,' must be quite obscured."

(13:7) Ltr 566, *LTRS*, II, 620: "I fear you think your sweetness 'fell among Thorns.'"

(13:15) Ltr 11, *LTRS*, I, 31: "'When our eyes are dull of seeing & our ears of hearing.'"

(13:32) Ltr 481, *LTRS*, II, 569: "the Heart is the 'seed' of which we read that 'the Birds of Heaven lodge in it's Branches.'"

(14:29) Ltr 965, *LTRS*, III, 858: "Peter took the Marine Walk at the great risk."

(16:28) P 432, *Poems*, I, 335 (also Mark 9:1; Luke 9:27): "I say to you, said Jesus –/That there be standing here –/A Sort, that shall not taste of Death."

(18:3) Ltr 425, *LTRS*, II, 531: "Father had 'Become as Little Children.'"

(18:12–13) Ltr 109, *LTRS*, I, 233: "I read of the one come back, worth all the 'ninety and nine.'" Ltr 154, *LTRS*, I, 285: "The one that returns . . . is dearer than 'ninety and nine' that did not go away."

(18:20) Ltr 77, *LTRS*, I, 183: "that 'two or three' are gathered in your name." Ltr 655, *LTRS*, III, 670: "a 'two or three in my name' a confiding multitude."

(19:14) Ltr 190, *LTRS*, II, 336: "'little children,' of whom is the 'Kingdom of Heaven.'" Ltr 353, *LTRS*, II, 482: "'Suffer little Children.'" P 70, *Poems*, I, 56: "Perhaps the 'Kingdom of Heaven's' changed –/I hope the 'Children' there/Wont be 'new fashioned' when I come." P 227, *Poems*, I, 162–163: "As should sound –/'Forbid us not' –/Some like 'Emily.'"

(19:26) P 1260, *Poems*, III, 876 (also Mark 10:27): "If 'All is possible with' him."

(19:28–30) P 964, *Poems*, II, 698: "I am small – 'The Least/ Is esteemed in Heaven the Chiefest –/Occupy my House.' "

(20:16) Ltr 178, *LTRS*, II, 317: "but 'the last shall be first, and the first last.' "

(22:4) Ltr 57, *LTRS*, I, 146: "for 'behold all things are ready'!"

(24:44) Ltr 471, *LTRS*, II, 560: " 'In such an hour as ye think not' means something when you try it."

(25:23) Ltr 702, *LTRS*, III, 697–698: "To have 'been faithful in a few things' was the delicate compliment."

(25:14–28) Ltr 285, *LTRS*, II, 427: "read at devotions the chapter of the gentleman with one talent."

(25:29) Ltr 551, *LTRS*, II, 609: " 'To him that hath, shall be given.' " Ltr 788, *LTRS*, III, 751 (also Mark 4:25): " 'from him that hath not, shall be taken even that he hath.' "

(25:35) Ltr 1004, *LTRS*, III, 882: "The Saviour's only signature . . . was, A Stranger and ye took me in."

(25:40) P 132, *Poems*, I, 95: " 'Unto the little, unto me.' "

(26:11) Ltr 222, *LTRS*, II, 365: "and Saviour tells us, Kate, 'the poor are always with us.' "

(26:35) P 193, *Poems*, I, 139: "He will tell me what 'Peter' promised."

(26:42) P 1736, *Poems*, III, 1168: "drunken without companion/Was the strong cup of anguish brewed for the Nazarene."

(27:46–48) P 313, *Poems*, I, 236 (also Mark 15:34–36): "That I could spell the Prayer/ . . . That Scalding One – Sabacthini."

(28:2) P 1530, *Poems*, III, 1055: "Why, Resurrection had to wait/Till they had moved a Stone."

(28:20) Ltr 52, *LTRS*, I, 135: "— we're 'with you alway, even unto the end'!" Ltr 501, *LTRS*, II, 581: "our Brother . . . we follow . . . 'even unto the end.' "

MARK

(4:25) Ltr 788, *LTRS*, III, 751 (also Matthew 25:29): " 'from him that hath not, shall be taken even that he hath.' "

(8:36) Ltr 979, *LTRS*, III, 870–871: "To 'gain the whole

MARK (continued)

World' . . . without the baleful forfeit hinted in the Scripture."

(9:1) P 432, *Poems*, I, 335 (also Matthew 16:28; Luke 9:27): "I say to you, said Jesus –/That there be standing here –/A Sort, that shall not taste of Death."

(10:27) P 1260, *Poems*, III, 876 (also Matthew 19:26): "If 'All is possible with' him."

(15:34–36) P 313, *Poems*, I, 236 (also Matthew 27:46–48): "That I could spell the Prayer/ . . . That Scalding One – Sabacthini."

LUKE

(1:28) Ltr 1042, *LTRS*, III, 903: "– Gabriel's Oration would adorn his Child." P 725, *Poems*, II, 555: "Tho' Gabriel – praise me – Sir."

(4:2–13) Ltr 36, *LTRS*, I, 98 (also Matthew 4:3–11): "I had read of Christ's temptations."

(4:10) Ltr 820, *LTRS*, III, 774 (also Psalm 91:11): "Tell her . . . 'I give my Angels charge.'" Ltr 975, *LTRS*, III, 865 (also Psalm 91:11): "I give his Angels Charge." Ltr 991, *LTRS*, III, 877 (also Psalm 91:11): " 'I give his angels charge!' " Ltr 1012, *LTRS*, III, 887 (also Psalm 91:11): "I give 'his Angels Charge.'"

(6:45) Ltr 30, *LTRS*, I, 83: "Out of a wicked heart cometh wicked words."

(9:27) P 432, *Poems*, I, 335 (also Matthew 16:28; Mark 9:1): "I say to you, said Jesus –/That there be standing here –/ A Sort, that shall not taste of Death."

(9:58) Ltr 979, *LTRS*, III, 871 (also Matthew 8:20): "Foxes have Tenements, and remember, the Speaker was a Carpenter." P 143, *Poems*, I, 102 (also Matthew 8:20): "For every Bird a Nest."

(11:9) Ltr 133, *LTRS*, I, 263–264 (also Matthew 7:7–8): "but I seek and I don't find and knock and it is not opened." Ltr 830, *LTRS*, III, 780 (also Matthew 7:7–8): "yet 'Seek and ye shall find' is the boon of faith." P 248, *Poems*, I, 179 (also Matthew 7:7–8): "Oh, if I – were the Gentleman/In the 'White Robe' –/And they – were the little Hand – that knocked."

(11:12) Ltr 133, *LTRS*, I, 264: "where when they ask an egg, they get a scorpion."

(12:6–7) P 141, *Poems*, I, 100 (also Matthew 10:29–31): "Sparrows, unnoticed by the Father." P 164, *Poems*, I, 120 (also Matthew 10:29): "If either of her 'sparrows fall',/She 'notices,' above." P 237, *Poems*, I, 171 (also Matthew 10:29–31): "That you – *so late* – 'Consider' *me* –/The '*Sparrow*' of your Care." P 690, *Poems*, II, 533 (also Matthew 10:29–31): "God kept His Oath to Sparrows."

(12:27) Ltr 119, *LTRS*, I, 246 (also Matthew 6:28): "please accept them – the 'Lily of the field.'" Ltr 213, *LTRS*, II, 358 (also Matthew 6:28): "Even the 'Lilies of the field' have their dignities." Ltr 683, *LTRS*, III, 686 (also Matthew 6:28): "Please 'consider' me – An antique request, though in behalf of Lilies." Ltr 824, *LTRS*, III, 776 (also Matthew 6:28): "Must it not have enthralled the Bible, . . . 'The lily of the field!'" Ltr 897, *LTRS*, III, 821 (also Matthew 6:28): "Thank you for 'considering the Lilies.'" Ltr 904, *LTRS*, III, 825 (also Matthew 6:28): "the only Commandment I ever obeyed – 'Consider the Lilies.'"

(15:24) Ltr 62, *LTRS*, I, 156: "'My son was dead, and lives again – he was lost and is found!'" Ltr 796, *LTRS*, III, 757: "the Bible . . . says of it's Truant, 'This was lost and is found.'"

(18:10–13) Ltr 39, *LTRS*, I, 103: "I would pray the prayer of the 'Pharisee,' but I am a poor little 'Publican.'"

(22:55–57) P 203, *Poems*, I, 144 (also John 18:18–27): "'Thou wert with him' – quoth 'the Damsel'?/'No' – said Peter, 'twas'nt me."

(23:42–43) Ltr 791, *LTRS*, III, 754: "the Thief cried 'Lord remember me when thou comest into thy Kingdom.'" P 1180, *Poems*, III, 823: "'Remember me' implored the Thief!"

(24:51) Ltr 185, *LTRS*, II, 329: "and those were 'parted' as we walked, and 'snatched up to Heaven.'"

JOHN

(1:11) Ltr 194, *LTRS*, II, 340: "You see they come to their own and their own do not receive them."

(1:14) PF 4, *LTRS*, III, 912: "The import of the Paragraph

JOHN (continued)

'The Word made Flesh' . . . 'made Flesh and dwelt among us.'" P 1651, *Poems*, III, 1129: "'Made Flesh and dwelt among us[']/Could condescension be."

(3:1–13) Ltr 1037, *LTRS*, III, 899: "are we not 'born again' every Day, without the distractions of Nicodemus?" P 1274, *Poems*, III, 886: "Old Nicodemus' Phantom/Confronting us again!"

(3:4) P 140, *Poems*, I, 100: "And Nicodemus' Mystery/Receives it's annual reply!"

(3:6) Ltr 458, *LTRS*, II, 552: "though you first teach us 'that which is born of the Spirit is Spirit.'" Ltr 558, *LTRS*, II, 614: "The Bible portentously says 'that which is Spirit is Spirit.'"

(3:16) P 573, *Poems*, II, 437: "Our Lord – 'so loved' – it saith."

(4:32) Ltr 820, *LTRS*, III, 774: "'Meat that we know not of,' perhaps slily handed them."

(5:2–4) Ltr 521, *LTRS*, II, 593: "Bathing in that heals her./How simple is Bethesda!"

(7:37) Ltr 712, *LTRS*, III, 701: "'And let him that is athirst come' – Jesus."

(8:51) Ltr 357, *LTRS*, II, 484: "There is a verse in the Bible that says there are those who shall not see death."

(9:4) Ltr 13, *LTRS*, I, 37: "'Work while the day lasts for the night is coming in the which no man can work.'"

(11:21) Ltr 895, *LTRS*, III, 820: "'If thou had'st been here,' Mary said, 'our Brother had not died.'"

(13) Ltr 385, *LTRS*, II, 502–503 (also Matthew 26; Mark 14; Luke 22): "The loveliest sermon I ever heard was the disappointment of Jesus in Judas."

(14:1) Ltr 113, *LTRS*, I, 239: "a beautiful verse in the Bible – 'Let not your heart be troubled.'"

(14:2) P 61, *Poems*, I, 46: "Papa above!/ . . . Reserve within thy kingdom/A 'Mansion' for the Rat!" P 127, *Poems*, I, 90: "'Many Mansions', by 'his Father',/I dont know him; snugly built!"

(14:3) Ltr 50, *LTRS*, I, 129: "that 'if I *go*, I *come* again, and ye shall be with me where I *am*.'"

(14:8-9) P 1202, *Poems*, III, 836: "To analyze perhaps/A Philip would prefer."

(14:19) Ltr 651, *LTRS*, III, 667: "'Because I live, ye shall live also,' was his physiognomy."

(15:16) P 85, *Poems*, I, 69: "'They have not chosen me,' he said,/'But I have chosen them!'"

(16:15) Ltr 899, *LTRS*, III, 823: "Ineffable Avarice of Jesus, who reminds a perhaps encroaching Father, 'All these are mine.'"

(16:16) Ltr 50, *LTRS*, I, 129: "'Yet a little while I am with you, and again a little while and I am *not* with you.'" Ltr 726, *LTRS*, III, 710: "'And again a little while and ye shall not see me.'"

(16:19) Ltr 50, *LTRS*, I, 129: "'yet a little while ye shall see me and again a little while and ye shall *not* see me.'"

(17:24) Ltr 50, *LTRS*, I, 131: "'here am I my Father, and those whom thou has given me.'" Ltr 353, *LTRS*, II, 481: "and even in Our Lord's ['] that they be with me where I am.'" Ltr 785, *LTRS*, III, 750: "'Thou gavest it to me from the foundation of the world.'"

(17:25) Ltr 1024, *LTRS*, III, 893: "The World hath not known her, but I have known her."

(18:18-27) P 203, *Poems*, I, 144 (also Luke 22:55-56): "'Thou wert with him' – quoth 'the Damsel'?/'No' – said Peter, 'twas'nt me."

(19:30) Ltr 555, *LTRS*, II, 613: "'It is finished' can never be said of us."

(20:2) Ltr 560, *LTRS*, II, 616: "and I 'know not where' you 'have laid' it?"

(20:24-25) P 861, *Poems*, II, 644: "Scarlet Experiment! Sceptic Thomas!/Now, do you doubt that your Bird was true?"

(20:29) P 555, *Poems*, II, 424: "The Same – afflicted Thomas –/When Deity assured."

ACTS

(5:1-5) P 1201, *Poems*, III, 835: "Moses was'nt fairly used –/Ananias was'nt."

ACTS (continued)

(7:59) P 597, *Poems*, II, 458: "Of Stephen – or of Paul –/ For these – were only put to death."

(9) Ltr 979, *LTRS*, III, 871: "Saul criticized his Saviour till he became enamored of him."

(9:36–43) Ltr 9, *LTRS*, I, 24: "pin-cushions and needle-books, which . . . would rival the works of Scripture Dorcas."

(16:23–40) P 1166, *Poems*, II, 814: "Of Paul and Silas it is said/They were in Prison laid."

ROMANS

(8:18) Ltr 63, *LTRS*, I, 158: " 'the griefs of the present moment are not to be compared with the joys which are here-after.' "

(8:31) Ltr 746, *LTRS*, III, 724: " 'When God is with us, who shall be against us.' "

(15:13) Ltr 1032, *LTRS*, III, 896: "the words 'found peace in believing' had other than a theological import?"

I CORINTHIANS

(1:26) Ltr 50, *LTRS*, I, 130: "dont it make you think of the Bible – 'not many mighty – not wise'?"

(2:9) Ltr 92, *LTRS*, I, 208: " 'Eye hath not seen, nor ear heard, nor can the heart conceive.' " Ltr 401, *LTRS*, II, 515: " 'eye hath not seen or ear heard the things that' I would do to you." Ltr 1035, *LTRS*, III, 898: " 'Eye hath not seen nor ear heard.' What a recompense!" P 160, *Poems*, I, 117: "Next time, the things to see/By Ear unheard,/Unscrutinized by Eye." P 1241, *Poems*, III, 863: " 'Eye hath not seen' may possibly/Be current with the Blind."

(3:21–22) Ltr 189, *LTRS*, II, 335: "for they are mine and 'all things are mine.' "

(10:31) Ltr 626, *LTRS*, II, 652: " 'Whatsoever ye do, do it unto the Glory.' "

(13:12) Ltr 96, *LTRS*, I, 215: "Shall I indeed behold you, not 'darkly, but face to face.' "

(15:35) Ltr 671, [P 1492], *LTRS*, III, 679: " 'And with what body do they come?' "

(15:41) Ltr 57, *LTRS*, I, 146: " – yet they 'differ as *stars*' in their distinctive glories." Ltr 669, *LTRS*, III, 677: "Did the 'stars differ' from each other in anything but 'glory.'"

(15:42–43) P 62, *Poems*, I, 47: "Corinthians I. 15. narrates/ A Circumstance or two!"

(15:51) Ltr 568, *LTRS*, II, 621: "Were the Statement 'We shall not all sleep, but we shall all be changed.'" Ltr 885, *LTRS*, III, 812: "'We shall not all sleep, but we shall all be changed.'"

(15:52) Ltr 1020, *LTRS*, III, 891: "But Corinthians' Bugle obliterates the Birds."

(15:53) Ltr 389, *LTRS*, II, 506: "in a few instances this 'mortal has already put on immortality.'"

(15:53–54) Ltr 391, *LTRS*, II, 508: "that 'this Corruption shall put on Incorruption.'"

(15:55) Ltr 732, *LTRS*, III, 714 (also Pope, "The Dying Christian to His Soul"): "Death has mislaid his sting — the grave forgot his victory." Ltr 967, *LTRS*, III, 860: "Oh, Death, where is thy Chancellor?"

II CORINTHIANS

(4:17) Ltr 52, *LTRS*, I, 135: "it shall work out for us a far more exceeding and 'eternal weight' of *presence!*" Ltr 815, *LTRS*, III, 771: "Paul's remark grows graphic, 'the *weight* of glory.'"

(5:1) Ltr 180, *LTRS*, II, 321: "we have *other* home – 'house not made with hands.'" Ltr 182, *LTRS*, II, 323: "We shall sit in a parlor 'not made with hands.'" Ltr 458, [P 1360], *LTRS*, II, 552: "'The House not made with Hands' it was." Ltr 866, *LTRS*, III, 797: "The first Abode 'not made with Hands' entices to the second."

GALATIANS

(5:22) Ltr 936, *LTRS*, III, 839–840: "We have no fruit this year, . . . except the 'Fruits of the Spirit.'"

EPHESIANS

(2:9) Ltr 850, *LTRS*, III, 789: "Lest any Bee should boast." Ltr 852, *LTRS*, III, 790: "'Lest any' Hen 'should boast.'"

(3:20) Ltr 820, *LTRS*, III, 774: "more love than 'we can ask or think.'"

(4:8) Ltr 937, *LTRS*, III, 840: "I infer from your Note you have 'taken Captivity Captive.'"

PHILIPPIANS

(1:23) Ltr 683, *LTRS*, III, 685: "Honey not born of Bee — but Constancy – which is 'far better.'"

I TIMOTHY

(1:17) Ltr 952, *LTRS*, III, 851: "The enemy 'eternal, invisible, and full of glory.'"

(3:16) Ltr 890, *LTRS*, III, 816: "he hastened away, 'seen,' we trust, 'of Angels.'"

(4:8) Ltr 184, *LTRS*, II, 328: "we have each a *pair* of lives, and need not chary be, of the one 'that *now* is.'" Ltr 685, *LTRS*, III, 687: "How sweet the 'Life that now is.'" P 1260, *Poems*, III, 876: "The 'Life that is to be,' to me."

II TIMOTHY

(1:12) Ltr 953, *LTRS*, III, 852: "To 'know in whom' we 'have believed,' is Immortality."

(3:16) Ltr 650, *LTRS*, III, 667: "She forgets that we are past 'Correction in Righteousness.'"

(4:7) Ltr 727, *LTRS*, III, 711: "'I have finished,' said Paul, 'the faith.'" PF 9, *LTRS*, III, 912: "'I have finished the faith,' he said; we rejoice he did not say *discarded* it."

HEBREWS

(12:6) Ltr 369, *LTRS*, II, 492: "'Whom he loveth, he punisheth' is doubtful solace." Ltr 976, *LTRS*, III, 866: "no solace in 'whom he loveth he chasteneth.'"

(12:23) Ltr 873, *LTRS*, III, 803: "May I go with you to the 'Church of the first born?'"

(13:8) Ltr 801, *LTRS*, III, 760: "'The first of April' 'Today, Yesterday, and Forever.'" Ltr 829, *LTRS*, III, 780: "'Yesterday, Today, and Forever,' then we will let you go."

JAMES

(2:17) Ltr 8, *LTRS*, I, 20: "of as much use as faith without works, which you know we are told is dead."

I PETER

(1:8) Ltr 671, *LTRS*, III, 679: "and your sweet wife, 'whom seeing not, we' trust." Ltr 747, *LTRS*, III, 724: "'Whom seeing not, we' clasp." Ltr 944, *LTRS*, III, 846: "The Apostle's inimitable apology for loving whom he saw not." P 1681, *Poems*, III, 1143: "Behold said the Apostle/Yet had not seen!"

(2:24) Ltr 689, *LTRS*, III, 689: "I have seen a Crow – 'in his own Body on the Tree.'"

II PETER

(1:21) Ltr 794, *LTRS*, III, 756: "my early question of 'Who made the Bible' – 'Holy Men moved by the Holy Ghost.'"

(3:18) Ltr 808, *LTRS*, III, 765: "the lovely Invalid is growing every Day, not in Grace but Vigor."

I JOHN

(3:10–11) Ltr 176, *LTRS*, I, 311: "'Little Children, love one another.'"

(4:10) Ltr 393, *LTRS*, II, 510: "'Not that we loved him but that he loved us'?" PF 5, *LTRS*, III, 912: "'Not that we first loved Him, but that He first loved us'?"

(4:16) P 1260, *Poems*, III, 876: "If 'God is Love' as he admits."

JUDE

(25) Ltr 194, *LTRS*, II, 340: "'Power and honor' are here today, and 'dominion and glory'!"

REVELATION

Ltr 261, *LTRS*, II, 404: "You inquire my Books . . . and the Revelations." P 168, *Poems*, I, 123: "Those who read the 'Revelations.'"

(1:9–11) Ltr 787, *LTRS*, III, 751: "as if I were . . . the Vision of John at Patmos."

(2:10) P 1357, *Poems*, III, 938: "'I will give' the base Proviso –/Spare Your 'Crown of Life.'"

(3:12) Ltr 185, *LTRS*, II, 329: "where friends should 'go no more out.'"

(4:4) P 81, *Poems*, I, 66: "The Bobolinks around the throne/ And Dandelions gold."

(6) Ltr 194, *LTRS*, II, 340: "*You* may tell, when 'the seal' is opened."

(7:3–8) P 322, *Poems*, I, 250. "Each was to each The Sealed Church."

REVELATION (continued)

(7:11) Ltr 194, *LTRS*, II, 340: "*Mat* may tell when they 'fall on their faces.'"

(7:13–14) P 325, *Poems*, I, 256: "Of Tribulation – these are They,/Denoted by the White."

(7:16) Ltr 352, *LTRS*, II, 479: "the men of the Revelations who 'shall not hunger any more.'" Ltr 593, *LTRS*, II, 635: "Home in the Revelations — 'Neither thirst any more.'" P 460, *Poems*, I, 354: "I read in an Old fashioned Book/That People 'thirst no more.'"

(14:3) Ltr 185, *LTRS*, II, 329: "the 'hundred and forty and four thousand' were chatting pleasantly."

(19:11) Ltr 804, *LTRS*, III, 762: "by the phrase in the Scripture 'And I saw the Heavens opened.'" Ltr 815, *LTRS*, III, 771: "'And I saw the Heavens opened.'"

(21:1) Ltr 683, *LTRS*, III, 686: "It is deep to live to experience 'And there was no more Sea.'" P 1200, *Poems*, III, 835: "To where the Strong assure me/Is 'no more Sea.'"

(21:4) Ltr 77, *LTRS*, I, 183: "The Bible tells us — 'there is no sickness there.'" Ltr 185, *LTRS*, II, 329: "and there were 'no tears.'"

(21:5) P 322, *Poems*, I, 249: "As if no soul the solstice passed/That maketh all things new."

(21:8) P 1598, *Poems*, III, 1100: "'All' Rogues 'shall have their part in' what."

(21:18–24) P 215, *Poems*, I, 151: "I shant walk the 'Jasper' – barefoot –/Ransomed folks – wont laugh at me."

(21:21) Ltr 399, *LTRS*, II, 514: "'Every several Gate was of one Pearl.'" Ltr 864, *LTRS*, III, 796: "'Every several Gate is one of Pearl.'" P 70, *Poems*, I, 56: "I hope the Father in the skies/Will lift his little girl –/ . . . Over the stile of 'Pearl.'"

(22:5) P 871, *Poems*, II, 648: "For the Zones of Paradise/The Lord alone is burned."

(22:16) Ltr 457, *LTRS*, II, 551: "'I – Jesus – have sent mine Angel.'"

(22:17) Ltr 57, *LTRS*, I, 146: "— home is bright and shining, 'and the spirit and the bride say *come*, and let him that' wandereth come."

Blind, Mathilde. *Life of George Eliot.* Ltr 813, *LTRS*, III, 768: "A base return indeed, for the delightful Book [received from Thomas Niles]." Ltr 814, *LTRS*, III, 769: "The Life of Marian Evans had much I never knew."

Brontë, Charlotte (Currer Bell). **Jane Eyre.* New York: Harper and Brothers, 1864. HCL. Inscribed to "Emily with the love of Mrs. Eastman, Sept 20th 1865." Ltr 28, *LTRS*, I, 77: "a prayer that Currer Bell might be saved." Ltr 475, *LTRS*, II, 562: " 'I find your Benefits no Burden, Jane.' "

——— **Villette.* New York: Harper and Brothers, 1859. HCL. Inscribed by Susan Dickinson, "Emily Dickinson."

——— "Biographical Notice" in 1850 edition of E. Brontë's *Wuthering Heights.* Ltr 742, *LTRS*, III, 721: "of whom Charlotte said 'Full of ruth for others, on herself she had no mercy.' "

Brontë, Emily (Ellis Bell). "No Coward Soul is Mine." Ltr 873, *LTRS*, III, 802–803: "– As Emily Bronte to her Maker, I write to my Lost 'Every Existence would exist in thee.' " Ltr 940, *LTRS*, III, 844: "Said that marvellous Emily Bronte ['] . . . Every Existence would Exist in thee.['] " Ltr 948, *LTRS*, III, 848: "Did you read Emily Bronte's marvellous verse?['] . . . Every existence would exist in Thee.['] "

——— **Wuthering Heights.* New York: Harper and Brothers, 1858. HCL. Ltr 742, *LTRS*, III, 721: see ED's quotation from C. Brontë's "Biographical Notice," cited above. Ltr 866, *LTRS*, III, 798: "and say with 'Heathcliff' to little Katrina."

Browne, Sir Thomas. *The Works of Sir Thomas Browne,* ed. Simon Wilkin, 3 vols. London: Henry G. Bohn, 1852. HCL. All volumes signed, "Susan H. Gilbert." Ltr 261, *LTRS*, II, 404: "You inquire my Books . . . For Prose – Mr Ruskin – Sir Thomas Browne – and the Revelations."

Browning, Elizabeth Barrett. **Aurora Leigh.* New York: C. S. Francis and Co., 1859. Amherst College Library, signed, "E. Dickinson." New York, Boston: C. S. Francis and Co., 1857. HCL, signed, "S. H. Dickinson." Ltr 234, *LTRS*, II, 376: "That Mrs. Browning fainted, we need not read *Aurora Leigh* to know." Ltr 372, *LTRS*, II, 495: "she will hate to leave it as badly as *Marian Erle* did." Ltr 696, *LTRS*, III, 695: "lain on

'Marian Erle's dim pallet.'" Ltr 950, *LTRS*, III, 849: "I did not forget the Anniversary . . . but cover it with Leaves."

Browning, Elizabeth Barrett. "Catarina to Camoens." Ltr 491, *LTRS*, II, 575: "I hope I have not tired 'Sweetest Eyes were ever seen.'" Ltr 801, *LTRS*, III, 759. "And for Katrina's Eyes, Camoens is sorry."

——— *Last Poems.* P 312, *Poems*, I, 234: "Her – 'last Poems.'"

——— "A Vision of Poets." P 449, *Poems*, I, 347: "I died for Beauty – . . . /And I – for Truth – Themself are One."

Browning, Robert. *By the Fireside.* Ltr 966, *LTRS*, III, 859: "'But the last Leaf fear to touch,' says the consummate Browning."

——— "Evelyn Hope." Ltr 669, *LTRS*, III, 677: "God, who certainly 'gave the love to reward the love.'"

——— "In Three Days." Ltr 547, *LTRS*, II, 607: "it is said there will be a Portrait – 'so I shall see it in just three Days.'"

——— "The Last Ride Together." Ltr 1015, *LTRS*, III, 889: "and one Day more I am deified, was the only impression she ever left." P 712, *Poems*, II, 546: "Because I could not stop for Death – "

——— "Love Among the Ruins." Ltr 891, *LTRS*, III, 817: "'Miles and miles away,' said Browning, 'there's a girl;' the colored end of evening smiles' on few so rare."

——— **Men and Women.* Boston: Ticknor and Fields, 1856. Amherst College Library. Signed, "E. Dickinson." Ltr 368, *LTRS*, II, 491. "You speak of 'Men and Women.' That is a broad Book – "

——— *The Ring and the Book*, 2 vols. Boston: Fields, Osgood, and Co., 1869. HCL. Both vols. signed, "S. H. Dickinson." P 1129, *Poems*, II, 792: "Tell all the Truth but tell it slant."

——— *Sordello.* Boston: Ticknor and Fields, 1864. HCL. Signed, "S. H. Dickinson." Ltr 337, *LTRS*, II, 466: "I suppose we must all 'ail till evening.'" Ltr 477, *LTRS*, II, 566: "Was it Browning's flower, that 'Ailed till Evening'?"

Bryant, William Cullen. *June.* Ltr 967, *LTRS*, III, 860: "I . . . cannot yet believe that 'his part in all the pomp that fills/The circuit of the Southern Hills/Is that his Grave is green.'"

——— "My Autumn Walk." P 131, *Poems*, I, 94: "Gone – Mr Bryant's 'Golden Rod.'"

—— *Poems by* . . . Philadelphia: Carey and Hart, 1849. HCL. Inscribed, "To Miss Gilbert . . . Dec 25th 51."

—— "Thanatopsis." Ltr 29, *LTRS*, I, 79: "five minutes in all – the 'wrapping the drapery of his couch about him – and lying down to pleasant dreams' included."

Bunyan, John. *The Pilgrim's Progress.* Boston: Phillips and Sampson, 1847. HCL. Signed, "Edw. Dickinson 1847." Ltr 110, *LTRS*, I, 234: "I . . . would recommend 'Pilgrim's Progress.'"

Burkitt, William. "Jerusalem! My Happy Home!" Ltr 42, *LTRS*, I, 111: "thinking of several future places 'where congregations ne'er break up.'" Ltr 110, *LTRS*, I, 235: "a favorite stanza of your's, 'where congregations ne'er break up, and Sabbaths have no end.'"

Burnett, Frances Hodgson. *The Fair Barbarian.* Ltr 689, *LTRS*, III, 690: "The neighborhood are much amused by the 'Fair Barbarian.'"

Burns, Robert. "Auld Lang Syne." Ltr 184, *LTRS*, II, 328: "Mid your momentous cares, pleasant to know – that 'Lang Syne' has it's own place."

—— *The Complete Works of* . . . Boston: Phillips, Sampson, and Company, 1853. HCL. Signed, "S. H. Gilbert."

—— "Despondency." P 23, *Poems*, I, 23: "That when I could not find it –/I sat me down to sigh."

—— "John Anderson, My Jo." Ltr 99, *LTRS*, I, 219: "the quiet cap, and the spectacles, and 'John Anderson my Joe.'"

—— "Here's to thy Health." Ltr 184, *LTRS*, II, 328: "John – Lad – and 'here's a health to *you*.'" P 23, *Poems*, I, 23: "Still, for my missing Troubadour/I kept the 'house at hame.'" P 192, *Poems*, I, 138: "Poor little Heart!/Did they forget thee?/Then dinna care! Then dinna care!"

—— "To a Louse." Ltr 128, *LTRS*, I, 256: "'Oh would some power the giftie gie' folks, to see themselves as we see them. Burns."

—— "To a Mouse." Ltr 118, *LTRS*, I, 244–245: "but this [is] a vexing world, and things 'aft gang aglay.'" Ltr 866, *LTRS*, III, 798: "Even my Puritan Spirit 'gangs' sometimes 'aglay.'"

Byron, George Gordon, Lord. "The Prisoner of Chillon." Ltr 233, *LTRS*, II, 374: "when I do not see – 'Chillon' is not funny."

Ltr 249, *LTRS*, II, 393: "To the people of 'Chillon' – this – is enoug[h]." Ltr 293, *LTRS*, II, 433: "You remember the Prisoner of Chillon did not know Liberty when it came." Ltr 1029, *LTRS*, III, 895: "This long, short penance 'Even I regain my freedom with a Sigh.'" Ltr 1042, *LTRS*, III, 903: "she will learn the Customs of Heaven, as the Prisoner of Chillon of Captivity."

Byron, George Gordon, Lord. *The Works of* . . . , 4 vols. New York: E. Duyckink and G. Long, 1821. HCL. Vol. II inscribed, "E. Dickinson, $2.80."

The Century Magazine. HCL. November 1881 through May 1886 (lacks Apr. 83).

Cervantes, Miguel. *Don Quixote,* 5 vols. Philadelphia: John Conrad and Co., 1803. HCL. Inscribed, "E. Dickinson 1827." Ltr 389, *LTRS*, II, 506: "It reminds me of Don Quixote demanding the surrender of the wind-mill."

Chambers, Robert, ed. *Cyclopaedia of English Literature,* 2 vols. HCL. Two editions: Boston, 1847, inscribed, "Edw. Dickinson."; Edinburgh, 1844, inscribed, "S. H. Gilbert. 1856."

Channing, William Ellery. "A Poet's Hope." P 1234, *Poems*, III, 858: "If my Bark sink/'Tis to another sea."

Clarke, Mrs. Cowden. **The Complete Concordance to Shakespeare.* Boston: Little, Brown and Company, 1877. HCL. Inscribed by Susan Dickinson, "Emily Dickinson from Judge Otis P. Lord."

Cowper, William. "Light Shining out of Darkness." Ltr 97, *LTRS*, I, 217: "Yet we should not repine – 'God moves in a mysterious way, his wonders to perform.'"

——— "John Gilpin's Ride." Ltr 213, *LTRS*, II, 359: "and can only sigh with one not present at 'John Gilpin.'" Ltr 888, *LTRS*, 814: "Baby's flight will embellish History with Gilpin's and Revere's."

——— *Poems,* 3 vols. Philadelphia: Thomas Desilver, 1818. HCL. Vol. I inscribed, "Emily Norcross . . . Monson 1828."

Cross, J. W. *The Life of George Eliot.* I (1885). ED's gift volume is in The Houghton Library, Harvard and is inscribed, "T. W. Higginson from Emily Dickinson, 1885." Ltr 972, *LTRS*, III, 863–864: "your consent to accept the Book [Cross's *Eliot*]."

Ltr 974, *LTRS*, III, 864–865: "how fitting (sweet) that his [Bowles's biography] and George Eliots . . . should be chosen so near."

Cross, Walter. *Life of Mrs. Cross.* Ltr 819, *LTRS*, III, 773: "May I ask the delight in advance, of sending you the 'Life of Mrs Cross' by her Husband." Ltr 962, *LTRS*, III, 856: "watching like a vulture for Walter Cross's life of his wife."

Cutter, Calvin. *A Treatise on Anatomy, Physiology, and Hygiene* . . . Boston: B. B. Mussey and Co. MHT. Ltr 20, *LTRS*, I, 59: "I am now studying 'Silliman's Chemistry' & Cutler's [*sic*] Physiology."

Dana, Charles Anderson, ed. *The Household Book of Poetry*, 6th ed. New York and London, 1860. HCL.

Davis, Rebecca Harding. "Life in the Iron Mills," *Atlantic Monthly* (Apr. 1861). Ltr 231, *LTRS*, II, 372: "Will Susan please lend Emily 'Life in the Iron Mills.'"

Day, Jeremiah. *An Introduction to Algebra* . . . New Haven: Durrie and Peck; Philadelphia: Smith & Peck, 1845. MHT. Philadelphia, New Haven, 1842. HCL. Ltr 19, *LTRS*, I, 57: "to tell you what my studies are now. . . . Chemistry, Physiology & quarter course in Algebra."

Defoe, Daniel. *Robinson Crusoe.* Ltr 685, *LTRS*, III, 687: "Many of us go farther. My pathetic Crusoe."

DeQuincey, Thomas. *The Works of* . . . , 10 of 12 vols. Boston: Ticknor, Reed, and Fields, 1853–1859. HCL. Ltr 191, *LTRS*, II, 336: "Have you . . . either *Klosterheim*, or 'Confessions of an Opium Eater,' by DeQuincey?"

Dickens, Charles. *Bleak House.* New York: G. W. Carleton and Co., 1880. HCL. Bookplate: Edward Dickinson. Ltr 85, *LTRS*, I, 195: "Vinnie and I had 'Bleak House' sent to us the other day."

——— *David Copperfield.* New York: G. W. Carleton and Co., 1879. HCL. Bookplate: Edward Dickinson. Ltr 42, *LTRS*, I, 111: "that 'Barkis is very willin.'" Ltr 49, *LTRS*, I, 126: "'I will never desert Micawber' however *he may* be forgetful." Ltr 86, *LTRS*, I, 196: "And what will dear Jennie say, if I tell her that selfsame minister." Ltr 107, *LTRS*, I, 229: "'Miss

Mills,' that is, Miss Julia, never *dreamed* of the depths." Ltr 204, *LTRS*, II, 350: "I did not suspect complacency in 'Mr Brown of Sheffield'!" Ltr 487, *LTRS*, II, 572: "Doctor's 'Child Wife' – indeed – if not Mr Copperfield's." Ltr 549, *LTRS*, II, 608: "[signed] 'Brooks of Sheffield.'" P 1020, *Poems*, II, 729. "Asked him his name – He lisped me 'Trotwood.'"

Dickens, Charles. *Dombey and Son*. New York: Burgess, Stringer, and Co., 1848. HCL. Ltr 409, *LTRS*, II, 522: "to me like Dickens's hero's dead mamma, 'too some weeks off' to risk." Ltr 692, *LTRS*, III, 693: "– the 'Cap'n Cuttle' of Amherst." Ltr 764, *LTRS*, III, 736: "It is 'Weeks off' as little Dombey said." Ltr 888, *LTRS*, III, 814: "'Weeks off,' as Dombey said." P 1078, *Poems*, II, 763: "The Bustle in a House."

——— *The Haunted Man and The Ghost's Bargain*. Ltr 31, *LTRS*, I, 89: "'Lord keep all our memories green.'"

——— *The Old Curiosity Shop*. Philadelphia, 184-. HCL. Inscribed, "Edw. Dickinson." Ltr 241, *LTRS*, II, 382: "but 'Swiveller' may be sure of the 'Marchioness.'" Ltr 491, *LTRS*, II, 575: "You remember Little Nell's Grandfather leaned on his Cane on the Knoll that contained her, with 'She will come tomorrow.'" P 78, *Poems*, I, 63: "A poor – torn heart – a tattered heart."

——— *The Pickwick Papers*. Ltr 30, *LTRS*, I, 82: "Pickwick himself could'nt have been more amazed when he found himself soul – body and – spirit incarcerated in the pound." P 91, *Poems*, I, 73. "For whom I robbed the Dingle –/For whom betrayed the Dell."

——— *The Uncommercial Traveller*. P 585, *Poems*, II, 448: "And neigh like Boanerges."

Disraeli, Benjamin (Lord Beaconsfield). **Endymion*. New York: D. Appleton and Company, 1880. HCL. Inscribed, "Emily, Whom not seeing I still love. Sue. Xmas 1880."

Eliot, George. **Adam Bede*. New York: Harper and Brothers, 1860. HCL. Inscribed, "Emily from Sue."

——— *Daniel Deronda*. Ltr 450, *LTRS*, II, 548: "please not to own 'Daniel Deronda' till I bring it, when it is done." Ltr 456, *LTRS*, II, 551: "Thank you, dear, for the 'Eliot.'" Ltr 457, *LTRS*, II, 551: "– To abstain from 'Daniel Deronda' is hard."

Ltr 802, *LTRS*, III, 761 (also John Milton, *Samson Agonistes*): "If the Spirits are fair as the Faces 'Nothing is here for Tears.' " Ltr 974, *LTRS*, III, 865: "have you read Daniel Deronda – That wise and tender Book."

——— *The Legend of Jubal and Other Poems.* Ltr 951, *LTRS*, III, 850. "when the 'Choir invisible' assemble in your Trees." Ltr 1042, *LTRS*, III, 903: "she had in her Hand as I entered, the 'Choir invisible.' "

——— *Middlemarch.* Ltr 389, *LTRS*, II, 506: " 'What do I think of *Middlemarch?*' What do I think of glory." Ltr 401, *LTRS*, II, 515: "also to her sweet sister *Mrs. Ladislaw.*"

——— **The Mill on the Floss.* New York: Harper and Brothers, 1860. HCL. Signed, "Emily E. Dickinson." Ltr 277, *LTRS*, II, 419: "for that can stand alone, like the best Brocade." Ltr 368, *LTRS*, II, 491: "but truth like Ancestor's Brocades can stand alone." Ltr 650, *LTRS*, III, 666: "I have a Letter from 'Aunt Glegg.' " Ltr 888, *LTRS*, III, 814: "Your flight from the 'Sewer' reminded me of the 'Mill on the Floss,' though 'Maggie Tulliver' was missing."

——— **The Spanish Gypsy: A Poem.* Boston: Ticknor and Fields, 1868. HCL. Inscribed by Susan Dickinson, "Emily Dickinson."

Emerson, Ralph W. "Bacchus." P 214, *Poems*, I, 149: "I taste a liquor never brewed."

——— "Concord Hymn." Ltr 436, *LTRS*, II, 539: "I have only a buttercup to offer for the centennial, as an 'embattled farmer.' "

——— "Fable." Ltr 794, *LTRS*, III, 756: "deathless as Emerson's 'Squirrel.' "

——— "The Humble-Bee." Ltr 1004, *LTRS*, III, 882: "an 'Humbler' Bee? 'I will sail by thee alone, thou animated Torrid Zone.' "

——— **Poems* (1847). Boston: James Munroe and Company, 1847. HCL. Ltr 30, *LTRS*, I, 84: "I had a letter – and Ralph Emerson's Poems – a beautiful copy – from Newton."

——— *Representative Men.* ED presented a copy of the new edition, J. R. Osgood, 1876 to Mrs. T. W. Higginson, inscribed, "To MCH from Emily Dickinson, Christmas, 1876." Ltr 481, *LTRS*, II, 569: "a little Granite Book you can lean upon."

Emerson, Ralph W. "The Snow Storm." PF 116, *LTRS*, III, 928: "'Tumultuous privacy of storm.'"

Emmons, Henry V. "The Words of Rock Rimmon," *Amherst Collegiate Magazine* (July 1854). Ltr 171, *LTRS*, I, 303: *"Then* 'golden morning's open flowings, *shall* sway the trees to murmurous bowings, in metric chant of blessed poems.'"

Fargus, Frederick John (Hugh Conway). *Called Back.* Ltr 962, *LTRS*, III, 856: "A friend sent me *Called Back.* It is a haunting story." Ltr 1046, *LTRS*, III, 906: "Little Cousins, Called back."

Fullerton, Lady Georgiana. *Ellen Middleton.* Ltr 90, *LTRS*, I, 205: "I have read 'Ellen Middleton.'" Ltr 94, *LTRS*, I, 212: "an hour with 'Edward' and 'Ellen Middleton.'"

Gaskell, E. C. *The Life of Charlotte Brontë.* New York: D. Appleton and Company, 1858. HCL. Inscribed by ED, "Sister from Sister." Ltr 471, *LTRS*, II, 559: "Vinnie has a new pussy the color of Branwell Brontë's hair."

Goldsmith, Oliver. *The Vicar of Wakefield.* Ltr 285, *LTRS*, II, 427: "Tell me precisely how Wakefield looks."

Gordon, Mary Wilson. *Memoir of John Wilson.* Ltr 409, *LTRS*, II 522: "I wish I could make you as long a call as DeQuincey made North."

Gray, Thomas. "Elegy in a Country Churchyard." Ltr 31, *LTRS*, I, 89: "I would have the 'long lingering look' which you cast behind."

Grimshaw, William. *The History of France from the Foundation of the Monarchy to the Death of Louis XVI. . .* Philadelphia: Grigg and Elliott, 1840. MHT. Ltr 18, *LTRS*, I, 54: "we read Goldsmith & Grimshaw."

Griswold, Rufus, ed. *The Sacred Poets of England and America.* New York and Philadelphia, 1849. HCL. Second copy, presented to Susan Gilbert December 22, 1848. HCL.

Halleck, Fitz-Greene. "Marco Bozzaris." Ltr 13, *LTRS*, I, 36: "& close their eyes 'calmly as to a nights repose or flowers at set of sun.'" Ltr 362, *LTRS*, II, 488: "'We conquered, but Bozzaris fell.'"

——— "On the Death of Joseph Rodman Drake." Ltr 875, *LTRS*, III, 804: "dear Mrs. Carmichael, whom 'to name is to praise.'"

APPENDIX A

The Hampshire and Franklin Express, September 1842–April 1868. (Published as *The Hampshire Express*, July 1866–April 1868.) See Chapter VI.

Harper's New Monthly Magazine. June 1850 to May 1886. May 1853; Jan and Sept 1869; May 1870. HCL.

Harte, Bret. *The Luck of Roaring Camp and Other Sketches.* Boston: Fields, Osgood, and Co., 1871. HCL. Signed, "S. H. Dickinson." Ltr 388, *LTRS*, II, 505: "Maggie preferred her home to 'Miggles' and 'Oakhurst.'"

Hawthorne, Nathaniel. *The House of the Seven Gables.* Boston: Ticknor, Reed, and Fields, 1851. HCL. Signed, "Wm A. Dickinson." Ltr 62, *LTRS*, I, 155: "then I thought of 'Hepzibah' how sorrowful *she* was . . . and for the sake of 'Clifford' she wearied on."

Heber, Reginald. "I see them on their winding way." Ltr 544, *LTRS*, II, 605: "'About' *which* 'Ranks the Sunbeams play,' is a touching question."

Herndon, William Lewis and Lardner Gibbon. *Exploration of the Valley of the Amazon*, 2 vols. Washington: Robert Armstrong, 1854. HCL. Vol. I inscribed, "Miss Emily Dickinson from her father."

Higginson, Mary Thacher [Mrs. Thomas Wentworth]. *Room for One More.* Ltr 641, *LTRS*, III, 661: "'Room for one more' was a plea for Heaven."

Higginson, Thomas Wentworth. *Army Life in a Black Regiment.* Ltr 487, *LTRS*, II, 573: "He seems the 'Child of the Regiment' since he was so sick." Ltr 653, *LTRS*, III, 669: "'Little Annie,' of whom you feared to make the mistake in saying 'Shoulder Arms' to the 'Colored Regiment.'"

——— *Atlantic Essays.* 1871. Ltr 368, *LTRS*, II, 491: "the 'Atlantic Essays.' They are a fine Joy."

——— "Carlyle's Laugh," *Atlantic Monthly* (October 1881). Ltr 728, *LTRS*, III, 711: "Does she coo with 'discraytion'?"

——— "Childhood Fancies," *Scribner's Monthly* (January 1876). Ltr 449, *LTRS*, II, 546: "I had read 'Childhood,' with compunction."

——— "Decoration," *Scribner's Monthly* (June 1874). Ltr 418,

LTRS, II, 528: "Your beautiful Hymn, was it not prophetic?" Ltr 503, *LTRS*, II, 583: "I was rereading your 'Decoration.'" Ltr 1042, *LTRS*, III, 903: "'Mars the sacred Loneliness'! What an Elegy!" P 1393, *Poems*, III, 960: "Lay this Laurel on the One."

Higginson, Thomas Wentworth. "Letter to a Young Contributor," *Atlantic Monthly* (April 1862). Ltr 260, *LTRS*, II, 403: "I enclose my name – asking you, if you please – Sir – to tell me what is true?" Ltr 488, *LTRS*, II, 573: "that paragraph of your's has saved me – 'Such being the Majesty of Art you presume to practice.'"

—— Unsigned review of Lowell's *Among My Books: Second Series*, *Scribner's Monthly* (March 1876). Ltr 457, *LTRS*, II, 551: "I inferred your touch in the Papers on Lowell and Emerson."

—— "The Life of Birds," *Atlantic Monthly* (September 1862). Ltr 692, *LTRS*, III, 693: "which is what the Essayist calls 'the Immortal Peewee.'" Ltr 1034, *LTRS*, III, 897: " – perhaps like Keats's bird, 'and hops and hops in little journeys'?"

—— *Malbone: An Oldport Romance*. Ltr 342a, *LTRS*, II, 473: "Malbone & OD Papers among other books." Ltr 450, *LTRS*, II, 548: "Did you not teach me that yourself, in the 'Prelude' to 'Malbone'?"

—— *Oldport Days*. Ltr 405, *LTRS*, II, 518: "I was re-reading 'Oldport.'"

—— *Outdoor Papers*. Ltr 342a, *LTRS*, II, 473: "Malbone & OD Papers among other books." Ltr 458, *LTRS*, II, 552: "as distinct as Paradise – the opening of your first Book."

—— "A Plea for Culture," *Atlantic Monthly* (January 1867). Ltr 323, *LTRS*, II, 457: "Bringing still my 'plea for Culture.'"

—— "The Procession of Flowers," *Atlantic Monthly* (February 1863). Ltr 280, *LTRS*, II, 424: "I trust the 'Procession of Flowers' was not a premonition."

—— "A Shadow," *Atlantic Monthly* (July 1870). Ltr 353, *LTRS*, II, 481: "I thought I spoke to you of the shadow – It affects me."

—— *Short Stories of American Authors*. Boston: Lee and Shepard; New York: Charles T. Dillingham, 1880. HCL. Inscribed, "Emily Dickinson from her friend the author, Christmas, 1879."

APPENDIX A

Ltr 622, *LTRS*, II, 649: "Mrs Jackson soars to your estimate
. . . but of Howells and James, one hesitates."

——— "To the Memory of H. H.," *Century Magazine* (May 1886).
Ltr 1042, *LTRS*, III, 903: "Thank you for 'the Sonnet'–I have
lain it at her loved feet."

——— "Water Lilies." P 1084, *Poems*, II, 766: "At Half past Three,
a single Bird."

Hitchcock, Edward. *Catalogue of Plants Growing in the Vicinity of
Amherst*. 1829. Ltr 488, *LTRS*, II, 573: "I used to read Dr
Hitchcock's Book on the Flowers of North America."

Holland, Josiah Gilbert. "To My Dog Blanco," *Scribner's Monthly*
(August 1881). Ltr 721, *LTRS*, III, 706: "Doctor's betrothal
to 'Blanco' . . .–I read it."

——— *Nicholas Minturn* (appeared serially, *Scribner's Monthly*,
1876–1877). Ltr 502, *LTRS*, II, 582: "our sacred Neighbors,
. . . were so enamored of 'Nicholas Minturn,' that they borrow
our Number."

Holmes, Oliver Wendell. **Poems*. Boston: William D. Ticknor,
1849. HCL. Inscribed, "Miss Emily E. Dickinson. From J. P.
K. 'Philopena.' Amherst, Jan 18th, 1849."

——— *Ralph Waldo Emerson*. Ltr 962, *LTRS*, III, 856: "Holmes's
Life of Emerson is sweetly commended."

Howells, William Dean. *A Fearful Responsibility* (appeared serially,
Scribner's Monthly, 1880). Ltr 714, *LTRS*, III, 702: "How
did you snare Howells?" Ltr 721, *LTRS*, III, 706: "Who wrote
Mr Howells' story? Certainly he did not."

——— *The Undiscovered Country* (appeared serially, *Atlantic
Monthly*, beginning January 1880). Ltr 629, *LTRS*, III, 656:
"Mr Howells implies in his 'Undiscovered Country,' that 'our
relation to Pie' will unfold in proportion." Ltr 752, *LTRS*, III,
730: "retraced almost from the 'Undiscovered Country.'"

Humphrey, Heman. *A Tribute to the Memory of Rev. Nathan W.
Fiske* . . . Ltr 1042, *LTRS*, III, 903: "'From Mount Zion
below to Mount Zion above'! said President Humphrey."

Huntington, F. D. **Christian Believing and Living*. Boston: Crosby,
Nichols, and Company, 1860. HCL. Inscribed, "A present to
Emily E. Dickinson from her father, April 4, 1860."

Irving, Washington. *Life of Columbus.* P 697, *Poems*, II, 538:
"Dower itself – for Bobadilo."
——— "Rip Van Winkle." Ltr 412, *LTRS*, II, 524: "someone has
been asleep! Suffer Rip – Van Winkle!"
Jackson, Helen Hunt (H. H., Mrs. William S. Jackson). **Bits of
Travel at Home.* Boston: Roberts Brothers, 1878. HCL. In-
scribed by Susan Dickinson, "Emily from the Author."
——— *Ramona.* Ltr 976, *LTRS*, III, 866: "Pity me, however, I
have finished Ramona."
——— *Verses by H. H.* Boston: Fields, Osgood, and Co., 1870. HCL.
Inscribed, "Sue from Vinnie." Ltr 368, *LTRS*, II, 491: "Mrs
Hunt's Poems are stronger than any . . . since Mrs — Brown-
ing."
James, Henry. *The Europeans* (appeared serially, *Atlantic Monthly*,
c. 1879). Boston: Houghton, Osgood, and Company, 1879.
HCL. Signed, "M. G. Dickinson." Ltr 619, *LTRS*, II, 647:
"I must ask with Mr Wentworth, 'Where are our moral founda-
tions?'"
Johnson, Samuel. *Rasselas.* Ltr 212, *LTRS*, II, 357: "and imitate,
and fail, like Mr 'Rasselas.'"
Keats, John. "Ode on a Grecian Urn." P 449, *Poems*, I, 347: "I
died for Beauty–. . ./And I – for Truth –Themself are One."
Kingsley, Charles. *Hypatia.* Ltr 162, *LTRS*, I, 295: "I thank you
for Hypatia, and ask you what it means?"
——— **Yeast: A Problem.* New York: Harper & Brothers, 1859.
HCL. Inscribed by Susan Dickinson, "Emily." Ltr 432, *LTRS*,
II, 537: "'Kingsley' rejoins 'Argemone.'"
Lathrop, George Parsons. "The Child's Wish Granted." Ltr 737,
LTRS, III, 717: "Mr. Lathrop's poem was piteously sweet."
The Light in the Valley. Philadelphia: American Baptist Publishing
Society, 1852. Ltr 85, *LTRS*, I, 195: "I have just read . . .
'The Light in the Valley.'"
Little Jennie. Boston: The American Tract Society, 1863. Ltr 188,
LTRS, II, 334: "Shall send 'Little Jennie' as soon as I know
where the Owner is."
Longfellow, Henry W. *The Courtship of Miles Standish.* Ltr 665,
LTRS, III, 673: "I fear Vinnie gave my message as John Alden

did the one from Miles Standish." PF 93, *LTRS*, III, 925: "Not
to send errands by John Alden." P 357, *Poems*, I, 284: "Verily,
a Vicarious Courtship–/'Miles', and 'Priscilla', were such an
One."

——— "The Day is Done." Ltr 372, *LTRS*, II, 495: "Folding her
own like the Arabs gives her no apprehension." Ltr 768, *LTRS*,
III, 739: "'Shall fold their Tents like Arabs, and as silently steal
away.'"

——— *Evangeline.* Ltr 23, *LTRS*, I, 66: "I had a feast in the reading
line, . . . *Evangeline.*"

——— "Footsteps of Angels." Ltr 36, *LTRS*, I, 99: "I have come
from 'to and *fro*, and walking up, and down.'"

——— *Kavanagh.* Ltr 30, *LTRS*, I, 85: "Kavanagh says 'there will
be mourning – mourning – mourning at the judgment seat of
Christ.'" Ltr 38, *LTRS*, I, 102: "your little 'Columbarium is
lined with warmth and softness, . . . so you differ from bonnie
'Alice.'" Ltr 102, *LTRS*, I, 221: "'At Dover dwells George
Brown Esq – Good Carlos Finch and David Fryer.'" Ltr 133,
LTRS, I, 264: "I kept my lofty letter for 'Adolphus Hawkins,
Esq.'" Ltr 342b, *LTRS*, II, 475: "One day her brother brought
home Kavanagh." Ltr 619, *LTRS*, II, 648: "they looked like
Mr and Mrs 'Pendexter,' turning their backs on Longfellow's
Parish."

——— "Paul Revere's Ride." Ltr 888, *LTRS*, III, 814: "Baby's flight
will embellish History with Gilpin's and Revere's."

——— "The Rainy Day." Ltr 36, *LTRS*, I, 97: "'the day is dark,
and dreary.'" Ltr 52, *LTRS*, I, 135: "it has been 'dark and
dreary' and winds 'are never weary.'" Ltr 54, *LTRS*, I, 140:
"'when the day is dark and drear and the wind is never weary.'"
Ltr 69, *LTRS*, I, 167: "for 'some days are dark and dreary, and
the wind is never weary.'" Ltr 74, *LTRS*, I, 177: "'into each
life some rain must fall.'" Ltr 88, *LTRS*, I, 201: "'some days
must be dark and dreary'!" Ltr 98, *LTRS*, I, 218: "upon this
stormy day – 'into each life some "*flakes*" must fall, some days
must be dark and dreary.'"

——— "The Reaper and the Flowers." Ltr 185, *LTRS*, II, 329:
"then a 'reaper whose name is Death' has come to get a few."

Lowell, James Russell. "After the Burial." Ltr 622, *LTRS*, II, 649: "fair as Lowell's 'Sweet Despair' in the Slipper Hymn."

—— *Among My Books*, 1st Series. Boston: Fields, Osgood, and Co., 1870. HCL. Signed, "S. H. Dickinson." Ltr 564, *LTRS*, II, 618: "Lowell quotes from the Stranger 'Live –live even to be unkind.'"

—— "A Good Word for Winter," *Atlantic Almanac* (1870). Ltr 337, *LTRS*, II, 466: "Read Mr. Lowell's *Winter*."

—— *My Study Windows*. Boston: James R. Osgood and Company, 1872. HCL. Inscribed by Emily: "Susan — Emily".

Mackarness, Matilda Anne. *A House upon a Rock*. Boston and Cambridge, Mass.: J. Monroe, 1850. Ltr 85, *LTRS*, I, 195: "I have just read . . . 'A House upon a Rock.'"

—— *Only*. Boston and Cambridge, Mass.: J. Monroe, 1850. Ltr 85, *LTRS*, I, 195: "I have just read . . . 'Only.'"

Manning, Ann. *The Maiden and Married Life of Mary Powell*. Ltr 181, *LTRS*, II, 322. "You will leave the 'maiden and married life of Mary Powell' behind."

Marsh, John. *An Epitome of General Ecclesiastical History, from the Earliest Period to the Present Time*. New York: J. Tilden, 1843. MHT. Ltr 15, *LTRS*, I, 45: "I go this term & am studying Algebra, Euclid, Ecc[lesiastical] History & reviewing Arithmetic again."

Milton, John. *Paradise Lost*. Philadelphia: Benjamin Warner, 1819. HCL. Inscribed, "E[dward] Dickinson." New York: Baker and Scribner, 1801. MHT. Ltr 29, *LTRS*, I, 79: "War Sir – 'my voice is for war!'" Ltr 693, *LTRS*, III, 694: "We read in a tremendous Book about 'an enemy,' . . . The time has passed, and years have come, and yet not any 'Satan.' I think he must be making war upon some other nation." Ltr 890, *LTRS*, III, 816: "'Who knows that secret deep'–'Alas, not I.'" Ltr 1038, *LTRS*, III, 899–900: "as the great florist says, 'The flower that never will in other climate grow.'"

—— *Samson Agonistes* (also George Eliot, *Daniel Deronda*). Ltr 802, *LTRS*, III, 761: "If the Spirits are fair as the Faces 'Nothing is here for Tears.'"

—— "To the Lord General Cromwell." Ltr 892, *LTRS*, III, 818: "'Peace hath her Victories, no less than War.'"

Mitchell, Donald G. (Ik Marvel). *Dream Life*. New York: Charles Scribner, 1851. HCL. Signed, "Wm. A. Dickinson." Ltr 75, *LTRS*, I, 178: "'Dream Life' is not near so great a book as 'Reveries of a Bachelor[']."

—— *Reveries of a Bachelor*. Ltr 56, *LTRS*, I, 144: "perhaps we would have a 'Reverie' after the form of 'Ik Marvel.'" Ltr 113, *LTRS*, I, 237: "there were 'somebody's *rev-e-ries*,' he didn't know whose they were." P 422, *Poems*, I, 327: "A Temperature just adequate/So Anthracite, to live."

Montgomery, James. "Servant of God, well done!" Ltr 414, *LTRS*, II, 526: "Almost the last tune that he heard was, 'Rest from thy loved employ.'"

—— "O where shall rest be found." Ltr 176, *LTRS*, I, 311: "Not all of life to live, is it, nor all of death to die."

Moore, Thomas. *The Epicurean*. Ltr 23, *LTRS*, I, 66: "while at home I had a feast in the reading line, . . . *The Epicurean*."

—— "The Last Rose of Summer." Ltr 337, *LTRS*, II, 466: "You have heard of 'the last rose of summer.'"

The New England Primer. Hartford: Ira Webster, 1843. HCL. Signed, "Edward Dickinson." Illustrations for "C" [Christ crucified], "T" [Young Timothy, Learn't sin to fly], and "X" [Xerxes did die, and so must I] have been cut out. Ltr 214, *LTRS*, II, 360. The illustration for "T" is pasted to this letter.

Newman, Samuel Phillips. *A Practical System of Rhetoric, or The Principles and Rules of Style, Inferred from Examples of Writing* . . . New York: Mark H. Newman and Co.; Cincinnati: W. H. Moore and Co. MHT. Ltr 23, *LTRS*, I, 67: "My studies for this series are Astronomy and Rhetoric."

Olmsted, Denison. *A Compedium of Astronomy; Containing the Elements of the Science, familiarly Explained and Illustrated with the Latest Discoveries*. New York: R. B. Collins, 184–. MHT. Ltr 23, *LTRS*, I, 67: "My studies for this series are Astronomy and Rhetoric."

Parker, Theodore. *The Two Christmas Celebrations*. 1859. Ltr.

213, *LTRS*, II, 358: "to thank dear Mrs Bowles for the little Book, . . . I never read before what Mr Parker wrote."

Payne, John Howard. "Home, Sweet Home." Ltr 542, *LTRS*, II, 604: " 'Home – sweet Home' – Austin's Baby sings – 'there is no place like Home.'" Ltr 929, *LTRS*, III, 836: "With the congratulatory trust that 'there is no place like Home.'"

Phelps, Mrs. Elizabeth Stuart (A. Trusta). **The Last Leaf from Sunny Side.* Boston: Phillips, Sampson, and Company, 1854. The Jones Library, Amherst. Inscribed: "For Misses E. & L. Dickinson from their friend Mrs. James Brown Washington Feb 19th 1855."

Pierpont, John. "My Child." Ltr 183, *LTRS*, II, 325–6. ED copies ten 6-line stanzas in a letter to Mary Warner, c. April 1856.

Pope, Alexander. "The Dying Christian to His Soul." Ltr 732, *LTRS*, III, 714 (also I Cor. 15:55): "Death has mislaid his sting – the grave forgot his victory." Ltr 967, *LTRS*, III, 860 (also I Cor. 15:55): "Oh, Death, where is thy Chancellor?"

——— *Essay on Man.* Ltr 18, *LTRS*, I, 54: "I recite a lesson in 'Pope's Essay on Man' which is merely transposition."

Porter, Jane. **Thaddeus of Warsaw.* New York: Everett Duyckinck, 1820. HCL. Signed, "E. Dickinson, 1827"; added, in pencil, "& Miss E. Dickinson."

Robinson, A. Mary F. *Emily Brontë.* Boston: Roberts Brothers, 1883. Ltr 822, *LTRS*, III, 775: "to let you read 'Emily Bronte' – more electric far than anything since 'Jane Eyre.'"

Robinson, William S. ("Warrington"). *Pen-Portraits.* Ltr 908, *LTRS*, III, 828: "I wish I could find the Warrington Words."

Sand, George. *Mauprat.* P 1167, *Poems*, II, 815: "That Larceny of time and mind." See Johnson's note, *Poems*, II, 816.

Saintine, X. B. (Joseph Xavier Boniface). *Picciola*, 2d ed. Philadelphia: Lea and Blanchard, 1839. Falconer's *Shipwreck* in the same volume. HCL. Ltr 27, *LTRS*, I, 75: "I'm a 'Fenestrellan captive,' if this world *be* 'Fenestrella,' . . . T'is 'Picciola.'"

Scribner's Monthly. November 1870 through October 1881 (lacks Dec. 70, Mar. 74, Aug. 75, Jun. 77). HCL.

Shakespeare, William. *The Comedies, Histories, Tragedies and Poems of William Shakespeare*, 8 vols. Boston: Little Brown and Company, 1853. HCL. Each volume inscribed, "Edw. Dickinson, 1857."

—— *Antony and Cleopatra.* Ltr 430, *LTRS,* II, 533: " 'Egypt — thou knew'st'." Ltr 488, *LTRS,* II, 573: "and Enobarbus said 'Leave that which leaves itself.' " Ltr 791, *LTRS,* III, 754: "Antony's remark to a friend, 'since Cleopatra died' is said to be the saddest ever lain in Language." Ltr 854, *LTRS,* III, 791: "like Antony's Supper—'And pays his Heart for what his Eyes eat, only.' " Ltr 978, *LTRS,* III, 870: " 'You knew, Oh Egypt' said the entangled Antony." Ltr 1026, *LTRS,* III, 894: " 'And pays his Heart for what his Eyes eat only!' " PF 56, *LTRS,* III, 920: "I send you Antony's Orchard, who paid his Heart for what his eyes ate, only."

—— *As You Like It.* Ltr 545, *LTRS,* II, 606: "With it, I enclose Love's 'remainder biscuit.' " Ltr 882, *LTRS,* III, 811: "Love's 'remainder Biscuit' is henceforth for us."

—— *Coriolanus.* Ltr 484, *LTRS,* II, 571: "Doth forget that ever he heard the name of Death."

—— *Hamlet.* Ltr 512, *LTRS,* II, 587: "Hamlet wavered for all of us." Ltr 547, *LTRS,* II, 607: "the 'Whips of Time' felt a long way off." Ltr 678, *LTRS,* III, 683: "it has saved too many to be assailed by an 'envious sliver.' " Ltr 724, *LTRS,* III, 708 (also Matthew 10:29): "Mr. Samuel's 'sparrow' does not 'fall' without the fervent 'notice.' " Ltr 865, [P 1768], *LTRS,* III, 797: "faithful be/To Thyself." Ltr 979, *LTRS,* III, 871: "her Maker must be her 'Crowner's Quest.' " Ltr 1006, *LTRS,* III, 883. " 'An envious Sliver broke' was a passage your Uncle peculiarly loved in the drowning Ophelia." Ltr 1012, *LTRS,* III, 888: "let me reply with the Laureate, 'Speak that I live to hear!' " Ltr 1028, *LTRS,* III, 895: "Do you remember what whispered to 'Horatio'?" P 741, *Poems,* II, 565: " 'Hamlet' to Himself were Hamlet."

—— *I Henry VI.* Ltr 304, *LTRS,* II, 440: "I read a few words since I came home—John Talbot's parting with his son, and Margaret's with Suffolk."

—— *Julius Caesar.* Ltr 448, *LTRS,* II, 546: " 'For Brutus, as you know, was Caesar's Angel.' " Ltr 907, *LTRS,* III, 824: "Ask some kind Voice to read to you Mark Antony's Oration over his Playmate Caesar." P 102, *Poems*, I, 78: "Great Caesar! Condescend/The Daisy, to receive,/Gathered by Cato's Daughter."

Shakespeare, William. *King Lear.* Ltr 544, *LTRS*, II, 605: "for those ways 'Madness lies.'"

—— *Macbeth.* Ltr 8, *LTRS*, I, 20: "autumn with the sere and yellow leaf is already upon us." Ltr 29, *LTRS*, I, 79–80: "'Burn flame – simmer heat – swelter toad – I have cursed thee'. . . . but if I stab you while sleeping the dagger's to blame." Ltr 31, *LTRS*, I, 89: "I put my treasures away till 'we *two* meet again.'" Ltr 73, *LTRS*, I, 175: "Vinnie expresses her sympathy at my 'sere and yellow leaf.'" Ltr 332, *LTRS*, II, 463: "the Physician said to Macbeth? 'That sort must heal itself.'" Ltr 339, *LTRS*, II, 470: "'Tis said that 'nothing in her life became her like the leaving it.'" Ltr 352, *LTRS*, II, 479: "I took Macbeth and turned to 'Birnam Wood.'" Ltr 551, *LTRS*, II, 609: "'I thought that Birnam Wood' had 'come to Dunsinane.'" Ltr 669, *LTRS*, III, 677: "The mighty answer, 'That sort must heal itself.'" Ltr 882, *LTRS*, III, 811: "That nothing in her Life became her like it's last event." Ltr 950, *LTRS*, III, 849: "I trust 'the Airs were delicate' the Day they made their flight." Ltr 966, *LTRS*, III, 859: "I shall then seek the 'Letter' which the 'Weird Woman promised' me." Ltr 986, *LTRS*, III, 874: "Macbeth said 'that sort must heal itself.'"

—— *Merchant of Venice.* Ltr 48, *LTRS*, I 126: "when he has oped his mouth I *think* no dog has barked." Ltr 958, *LTRS*, III, 854: "the 'Children' for whom the Cakes were founded are 'Merchants of Venice.'" P 247, *Poems*, I, 178: "'Shylock'? Say!/Sign me the Bond!"

—— *Othello.* Ltr 478, *LTRS*, II, 567: "Beloved Shakespeare says, 'He that is robbed and smiles, steals something from the thief.'" Ltr 506, *LTRS*, II, 585: "we think of others possessing you with the throe of Othello." Ltr 538, *LTRS*, II, 602–603: "Brabantio's resignation is the only one –'I here do give thee that with all my heart.'" Ltr 560, *LTRS*, II, 616: "'And very Sea – Mark of my utmost Sail.'" Ltr 622, *LTRS*, II, 649: "Brabantio's Gift was not more fair than your's . . . 'Which but thou hast.'" Ltr 882, *LTRS*, III, 811: "We will try to bear it as divinely as Othello did." Ltr 937, *LTRS*, III, 840: "He who is 'slain and smiles, steals something from the' Sword." Ltr 948, *LTRS*, III, 847: "Othello is uneasy, but then Othellos always are." Ltr 958, *LTRS*, III, 854: "the 'Children' . . . are 'Merchants of Venice' and 'Desdemonas.'" Ltr 1010, *LTRS*, III, 886: "when they ask who slew her, 'Nobody – I myself.'" Ltr 1016, *LTRS*, III, 889: "Why should we censure Othello."

—— *Romeo and Juliet.* Ltr 737, *LTRS*, III, 717: "quaint as a druggist's formula – 'I do remember an apothecary.'" Ltr 746, *LTRS*, III, 724: "An 'Envious Worm' attacked them." Ltr 1041, *LTRS*, III, 902: "'I do remember an Apothecary,' said that sweeter Robin than Shakespeare." P 741, *Poems*, II, 565: "Though the 'Romeo' left no Record."

—— *Tempest.* Ltr 889, *LTRS*, III, 815: "Caliban's 'clustring filberds' were not so luscious nor so brown." P 1463, *Poems*, III, 1010: "The mail from Tunis, probably."

Silliman, Benjamin. *Elements of Chemistry, in the Order of the Lectures Given in Yale College.* New Haven: H. Howe, 1830– 31. MHT.

—— *First Principles of Chemistry, for the Use of Colleges and Schools.* Philadelphia: H. C. Peck and T. Bliss, 184–. MHT. Ltr 19, *LTRS*, I, 57: "They are, Chemistry, Physiology & quarter course in Algebra." Ltr 20, *LTRS*, I, 59: "I am now studying 'Silliman's Chemistry.'"

Smedley, Marcella Bute. *The Maiden Aunt.* Ltr 23, *LTRS*, I, 66: "while at home I had a feast in the reading line, . . . *The Maiden Aunt.*"

Smith, Alexander. *A Life Drama and Other Poems.* Ltr 128, *LTRS*, I, 256: "I must read them again before I know just [what] I think of 'Alexander Smith.'" Ltr 130, *LTRS*, I, 260: "I admire the Poems very much."

[Spofford], Harriet Prescott. "Circumstance." Ltr 261, *LTRS*, II, 404: "I read Miss Prescott's 'Circumstance,' but it followed me, in the Dark."

Sprague, William B. *Letters on Practical Subjects to a Daughter.* Albany: E. H. Pearse and Co., 1851. HCL. Inscribed, "Emily from her father April 18, 1862."

The Springfield Republican, 1844–1886. See Chapter VI.

Stephens, John L. *Incidents of Travel in Central America, Chiapas, and Yucatan,* 2 vols. New York: Harper and Brothers, 1841. HCL. Signed, "E[dward] Dickinson 1843." P 1148, *Poems,* II, 804: "Fresh as a Cargo from Batize."

Stoddard, Solomon and Ethan Allen Andrews. *A Grammar of the Latin Language,* Boston, 1837. Ltr 92, *LTRS,* I, 208: "I made up the Latin . . . for I could'nt think how it went, according to Stoddard and Andrew!"

Stowe, Harriet Beecher. *Uncle Tom's Cabin,* 2 vols. Boston: John P. Jewett and Company, 1852. HCL. Both volumes inscribed, "Dickinson." Ltr 113, *LTRS,* I, 237: "he gave me quite a trimming about 'Uncle Tom' and 'Charles Dickens' and these 'modern Literati.' "

Taylor, Henry. *Philip Van Artevelde.* Boston: Ticknor and Fields, 1863. HCL. Signed, "Emily." P 29, *Poems,* I, 27: "If those I loved were found/The bells of Ghent w'd ring–/. . . Philip–when bewildered/Bore his riddle in!"

Tennyson, Alfred. *Harold, A Drama.* Ltr 486, *LTRS,* II, 571: "designed 'Harold' to accompany Emerson, but Tennyson declines."

——— *The Idylls of the King.* Ltr 506, *LTRS,* II, 585: "to fall asleep in Tennyson's Verse, seems almost a Pillow. 'To where beyond these voices there is peace.' "

——— *Love and Duty.* Ltr 801, *LTRS,* III, 760: " 'Can Trouble dwell with April Days?'/'Of Love that never found it's earthly close, what sequel?' Both in the same Book." (Second quotation is from *Love and Duty.*)

——— *In Memoriam.* Ltr 801, *LTRS,* III, 760: " 'Can Trouble dwell with April Days?'/'Of Love that never found it's earthly close, what sequel?' Both in the same Book." (First quotation is from *In Memoriam,* No. 83.)

——— *The Princess.* Boston: William D. Ticknor and Co., 1848. HCL. Inscribed, "Susan H. Gilbert . . Dec 22/48." Ltr 23,

LTRS, I, 66: "while at home I had a feast in the reading line, . . . *The Princess*."

Thackeray, William M. *Vanity Fair.* Ltr 194, *LTRS*, II, 340: "Ah – Dobbin – Dobbin – you little know the chink which your dear face makes."

Thomas á Kempis. **Of the Imitation of Christ*. London: Roving-ton's, 1876. American Literature Collection, Yale University. Inscribed, "Emily wi[th] love Dec 26th 76."

Thomson, James. *The Seasons.* Philadelphia: Edwin T. Scott, 1828. HCL. P 131, *Poems*, I, 94: "Gone – Mr Bryant's 'Golden Rod' –/And Mr Thomson's 'sheaves.'"

Trelawny, E. J. **Recollections of the Last Days of Shelley and Byron*, 2d edition. Boston: Ticknor and Fields, 1859. HCL. Inscribed by Susan Dickinson, "Emily Dickinson."

Tupper, Martin. **Proverbial Philosophy*. New York: Wiley and Putnam, 1846. HCL. Signed, "E. Dickinson, 1846."

——— *The Twins* and *The Heart.* Ltr 23, *LTRS*, I, 66–67: "while at home I had a feast in the reading line, . . . and *The Twins and Heart* by Tupper."

Vane, Florence. "Are We Almost There?" Ltr 12, *LTRS*, I, 33: "*Are we almost there?* is the title of it."

Vaughan, Henry. "They are all gone into the world of light." Ltr 653, *LTRS*, III, 669: "such Scene made Vaughn humbly say 'My Days that are at best but dim and hoary.'"

Waller, Edmund. "The Last Prospect." Ltr 544, *LTRS*, II, 605: "when we recall that the 'Soul's poor Cottage, battered and dismayed, lets in new light through chinks that time has made.'" Ltr 888, *LTRS*, III, 814. "the 'Soul's poor Cottage' may lose it's Tenant."

Watts, Isaac. *The Psalms, Hymns and Spiritual Songs of the Rev. Isaac Watts, D.D.*, new edition. Boston: Crocker and Brewster, 1834. HCL. Signed, "Edward Dickinson."

——— "There is a land of pure delight." P 112, *Poems*, I, 83: "'Oh could we climb where Moses stood,/And view the Landscape o'er.'"

Worcester, J. E. *Elements of History, Ancient and Modern*. Boston: Hilliard, Gray, Little, and Wilkins, 1828. Ltr 352, *LTRS*,

II, 480: "I have but to lift my Hands to touch the 'Hights of Abraham.'" Ltr 906, *LTRS*, III, 826: "We die, said the Deathless of Thermopylae, in obedience to Law." P 444, *Poems*, I, 343: "The Stone – that tells defending Whom/This Spartan put away." P 678, *Poems*, II, 524: "Wolfe demanded during dying/. . ./Montcalm, his opposing Spirit." P 1321, *Poems*, III, 914: "Elizabeth told Essex." P 1554, *Poems*, III, 1071: "To Law – said sweet Thermopylae/I give my dying Kiss."

Wordsworth, William. *Elegiac Stanzas*. Ltr 315, *LTRS*, II, 449: "Here is the 'light' the Stranger said 'was not on land or sea.'" Ltr 394, *LTRS*, II, 510: "'The light that never was on sea or land' might just as soon be had for the knocking."

––– "We are Seven." Ltr 96, *LTRS*, I, 215: "'We are seven, and one in heaven.'"

The Wreath: A Collection of Poems. Hartford: Silas Andrus, 1824. HCL. Inscribed, "E Dickinson, 1826."

Young, Edward. *The Complaint: or, Night Thoughts*. Philadelphia: Uriah Hunt and Son, 1845. HCL. Ltr 11, *LTRS*, I, 31: "as Dr Young when he exclaimed, O! what a miracle to man is man." Ltr 13, *LTRS*, I, 37: "the poet has said, 'We take no note of Time, but from its loss. T'were wise in man to give it then a tongue . . . Part with it as with life reluctantly.'" Ltr 979, *LTRS*, III, 871: "Contention 'loves a shining Mark.'"

Appendix B

Emily Dickinson's Mount Holyoke Textbooks

The *Eleventh Annual Catalogue of Mount Holyoke Female Seminary* (1847–1848) lists Emily E. Dickinson of Amherst as a member of the Middle Class. The catalogue also indicates the course of study for each class:

STUDIES OF THE JUNIOR CLASS

Review of English Grammar, Latin (Cornelius Nepos), History (Worcester's Elements, Goldsmith's Greece, Rome, and Grimshaw's France), Day's Algebra, Playfair's Euclid, (old edition) and Wood's Botany commenced; also Smellie's Philosophy of Natural History,* and Marsh's Ecclesiastical History.*

STUDIES OF THE SENIOR CLASS

Latin, Cutter's Physiology, Silliman's Chemistry, Olmsted's Natural Philosophy, Olmsted's Astronomy, Wood's Botany continued, Newman's Rhetoric; also Alexander's Evidences of Christianity.*

* Not strictly required of those who have a good knowledge of Latin.

The following textbooks were in use at the seminary during the period 1847–1848:

Alexander, Archibald. *The Evidences of the Christian Religion*, 6th ed. New York: Jonathan Leavitt, 1832.
Butler, Joseph. *The Analogy of Religion, Natural and Revealed, to the constitution and course of nature.* New York: Jonathan Leavitt; Boston: Crocker & Brewster, 1833, 1843, 1847.
Cutter, Calvin. *A Treatise on Anatomy, Physiology, and Hygiene* . . . Boston: B. B. Mussey and Co.; New York: Clark, Austin, and Co., n.d.

Day, Jeremiah. *An Introduction to Algebra,* 52nd ed. New Haven: Durrie and Peck; Philadelphia: Smith and Peck, 1845.

Goldsmith, Oliver. *An Abridgement of the History of England.* Boston: T. Bedlington, 1825.

——— *Dr. Goldsmith's Roman History.* Philadelphia: printed for Ogilvie, 1793.

——— *The Grecian History,* 2 vols. in one. Hartford: Judd, Loomis and Co., 1837.

Grimshaw, William. *The History of France.* Philadelphia: Grigg and Elliott, 1840.

Hitchcock, Edward. *Elementary Geology.* New York: M. H. Newman, [1847].

Marsh, John. *An Epitome of General Ecclesiastical History.* New York: J. Tilden, 1843.

Milton, John. *The Paradise Lost.* New York: Baker and Scribner, 1801.

Nepos, Cornelius. *Cornelius Nepos: with answered questions, and imitative exercises* [Latin], new ed. New York: D. Appleton and Co.

Newman, Samuel Phillips. *A Practical System of Rhetoric,* 50th ed. New York: Mark H. Newman and Co.; Cincinnati: W. H. Moore and Co., [c. 1834].

Olmsted, Denison. *A Compendium of Astronomy.* New York: R. B. Collins.

——— *A Compendium of Natural Philosophy.* New Haven: S. Babcock.

——— *An Introduction to Natural Philosophy.* New Haven: 1831–32.

Paley, William. *Natural Theology: or, Evidences of the Existence and Attributes of the Deity.* Boston: Gould, Kendall, and Lincoln, 1831, 1835.

Playfair, John. *Elements of Geometry.* New York: W. E. Dean, 1824, 1844.

Silliman, Benjamin. *Elements of Chemistry.* Philadelphia: H. C. Peck and T. Bliss, 184– .

Smellie, William. *The Philosophy of Natural History.* Boston: Simpkins, 1835, 1841.

Upham, Thomas Cogswell. *Elements of Mental Philosophy.* New York: Harper and Brothers.

Wayland, Francis. *Elements of Moral Science.* Boston: Gould, Kendall and Lincoln, 1835.

Whately, Richard. *Elements of Logic.* Boston and Cambridge, Mass.: James Munroe and Co.

Wood, Alphonso. *A Class-book of Botany.* Claremont, N.H.: Claremont Manufacturing Company.

Worcester, Joseph Emerson. *Elements of History, Ancient and Modern.* Boston: Hilliard, Gray, Little and Wilkins, 1828.

Appendix C

Emily Dickinson's Allusions to the Bible

Old Testament	Poems	Letters	Total
Genesis	10	13	23
Exodus	6	4	10
Deuteronomy	4	3	7
Joshua	1	1	2
Judges	0	1	1
Ruth	0	1	1
I Samuel	1	2	3
II Samuel	0	3	3
I Kings	0	4	4
II Kings	2	2	4
Job	0	5	5
Psalms	2	14	16
Proverbs	0	3	3
Ecclesiastes	0	3	3
Isaiah	1	9	10
Jeremiah	0	1	1
Lamentations	0	1	1
Daniel	0	3	3
	27	73	100

New Testament	Poems	Letters	Total
Matthew	20	54	74
Mark	3	2	5
Luke	10	23	33
John	11	24	35

New Testament	Poems	Letters	Total
Acts	3	2	5
Romans	0	3	3
I Corinthians	3	17	20
II Corinthians	1	5	6
Galatians	0	1	1
Ephesians	0	4	4
Philippians	0	1	1
I Timothy	1	4	5
II Timothy	0	3	3
Hebrews	0	5	5
James	0	1	1
I Peter	1	4	5
II Peter	0	2	2
I John	1	2	3
Jude	0	1	1
Revelation	12	17	29
	66	175	241

BIBLIOGRAPHY

NOTES

INDEX OF FIRST LINES

SUBJECT INDEX

Bibliography

Primary Sources

Bolts of Melody, ed. Mabel Loomis Todd and Millicent Todd Bingham. New York: Harper and Brothers, 1945.

Emily Dickinson's Letters to Dr. and Mrs. Josiah Gilbert Holland,
ed. Theodora Van Wagenen Ward. Cambridge, Mass.: Harvard
University Press, 1951.

*Emily Dickinson Face to Face: Unpublished Letters with Notes
and Reminiscences* by Martha Dickinson Bianchi. Boston:
Houghton Mifflin, 1932.

The Letters of Emily Dickinson, ed. Mabel Loomis Todd, 2 vols.
Boston: Roberts Brothers, 1894.

The Letters of Emily Dickinson, ed. Thomas H. Johnson, 3 vols.
Cambridge, Mass.: Harvard University Press, 1958.

The Life and Letters of Emily Dickinson by Martha Dickinson
Bianchi. Boston: Houghton Mifflin, 1924.

Poems by Emily Dickinson, ed. Martha Dickinson Bianchi and
Alfred Leete Hampson. Boston: Little, Brown and Company,
1937.

The Poems of Emily Dickinson, ed. Thomas H. Johnson, 3 vols.
Cambridge, Mass.: Harvard University Press, 1955.

Secondary Sources

Allen, Caroline C. "The Homestead in Amherst," *Horn Book,* 33:
30–34 (February 1957).

Anderson, Charles R. "From a Window in Amherst: E. D. Looks
at the American Scene," *NEQ,* 31:147–171 (June 1958).

——— *Emily Dickinson's Poetry, Stairway of Surprise.* New York:
Holt, Rinehart and Winston, 1960.

Banzer, Judith. "'Compound Manner': Emily Dickinson and the Metaphysical Poets," *AL*, 32:417–433 (January 1961).

Barbot, Mary Elizabeth. "Emily Dickinson Parallels," *NEQ*, 14: 689–696 (December 1941).

Bingham, Millicent Todd. *Ancestors' Brocades: The Literary Debut of Emily Dickinson.* New York: Harper and Brothers, 1945.

––– *Emily Dickinson's Home.* New York: Harper and Brothers, 1955.

Blackmur, R. P. "Emily Dickinson's Notation," *KR*, 18:224–237 (Spring 1956).

––– *The Expense of Greatness.* New York: Arrow Editions, 1940.

––– "Religious Poetry in the United States," *Religion in American Life*, II, Princeton, N.J.: Princeton University Press, 1961.

Boynton, Percy H. *Literature and American Life.* New York: Ginn and Company, 1936.

Chase, Richard. *Emily Dickinson.* New York: William Sloane Associates, 1951.

Childs, Herbert E. "Emily Dickinson and Sir Thomas Browne," *AL*, 22: 455–465 (January 1951).

[Cridland], Margery McKay. "'Amazing Sense,' The Application of a New Method to the Poetry of Emily Dickinson." Unpublished Swarthmore College Honors Thesis, 1936.

Davidson, Frank. "A Note on Emily Dickinson's Use of Shakespeare," *NEQ*, 18:407–408 (September 1959).

Davidson, J. "Emily Dickinson and Isaac Watts," *BPLQ*, 6:141–149 (July 1954).

Dickinson, Ellen E. "Emily Dickinson," *Boston Evening Transcript*, Friday, September 28, 1894.

Frye, Northrop, ed. "Emily Dickinson," *Major Writers of America*, II. New York: Harcourt, Brace and World, 1962.

Howard, William. "Emily Dickinson's Poetic Vocabulary," *PMLA*, 72:225–248 (March 1957).

––– "Dickinson's I NEVER SAW A MOOR," *The Explicator*, 21:13 (October 1962).

Johnson, Thomas H. *Emily Dickinson: An Interpretive Biography.* Cambridge, Mass.: Harvard University Press, 1955.

198

Leary, Lewis. "The Poems of Emily Dickinson," *Thought*, 31:282–286 (Summer 1956).

Leyda, Jay. *The Years and Hours of Emily Dickinson*, 2 vols. New Haven: Yale University Press, 1960.

——— "Late Thaw of a Frozen Image," *New Republic*, 132:22–24 (February 21, 1955).

McLean, Sidney R. "Emily Dickinson at Mount Holyoke," *NEQ*, 7:25–42 (March 1934).

MacLeish, Archibald, Louise Bogan, and Richard Wilbur. *Emily Dickinson: Three Views.* Amherst: Amherst College Press, 1960.

Marcellino, Ralph. "Horace and Emily Dickinson," *CJ*, 52:221–222 (February 1957).

Martz, Louis L. "In 'Being's Centre,'" *UTQ*, 27:556–565 (July 1957).

Newell, Kenneth B. "Dickinson's AURORA IS THE EFFORT," *The Explicator*, 20:5 (October 1961).

——— "Dickinson's WE SHOULD NOT MIND SO SMALL A FLOWER," *The Explicator*, 19:65 (April 1961).

Parks, Edd Winfield. "The Public and the Private Poet," *SAQ*, 56:480–485 (Autumn 1957).

Patterson, Rebecca. "Elizabeth Browning and Emily Dickinson," *Educational Leader*, 20:21–48 (July 1956).

Pearce, Roy Harvey. *The Continuity of American Poetry.* Princeton, N.J.: Princeton University Press, 1961.

Pollitt, Josephine. *Emily Dickinson: The Human Background of Her Poetry.* New York: Harper and Brothers, 1930.

Ransom, John Crowe. "Emily Dickinson," *Perspectives USA*, 15:5–20 (Spring 1956).

Scott, Aurelia G. "Emily Dickinson's 'Three Gems,'" *NEQ*, 16:627–628 (December 1943).

Taggard, Genevieve. *The Life and Mind of Emily Dickinson.* New York: Alfred A. Knopf, 1930.

Tate, Allen. *On the Limits of Poetry.* New York: Swallow Press and William and Morrow, 1948.

Turner, Clara Newman. "My Personal Acquaintance with Emily

Dickinson." Unpublished MS in the Jones Library, Amherst, Mass.

Ward, Theodora Van Wagenen. *The Capsule of the Mind*. Cambridge, Mass.: Harvard University Press, 1961.

Warren, Austin. "Emily Dickinson," *SR*, 65:565–586 (Autumn 1957).

Wells, Henry W. *Introduction to Emily Dickinson*. Chicago: Packard and Company, 1947.

Whicher, George Frisbie. *This Was a Poet*. New York: Charles Scribner's Sons, 1938.

Whiteside, M. B. "Poe and Dickinson," *Personalist*, 15:315–326 (Autumn 1934).

Winters, Yvor. *Maule's Curse*. Norfolk, Conn.: New Directions, 1938.

Wright, Nathalia. "Emily Dickinson's Boanerges and Thoreau's Atropos; Locomotives of the Same Line?" *MLN*, 72:101–103 (February 1957).

Zabel, Morton D. "Christina Rosetti and Emily Dickinson," *Poetry*, 37:213–216 (January 1931).

Reference Works

Addison, Joseph. *The Spectator*, 12 vols. Philadelphia: Thomas DeSilver, 1819.

Adler, G. J. *Ollendorff's New Method of Learning . . . The German Language* . . . New York: D. Appleton and Co., 1846.

Alexander, Archibald. *The Evidences of Christian Religion*, 6th ed. New York: Jonathan Leavitt, 1832.

Alexander, Francesca. *The Story of Ida*. Boston: Mosher, 1883.

The Amherst Record. May 1868 to May 1886.

The Atlantic Monthly. November 1857 to May 1886.

Bartlett, John. *A Complete Concordance [of] Shakespeare*. New York: St. Martin's Press, 1953.

Baugh, Albert C. *A Literary History of England*. New York: Appleton-Century-Crofts, 1948.

Beaconsfield, Benjamin Disraeli Lord. *Endymion*. New York: D. Appleton and Co., 1880.

Beauties of the British Poets. New York: J. S. Andersen, 1826.

BIBLIOGRAPHY

BIBLIOGRAPHY

BIBLIOGRAPHY

Bowles, Samuel. *Across the Continent.* New York: Houghton & Hurd, 1865.

——— *A Summer Vacation in the Parks and Mountains of Colorado.* Boston: Lee and Shepard, 1869.

——— *Our New West.* Hartford: Hartford Publishing Company, 1869.

Brontë, Anne (Acton Bell). *The Tenant of Wildfell Hall.* New York: Harper and Brothers, 1858.

Brontë, Charlotte (Currer Bell). *Jane Eyre.* New York: Harper and Brothers, 1864.

——— *The Professor.* New York: Harper and Brothers, 1857.

——— *Villette.* New York: Harper and Brothers, 1859.

Brontë, Emily (Ellis Bell). *Wuthering Heights.* New York: Harper and Brothers, 1858.

Broughton, L. N., and B. F. Stelter. *Concordance to the Poems of Robert Browning.* New York: G. E. Stechert and Company, 1954.

Browne, Sir Thomas. *The Works of Sir Thomas Browne,* ed. Simon Wilkin, 3 vols. London: Henry G. Bohn, 1852.

Browning, E. B. *Aurora Leigh.* New York: C. S. Francis and Co., 1859.

——— *The Complete Poetical Works of Elizabeth Barrett Browning,* ed. Harriet Waters Preston. Boston: Houghton Mifflin Company, 1900.

——— *Essays on the Greek Christian Poets and English Poets.* New York: James Miller, 1863.

——— *Prometheus Bound, and Other Poems.* New York and Boston: Francis and Co., 1851.

Browning, Robert. *The Complete Poetic and Dramatic Works of Robert Browning,* ed. Horace E. Scudder. Boston: Houghton Mifflin Company, 1895.

——— *Men and Women.* Boston: Ticknor and Fields, 1856.

——— *Dramatis Personae.* Boston: Ticknor and Fields, 1864.

——— *The Ring and the Book,* 2 vols. Boston: Fields, Osgood, and Co., 1869.

——— *Sordello, Strafford, Christmas-Eve and Easter-Day.* Boston: Ticknor and Fields, 1864.

Bryant, William Cullen. *Poems.* Philadelphia: Carey and Hart, 1849.

Bunyan, John. *The Pilgrim's Progress.* Boston: Phillips and Sampson, 1847.

Burns, Robert. *The Complete Poetical Works of . . .* , ed. W. E. Henley and T. F. Henderson. Boston: Houghton Mifflin Company, 1897.

――― *The Complete Works of Robert Burns.* Boston: Phillips, Sampson, and Company, 1853.

Butler, Joseph. *The Analogy of Religion, Natural and Revealed.* Boston: Crocker and Brewster, 1833.

Byron, George Gordon Lord. *The Works of Lord Byron,* 4 vols. New York: E. Duyckinck and G. Long, 1821.

The Century Magazine. November 1881 to May 1886.

Cervantes Saavedra, Miguel de. *The History and Adventures of The Renowned Don Quixote,* 5 vols. Philadelphia: John Conrad, 1803.

Chambers, Robert, ed. *Cyclopaedia of English Literature,* 2 vols. Boston: Gould, Kendall and Lincoln, 1847.

Chaucer, Geoffrey. *The Poetical Works of Geoffrey Chaucer,* ed. Authur Gilman, 3 vols. Boston: Houghton Mifflin, 1880.

Clarke, Mrs. Cowden. *The Complete Concordance to Shakespeare.* Boston: Little, Brown and Company, 1877.

Clough, Arthur Hugh. *The Poems and Prose Remains of Arthur Hugh Clough,* 2 vols. London: Macmillan and Co., 1869.

Cowper, William. *Poems,* 3 vols. Philadelphia: Thomas DeSilver, 1818.

Crabb, George. *English Synonymes.* Boston: Charles Ewer, 1819.

Cutter, Calvin. *A Treatise on Anatomy, Physiology, and Hygiene.* Boston: B. B. Mussey and Co., 1850.

Dana, Charles A., ed. *The Household Book of Poetry,* 6th ed. New York: D. Appleton and Company, 1860.

Day, Jeremiah. *An Introduction to Algebra,* 52nd ed. Philadelphia: Smith and Peck, 1845.

De Quincey, Thomas. *The Works of . . .* , 12 vols. Boston: Ticknor, Reed, and Fields, 1853–59.

Dickens, Charles. *Bleak House*. New York: G. W. Carleton and Co., 1880.

—— *David Copperfield*. New York: G. W. Carleton and Co., 1879.

—— *Dealings with the Firm of Dombey and Son*. New York: Burgess, Stringer and Co., 1848.

—— *The Pickwick Papers*. New York: G. W. Carleton and Co., 1874.

—— *The Works of* . . . , 20 vols. New York: Bigelow, Brown and Company, n.d.

Eliot, George. *George Eliot's Works*, 15 vols. Boston: Estes and Lauriat, 1883.

Elegant Extracts, 6 vols. Boston: Wells and Lilly, 1826.

Eleventh Annual Catalogue of Mount Holyoke Female Seminary. 1848.

Eliot, George. *Adam Bede*. New York: Harper and Brothers, 1860.

—— *The Mill on the Floss*. New York: Harper and Brothers, 1860.

—— *The Spanish Gypsy*. Boston: Ticknor and Fields, 1868.

—— *Wit and Wisdom of George Eliot*. Boston: Roberts Brothers, 1878.

Emerson, Ralph Waldo. *The Complete Works of* . . . , ed. E. W. Emerson. Boston: Houghton Mifflin Company, 1903–1932.

—— *Essays, First Series*. Boston: Ticknor and Fields, 1861.

—— *Essays, Second Series*. Boston: Ticknor and Fields, 1862.

—— *Poems*. Boston: James Munroe and Company, 1847.

Franklin, Benjamin. *Franklin's Essays and Letters*, 2 vols. New York: R. and W. A. Bartow, 1822.

Gaskell, E. C. *The Life of Charlotte Brontë*. New York: D. Appleton and Company, 1858.

Goldsmith, Oliver. *An Abridgement of the History of England*. Boston: T. Bedlington, 1825.

—— *The Miscellaneous Works of Oliver Goldsmith, M.B.*, 6 vols. Boston: Hastings, Etheredge, and Bliss, 1809.

—— *Dr. Goldsmith's Roman History*. Philadelphia: printed for Ogilvie, et al., 1793.

—— *The Grecian History*. Hartford: Judd, Loomis and Co., 1837.

Gordon, Mary. *Christopher North, a Memoir of John Wilson.* New York: W. J. Middleton, 1863.

Grimshaw, William. *The History of France.* Philadelphia: Grigg & Elliott, 1840.

Griswold, Rufus W., ed. *Gems from the American Poets.* Philadelphia: H. Hooker, 1844.

——— ed. *The Sacred Poets of England and America.* New York: D. Appleton and Co., 1849.

The Hampshire and Franklin Express. September 1842 to April 1868. (Published as *The Hampshire Express,* July 1866 to April 1868.)

Harper's New Monthly Magazine. June 1850 to May 1886.

Hart, James D. *The Oxford Companion to American Literature,* 3d ed. New York: Oxford University Press, 1956.

Harte, Francis Bret. *The Luck of Roaring Camp and Other Sketches.* Boston: Fields, Osgood, and Co., 1871.

Harvey, Sir Paul. *The Oxford Companion to English Literature,* 3d ed. London: Oxford University Press, 1946.

Hawthorne, Nathaniel. *The House of the Seven Gables.* Boston: Ticknor, Reed, and Fields, 1851.

Herbert, George. *The Poetical Works of* . . . New York: D. Appleton, 1857.

Herndon, William Lewis, and Lardner Gibbon. *Exploration of the Valley of the Amazon,* 2 vols. Washington: Robert Armstrong, 1854.

Higginson, Thomas Wentworth. *Army Life in a Black Regiment.* New York: Collier Books, 1962.

——— *Short Stories of American Authors.* Boston: Lee and Shepard, 1880.

Hitchcock, Edward. *Elementary Geology,* new rev. ed. New York: M. H. Newman, 1842.

The Holy Bible. Philadelphia: J. B. Lippincott & Co., 1843.

——— Authorized King James Version. Oxford: Geoffrey Cumberlege, 1950.

Holland, Josiah Gilbert. *Bittersweet, A Poem,* 5th ed. New York: Charles Scribner, 1859.

——— *Kathrina.* New York: Charles Scribner, 1867.

——— *Miss Gilbert's Career*. New York: Charles Scribner, 1860.

Holmes, Oliver Wendell. *Poems*. Boston: William D. Ticknor, 1849.

——— *Ralph Waldo Emerson*. AML Series. Boston: Houghton Mifflin and Company, 1885.

Huntington, F. D. *Christian Believing and Living*. Boston: Crosby, Nichols, and Company, 1860.

Irving, Washington. *A History of the Life and Voyages of Christopher Columbus*, 5 vols. New York: G. P. Putnam's Sons, 1902.

Jackson, Mrs. Helen Hunt (H.H.). *Verses by H.H.* Boston: Fields, Osgood, and Co., 1870.

——— *Bits of Travel at Home*. Boston: Roberts Brothers, 1878.

James, Henry. *The Europeans*. Boston: Houghton, Osgood, and Company, 1879.

Johnson, Samuel. *Rasselas, Poems, and Selected Prose*, ed. Bertrand H. Bronson. New York: Rinehart, 1958.

Kingsley, Charles. *Yeast: A Problem*. New York: Harper and Brothers, 1859.

Lowell, James Russell. *Among My Books*. Boston: Fields, Osgood, and Co., 1870.

——— *My Study Windows*. Boston: James R. Osgood and Company, 1872.

Longfellow, Henry W. *Hyperion, a Romance*. Boston: Ticknor, Reed, and Fields, 1852.

——— *Poems*. 2 vols. Boston: Ticknor and Fields, 1863.

Marsh, John. *An Epitome of General Ecclesiastical History*. New York: J. Tilden, 1843.

Matthiessen, F. O., ed. *The Oxford Book of American Verse*. New York: Oxford University Press, 1950.

Milton, John. *Paradise Lost*. Philadelphia, Benjamin Warner, 1819.

——— *The Complete Poetical Works of John Milton*, ed. W. H. D. Rouse. Boston: Houghton Mifflin and Company, 1899.

Mitchell, Donald Grant (Ik Marvel). *Dream Life: A Fable of the Seasons*. New York: Charles Scribner, 1851.

——— *My Farm of Edgewood: A Country Book*. New York: Charles Scribner, 1863.

——— *Reveries of a Bachelor*. Indianapolis: Bobbs-Merrill Co., 1906.

Moore, Thomas. *Irish Melodies*. Philadelphia: E. H. Butler and Co., 1865.

———, ed. *Letters and Journals of Lord Byron*, 2 vols. New York: J. and J. Harper, 1830.

The New England Primer. Hartford: Ira Webster, 1843.

Newman, Samuel Phillips. *A Practical System of Rhetoric*, 50th ed. New York: Mark H. Newman, n.d.

Olmsted, Denison. *A Compendium of Astronomy*. New York: R. B. Collins, 1848.

——— *A Compendium of Natural Philosophy*. New Haven: S. Babcock, 1850.

——— *An Introduction to Natural Philosophy*. New Haven, 1831–32.

Page, Curtis H., ed. *The Chief American Poets*. Boston: Houghton Mifflin, 1905.

Paley, William. *Natural Theology: or Evidences of the Existence of the Deity*. Boston: Gould, Kendall, and Lincoln, 1831.

[Patmore, Coventry.] *The Angel in the House. The Espousals*. Boston: Ticknor and Fields, 1856.

Phelps, E. Stuart (A. Trusta). *The Last Leaf from Sunny Side*. Boston: Phillips, Sampson, and Company, 1854.

Playfair, John. *Elements of Geometry*. New York: W. E. Dean, 1844.

Pope, Alexander. *The Iliad of Homer*, 2 vols. Boston: Edward Cotton, 1806.

Porter, Jane. *Thaddeus of Warsaw*. New York: Everett Duyckinck, 1820.

Reid, J. B. *A Complete Word and Phrase Concordance . . . of Robert Burns*. Glasgow: Kerr and Richardson, 1889.

Saintine, M. D. *Picciola*, 2d ed. Philadelphia: Lea and Blanchard, 1839.

Scribner's Monthly. November 1870 to October 1881.

Shakespeare, William. *The Complete Plays and Poems of William Shakespeare*, ed. William A. Neilsen and Charles J. Hill. Boston: Houghton Mifflin Company, 1942.

Silliman, Benjamin. *First Principles of Chemistry*. Philadelphia: H. C. Peck and T. Bliss, 1850.

——— *Elements of Chemistry*. New Haven: H. Howe, 1830.

Smellie, William. *The Philosophy of Natural History*. Boston: Simpkins, 1841.

Smith, Alexander. *A Life Drama and Other Poems*. Boston: Ticknor, Reed, and Fields, 1853.

Sprague, William B. *Letters on Practical Subjects to a Daughter*. Albany, N.Y.: E. H. Pease and Co., 1851.

Spiller, Robert E. *The Cycle of American Literature*. New York: The Macmillan Company, 1955.

——— et al., eds. *Literary History of the United States*, rev. ed. New York: The Macmillan Company, 1959.

The Springfield Republican. March 1844 to May 1886.

Stephens, John L. *Incidents of Travel in Central America, Chiapas, and Yucatan*, 2 vols. New York: Harper and Brothers, 1841.

Stowe, Harriet B. *Uncle Tom's Cabin*, 2 vols. Boston: John P. Jewett and Company, 1852.

Strong, James. *The Exhaustive Concordance of the Bible*. New York: Hunt and Eaton, 1894.

Taylor, Sir Henry. *Philip Van Artevelde*. Boston: Ticknor and Fields, 1863.

Tennyson, Alfred Lord. *The Poetical Works of Alfred Tennyson*, 2 vols. Boston: Ticknor and Fields, 1862.

——— *The Princess*. Boston: William D. Ticknor and Co., 1848.

——— *The Works of . . .* , ed. W. J. Rolfe. New York: The Macmillan Company, 1911.

Thomas à Kempis. *Of the Imitation of Christ*. London: Rovington's, 1876.

Thomson, James. *The Seasons*. Philadelphia: Edwin T. Scott, 1828.

Thoreau, Henry D. *Walden*. Boston: Ticknor and Fields, 1862.

Tupper, Martin F. *Proverbial Philosophy*. New York: Wiley and Putnam, 1846.

Upham, Thomas C. *Elements of Mental Philosophy*. New York: Harper and Brothers, 1850.

Watts, Isaac. *The Psalms, Hymns and Spiritual Songs of the Rev. Isaac Watts, D.D.*, ed. Samuel N. Worcester. Boston: Crocker and Brewster, 1834.

[———] *Watts's Improvement of the Mind*, ed. Joseph Emerson. Boston: James Loring, 1833.

BIBLIOGRAPHY

Wayland, Francis. *Elements of Moral Science*. Boston: Gould, Kendall and Lincoln, 1835.

Whately, Richard. *Elements of Logic*. Boston and Cambridge, Mass.: James Munroe and Co., 1855.

Wood, Alphonso. *A Class-book of Botany*. Claremont, N.H.: Claremont Manufacturing Company, 1853.

Woods, George B., ed. *English Poetry and Prose of the Romantic Movement*, rev. ed. Chicago: Scott, Foresman and Company, 1950.

Worcester, Joseph E. *Elements of History, Ancient and Modern*. Boston: Hilliard, Gray, Little and Wilkins, 1828.

The Wreath, A Collection of Poems. Hartford: Silas Andrus, 1824.

Young, Edward. *The Complaint: or, Night Thoughts*. Philadelphia: Uriah Hunt and Son, 1845.

Notes

Introduction

1. Citations from Dickinson are from *The Poems of Emily Dickinson* (Cambridge, Mass., 1955) and *The Letters of Emily Dickinson* (Cambridge, Mass., 1958), both edited by Thomas H. Johnson. Poems and letters are cited by the Johnson edition numbers. Poem numbers appear in notes only if the first line is not included in the quoted passage.

2. Ltr 268.

3. *This Was a Poet* (New York, 1938), p. 103.

4. Whicher, p. 224.

5. *Emily Dickinson* (New York, 1951), p. 206.

6. Ltr 271.

7. *The Continuity of American Poetry* (Princeton, N.J., 1961), p. 175.

8. Ltr 503.

9. Letter from Thomas Wentworth Higginson to Mabel Loomis Todd, quoted by Millicent Todd Bingham, *Ancestors' Brocades* (New York, 1945), p. 130.

10. Ltr 503.

11. *This Was a Poet*, p. 237.

12. The spelling has since been changed to "Belize."

Chapter I. Emily Dickinson on Books and Reading

1. Higginson, Ltr 342a.

2. Jay Leyda, *The Hours and Years of Emily Dickinson* (New Haven, 1960), I, 30.

3. Leyda, I, 45.

4. *Ibid.*, I, 52.

5. Ltr 200. Edward Dickinson's reading was probably part of the twelve-volume *Works of Thomas De Quincey* published in Boston, 1853–1859, ten volumes of which are in the Dickinson Collection at Harvard.

6. Higginson, Ltr 342a.

7. Higginson, Ltr 342b.

8. *Ibid.*

9. Ltr 261.

10. Ltr 113.

11. Legal terms do not appear frequently in the personal letters of either Austin or Edward Dickinson. Consequently, it is unlikely that ED's vocabulary of such terms came from either these letters or family conversation. The law books which belonged to the family are still in the possession of Mrs. Alfred Leete Hampson at The Evergreens in Amherst.

12. Ltr 418.

13. In *This Was a Poet* (New York, 1938), Whicher devotes two chapters, "Amherst Academy" and "Mount Holyoke Female Seminary," to the presentation of a clear picture of the schools and of ED as a student.

14. Ltr 3.

15. Leyda, I, 81.

16. Ltrs 15 and 18.

17. Ltrs 16 and 18.

18. Lavinia to Austin Dickinson, 1850. Millicent Todd Bingham, *Emily Dickinson's Home* (New York, 1955), p. 89.

19. Ltr 23.

20. Ltr 16.

21. Ltr 23.

22. Ltr 153.

23. Ltr 258.

24. See Whicher, p. 92.

25. P 360.

26. Ltr 44.

27. Whicher, p. 9.

28. Ltr 56.

29. P 1587.

30. Ltr 450.

31. Ltr 304.

32. Ltr 413.

33. P 299.

34. Ltr 261.

35. *The Atlantic Monthly*, 9: 401–411 (April 1862).

36. Ltr 261.

37. Martha Dickinson Bianchi, *The Life and Letters of Emily Dickinson* (Boston, 1924), p. 80.

38. Ltrs 622, 962, and 337.

39. Higginson, Ltr 342a.

40. Ltr 368.

Chapter II. The King James Version

1. Ltr 285.

2. Ltr 23.

3. Ltr 794.
4. Ltr 395.
5. A few references, usually to the Gospels, are related to verses that appear in two or more places in the Bible. Such cases are individually noted in Appendix A. A table indicating the number and distribution of biblical allusions in Dickinson letters and poems appears in Appendix C.
6. P 1569 and P 1369.
7. Ltr 911.
8. P 159.
9. Ltr 946.
10. P 13.
11. P 53.
12. P 1119.
13. P 1195.
14. Book XI, lines 265–290.
15. Ltr 9.
16. *Ibid.*
17. P 195.
18. Ltr 1042.
19. P 1483.
20. P 1201.
21. P 168.
22. P 1733.
23. Ltr 339.
24. P 48. The dove carried the olive branch at the end of its second flight from the ark. Sent out the third time, it did not return. Genesis 8:8–12.
25. P 403.
26. Ltrs 1035 and 1042. My italics.
27. P 540.
28. *Religion in American Life* (Princeton, N.J., 1961), II, 273–287.
29. P 1342. " 'Was not' was all the Statement."
30. Ltr 98.
31. "Covert" is used here in the sense of the legal term meaning "protection."
32. P 1310.
33. Ltr 883.
34. Leyda, II, 463–464.
35. Ltr 481.
36. See Ltr 444a and Thomas H. Johnson's *Emily Dickinson, An Interpretive Biography* (Cambridge, Mass., 1955), pp. 160–161.
37. Ltr 425.
38. Ltr 824.
39. Ltr 595.

40. Ltr 951.
41. Ltr 133. The scripture reference is to Matthew 7:7–8.
42. Ltr 979.
43. Matthew 25:29. Quoted in Ltr 551.
44. Ltr 788.
45. Ltr 471.
46. Ltr 843.
47. According to Whicher (*This Was a Poet*, p. 156), "The New Testament gave her material for but one poem, on the repentant Thief at the crucifixion."
48. P 127.
49. Ltr 50.
50. P 1166 and P 597.
51. P 1241.
52. Ltr 401.
53. P 62.
54. *The Atlantic Monthly*, 9:401–411 (April 1862).
55. P 460. Cf. Revelation 7:16–17.
56. P 168.
57. P 1598. See *Poems*, III, 1100–1101.
58. Millicent Todd Bingham has published a considerable amount of Dickinson family correspondence in *Ancestors' Brocades* (New York, 1945) and *Emily Dickinson's Home* (New York, 1955).
59. Ltrs 950 and 268.

Chapter III. British Literature: Renaissance and Eighteenth Century

1. There are, in the Dickinson Collection at Harvard, nineteen Bibles and six various editions of Shakespeare, all of which belonged to the family.
2. London: Rovington's, 1876.
3. Ltrs 402 and 721.
4. *Letters of Emily Dickinson* (Boston, 1894), ed. Mabel Loomis Todd, I, 129–130.
5. P 593.
6. *Hamlet*, I, iii.
7. Ltr 865.
8. II, i, 170.
9. P 322.
10. *This Was a Poet* (New York, 1938), p. 223; *Introduction to Emily Dickinson* (Chicago, 1947), pp. 126–127; Frank Davidson, "A Note on Emily Dickinson's Use of Shakespeare," *NEQ*, 18: 407–408 (1945).

11. Ltrs 553, 1004, and 340.
12. Samuel Phillips Newman, *A Practical System of Rhetoric* (New York, 1834), p. 296.
13. 9: 405 (April 1862).
14. "Emily Dickinson and Sir Thomas Browne," *AL*, 22: 455–465 (1951). The connection between Browne and Dickinson was first pointed out by Margery McKay Cridland in a 1936 Swarthmore College thesis entitled, "'Amazing Sense,' The Application of a New Method to the Poetry of Emily Dickinson."
15. *Religio Medici*, part I, section 13; ED's reference is in P 576. See *This Was a Poet*, pp. 222–223.
16. *Christian Morals*, part II, section 7.
17. P 964, P 1737, and P 242.
18. *Religio Medici*, part II, section 8.
19. *Christian Morals*, part III, section 9.
20. Charles Anderson, *Emily Dickinson's Poetry: Stairway of Surprise* (Princeton, N.J., 1960), p. 299; Judith Banzer, "'Compound Manner': Emily Dickinson and the Metaphysical Poets," *AL*, 32: 417–433 (1961).
21. (Boston, 1847), I, 149–150.
22. (New York, 1945), p. 125.
23. I, 318–319.
24. P 59.
25. Ltr 653.
26. Page 2, col. 1.
27. Ltrs 544 and 888.
28. Ltrs 110 and 564.
29. Ltr 693.
30. Ltr 304, P 503.
31. Book XI, lines 265–290.
32. Ltr 802.
33. Line 1721.
34. Ltr 141.
35. Ltrs 685 and 285.
36. Ltr 212.
37. See Genevieve Taggard, *The Life and Mind of Emily Dickinson* (New York, 1930), p. 96.
38. Ltrs 731 and 737, P 1439.
39. Ltrs 18, 732, and 967.
40. See Thomas H. Johnson, *Emily Dickinson: An Interpretive Biography* (Cambridge, Mass., 1955), pp. 84–86; and J. Davidson, "Emily Dickinson and Isaac Watts," *BPLQ*, 6: 141–149 (July 1954).
41. Ltr 110.
42. Ltr 42.

43. Ltr 414. The hymn is by James Montgomery and begins: "Servant of God, well done!"
44. Ltr 97.
45. Ltrs 213 and 888.
46. P 131, Ltrs 11 and 13 (1846), and Ltr 31.
47. Ltrs 39, 77, and 624.
48. P 285.
49. Ltr 261.

Chapter IV. British Literature: Romantic and Victorian

1. "Auguries of Innocence."
2. Ltr 400.
3. Ltrs 261 and 1034. The essay was "The Life of Birds," September 1862.
4. Ltr 1018. When Keats died in Rome, Joseph Severn was with him and reported the details of his death, including his last words.
5. Ltr 227.
6. Ltr 1029.
7. Ltr 337.
8. See Jay Leyda, *The Years and Hours of Emily Dickinson* (New Haven, 1960), I, 161.
9. *Christopher North, a Memoir of John Wilson* (New York, 1863), p. 327. ED's reference is in Ltr 409.
10. (Boston, 1853–1859.) *Confessions of an Opium Eater* is included, but *Klosterheim* is in one of the volumes now missing from the set. ED's request is in Ltr 191.
11. Ltr 200.
12. Archibald MacLeish, Louise Bogan, and Richard Wilbur, *Emily Dickinson: Three Views* (Amherst, 1960), p. 29.
13. Ltr 261.
14. 8: 368–376 (1861).
15. Lines 289–291. The complete line 289 reads: "The current. These were poets true."
16. Ltr 1019.
17. P 408.
18. P 700.
19. Ltr 271; *The Life and Letters of Emily Dickinson* (Boston, 1924), p. 83; Ltr 266.
20. Ltr 244.
21. Ltrs 261 and 298.
22. This is almost certainly the volume of *"Mr Browning"* that ED offered Samuel Bowles (Ltr 300); and, if so, she probably read it before making the offer.

23. *The Ring and the Book*, lines 855–866.

24. Ltrs 368, 966, and 1015.

25. The idea of death's calling at sunset may have come from a poem published in *The Hampshire and Franklin Express*. See Chapter VI.

26. See *The Capsule of the Mind* (Cambridge, Mass., 1961), pp. 61–63.

27. Ltrs 942 and 669.

28. See Johnson, *Poems*, I, 27–28.

29. One of these was a signed volume given ED by Mrs. Edward Dwight. It has since disappeared. See Ltr 243.

30. Ltr 801.

31. Leyda, I, 351.

32. Ltrs 449 and 368.

33. Ltrs 401 and 650.

34. Book I, chapter 12.

35. Ltrs 368 and 277.

36. Ltrs 389, 456, and 974.

37. Ltrs 814 and 962.

38. Ltr 972. The poem was one she had included in a letter (Ltr 868) to Sue written after Gilbert Dickinson's death in October 1883.

39. Ltr 710.

40. Ltr 389.

41. Ltr 28.

42. Ltr 113.

43. *The Life and Letters of Emily Dickinson*, p. 81.

44. *A Child's History of England, A Tale of Two Cities, Great Expectations, Nicholas Nickleby,* and *Oliver Twist.*

45. *The Life and Letters of Emily Dickinson*, p. 81.

46. Ltrs 692 and 723.

47. Ltr 241.

48. See Johnson's note on Ltr 515, *Letters*, II, 589–590.

49. P 91.

50. Ltr 291.

51. See Thomas H. Johnson, *Emily Dickinson: An Interpretive Biography* (Cambridge, Mass., 1955), pp. 207–208.

52. (New York, 1820), pp. 42, 189.

53. Ltr 955.

54. Ltrs 962 and 1046.

Chapter V. American Reading: Colonial and Contemporary

1. Ltr 712.

2. Thomas H. Johnson, *Emily Dickinson: An Interpretive Biography* (Cambridge, Mass., 1955), pp. 145–146.

3. Ltrs 33 and 214.
4. Ltr 15.
5. *Eleventh Annual Catalogue of Mount Holyoke Female Seminary,*
1847–1848, appendix, p. 6.
6. Revised by Rev. Joseph Emerson (Boston, 1833), p. iii.
7. *Ibid.,* pp. ii, 231–232.
8. ED's German text, Adler's *Ollendorff's New Method of Learning*
. . . the German Language, is in the Harvard Collection.
9. *Eleventh Annual Catalogue of Mount Holyoke Female Seminary,*
p. 5.
10. Ltr 92. The text to which ED referred was probably *A Grammar*
of the Latin Language for Schools and Colleges by Solomon Stoddard
and Ethan Allen Andrews.
11. P 600.
12. Denison Olmsted's *A Compendium of Astronomy.*
13. P 1299.
14. Newman, p. 69.
15. *Ibid.,* p. 38.
16. Ltr 906. See also Ltr 519.
17. Worcester, p. 25.
18. *Ibid.,* pp. 195–196.
19. Ltr 352.
20. Worcester, p. 256.
21. (Philadelphia, 1844).
22. Ltrs 13 and 362. Stearns was the son of the president of Amherst
College and a friend of Austin Dickinson and his sisters.
23. Ltr 875, P 131.
24. Ltr 214. See Johnson's note, *Letters,* II, 360.
25. *Introduction to Emily Dickinson* (Chicago, 1947), p. 46.
26. Ltr 153.
27. P 67, published in *A Masque of Poems* (Boston, 1878). See
Thomas Niles, Ltr 573d.
28. *This Was a Poet* (New York, 1938), p. 205.
29. *Emily Dickinson* (New York, 1951), p. 67.
30. P 526.
31. Ltr 353.
32. In *The Years and Hours of Emily Dickinson* (New Haven,
1960), II, 20–21, Jay Leyda calls this poem a "comment" on the Emerson essay.
33. Ltr 481.
34. *Emily Dickinson* (New York, 1951), p. 112.
35. Ltr 794.
36. Prose fragment 116, *Letters,* III, 928.
37. Ltr 691.

38. *Boston Evening Transcript*, September 28, 1894; *The Brooklyn Eagle*, April 28, 1892.

39. See Whicher, p. 192. ED's reference to Parker is in Ltr 213.

40. See Johnson's note, *Poems*, I, 284–285.

41. Ltrs 622, 337, and 564. The copy of *My Study Windows* is in the Harvard Collection.

42. Ltrs 962, 261, 368, and 622.

43. "Emily Dickinson's 'Three Gems,'" *NEQ*, 16: 627–628 (December 1943). ED's note is in Ltr 171.

44. Ltrs 737, 183, 128, and 12.

45. Reprinted in Leyda, I, 110. This source complements ED's reference to Elizabeth Barrett Browning's *Aurora Leigh*.

46. *The Springfield Republican*, Saturday, December 16, 1860.

47. Ltr 412.

48. Martha Dickinson Bianchi, *Emily Dickinson Face to Face* (Boston, 1932), p. 113.

49. Ltrs 62, 290, and 622.

50. Ltr 56.

51. Ltr 75.

52. Richard Chase, *Emily Dickinson* (New York, 1951), pp. 48–50.

53. Ltr 388.

54. Ltr 976.

55. See Johnson, *Emily Dickinson: An Interpretive Biography*, chapter VII.

56. This important relationship is thoroughly discussed by Theodora Ward in the concluding chapter of *The Capsule of the Mind* (Cambridge, Mass., 1961).

57. Ltr 261.

58. Ltrs 513, 622, and 458.

Chapter VI. Readings in Newspapers and Periodicals

1. Jay Leyda, *The Years and Hours of Emily Dickinson* (New Haven, 1960), I, *passim*.

2. Ltrs 109 and 42.

3. 3: 459 (October 1851).

4. Ltr 234.

5. Ltr 502.

6. Ltr 721.

7. Ltrs 714 and 721. The Howells novel is *The Undiscovered Country*, beginning in January 1880.

8. Ltrs 619 and 629.

9. Ltr 231. The Davis story appeared in the April 1861 issue.

10. *The Capsule of the Mind* (Cambridge, Mass., 1961), p. 190.

11. XI, 403.
12. Ltr 1018. See Chapter IV.
13. George F. Whicher, *This Was a Poet* (New York, 1938), pp. 9–10.
14. Reprinted in Johnson's note on Ltr 60, *Letters*, I, 154.
15. Ltrs 103 and 60.
16. *This Was a Poet*, p. 170.
17. Josephine Pollitt, *Emily Dickinson, The Human Background of Her Poetry* (New York, 1930), p. 345.
18. Ltr 133.
19. Saturday, June 16, 1860.
20. Martha Dickinson Bianchi, *The Life and Letters of Emily Dickinson* (Boston, 1924), p. 80.
21. Ltr 149.
22. Saturday, December 16, 1860.
23. See Johnson, *Poems*, I, 207.
24. Wednesday, September 14, 1864.
25. Ltrs 683 and 457.
26. P 1396.
27. *Poems*, III, 965–966.
28. Ltr 908.
29. See Millicent Todd Bingham, *Ancestors' Brocades* (New York, 1945), pp. 16–17.
30. Wednesday, September 14, 1864.
31. Ltr 381.
32. *The Springfield Republican*, Saturday, June 29, 1861.
33. Ltr 822.

INDEX OF FIRST LINES

INDEX OF FIRST LINES

Index

Abraham, 38
Adam, 31–33
Adams, Henry, 39
Adams, John S., 20, 134
Addison, Joseph, 72; *The Spectator,* 12
Adler, G. J., *Ollendorff's New Method of Learning . . . the German Language,* 147, 216
Aesop, 43
Alden, John, 119–120
Alexander, Francesca, *The Story of Ida,* 100, 147
Amherst, Massachusetts, 17, 20, 30, 94, 101–102, 131, 134
Amherst Academy, 15, 19, 28, 102, 105, 209
Amherst College, 15, 28
Amherst Record, The, 128, 134, 147
Anderson, Charles R., 213
Arnold, Benedict, 130
Atlantic Monthly, The, 83, 118, 128, 132–133, 148, 212

Badger, Mrs. C. M., *Wild Flowers,* 14
Balize (Batize), 7, 209
Banzer, Judith, 213
Bianchi, Martha Dickinson (ED's niece), 23, 86, 95, 100, 112, 209, 217, 218
Bible, 5, 13, 24, 27–59, 63, 77, 134, 140, 143, 145, 148–166, 212; tabulation of ED's biblical allusions, 192–193; Genesis, 30–34, 38–39, 57, 71; Exodus, 37–38; Deuteronomy, 30; Ruth, 34; II Kings, 38; Job, 40; Psalms, 30, 40; Isaiah, 30,

40; Daniel, 34; Matthew, 30, 40–51; Mark, 40–41, 49–50, 98; Luke, 30, 40, 42, 50–51; John, 30, 40, 51–55; Acts, 55; I Corinthians, 30, 55, 73; I Peter, 56; Revelation, 22, 30, 56–58, 140
Bingham, Millicent Todd, 69, 209, 212, 218
Blackmur, R. P., 39
Blake, William, 78
Blind, Mathilde, *Life of George Eliot,* 94, 167
Bobadilla (Bobadilo), 122–123
Bogan, Louise, 82, 214
Bowdoin, Elbridge, 95
Bowles, Samuel, 86, 93, 94, 96, 100, 101, 107, 137, 145, 214
Bowles, Mrs. Samuel, 44
Bradstreet, Anne, 39
Brontë, Anne, *The Tenant of Wildfell Hall,* 95
Brontë, Charlotte, 94, 99, 121, 123, 142, 167; *Jane Eyre,* 95, 124, 142; *Villette,* 95
Brontë, Emily, 94, 142, 167; "No Coward Soul is Mine," 94; *Wuthering Heights,* 95
Browne, Sir Thomas, 4, 22, 66–68, 106, 167, 213
Browning, Elizabeth Barrett, 4, 22, 24, 77, 83–87, 107, 123, 133, 167–168; *Aurora Leigh,* 84–86, 217; "Caterina to Camoens," 84; *Last Poems,* 87; "A Vision of Poets," 83
Browning, Robert, 22, 77, 87–91, 114, 135, 139, 145, 148, 214; *Bells and Pomegranates,* 24; *Dramatis Personnae,* 87; "Evelyn Hope,"

INDEX

Elizabeth I, 109–110

Eliot, George, 19, 24, 66, 77, 86, 92–94, 99, 121, 123, 145, 172–173; *Daniel Deronda*, 72, 93; *Middlemarch*, 93; *The Mill on the Floss*, 93

Emerson, Ralph W., 92, 101, 111–118, 121, 127, 145, 173–174; "Bacchus," 114–116; "Fable," 117–118; "The Humble-Bee," 117; *Poems* (1847), 18, 113; *Representative Men*, 117; "The Snow Storm," 118

Emmons, Henry V., 121, 174

Enoch, 39

Eve, 31–34, 71

Fargus, Frederick John (Hugh Conway), *Called Back*, 100, 174

Fiske, Daniel, 15

Fiske, Samuel (Mr. Dunne Browne), 138

Ford, Emily Fowler, 41, 63, 74

Franklin, Benjamin, 12, 102

Franklin, Sir John and Lady Jane, 129–130

Fuller, Margaret, *Gunderode*, 119

Fullerton, Lady Georgiana, *Ellen Middleton*, 100

Gabriel, 34–35

Gaskell, E. C., *The Life of Charlotte Brontë*, 94, 174

Gibbon, Lardner, *Exploration of the Valley of the Amazon*, 14

Goldsmith, Oliver, 60, 107–108; *The Vicar of Wakefield*, 72, 174

Goliath, 38–39

Gordon, Mary Wilson, *Memoir of John Wilson*, 81, 214

Gould, George, 18–19

Gray, Thomas, "Elegy in a Country Churchyard," 75, 106–107, 174

Griswold, Rufus, 102, 111, 174

Hale, Edward Everett, 18

Halleck, Fitz-Greene, "Marco Bozzaris," "On the Death of Joseph Rodman Drake," 111, 174

Hampshire and Franklin Express, The, 128, 134–136, 140, 143, 175

Hampshire Gazette, 136

Hampson, Mrs. Alfred Leete, 209

Harper's New Monthly Magazine, 93, 128–131, 175

Harte, Bret, *The Luck of Roaring Camp and Other Sketches*, 124–125, 175

Hawthorne, Nathaniel, 19, 25, 123; *The House of the Seven Gables*, 123, 175

Herbert, George, 68–71

Herndon, William Lewis, *Exploration of the Valley of the Amazon*, 14, 175

Herrick, Robert, 139

Herschel, Sir William and Sir John, 105–106

Higginson, Mary (Mrs. Thomas Wentworth), 43, 175

Higginson, Thomas Wentworth, 11–13, 22–23, 35, 66, 70, 76, 83, 87, 92, 94, 101, 120, 122, 125–127, 133, 141–142, 145, 175–177, 209; "Decoration," 5–6, 126, 136; "Letter to a Young Contributor," 22, 56, 66; "The Life of Birds," 126–127; *Oldport Days, Outdoor Papers*, 126; *Short Studies of American Authors*, 23, 123; "To the Memory of H. H.," 126

Hills, Mrs. Henry, 45

Hitchcock, Edward, *Catalogue of Plants Growing in the Vicinity of Amherst*, 133, 177; *Elements of Geology*, 84, 106

Holland, Josiah Gilbert, 46, 71, 101, 107, 122, 131–133, 138, 140, 145, 177; "To My Dog Blanco," 131; *Nicholas Minturn*, 131

Holland, Mrs. Josiah Gilbert, 29–30, 59, 95, 140, 142

Holmes, Oliver Wendell, *Poems*, 19, 120; *Ralph Waldo Emerson*, 23, 120

Holt, Jacob, 134–136, 140

Howells, William Dean, 126, 132, 177; *A Fearful Responsibility*, 132;

227

INDEX

INDEX

Whitney, Maria, 45

Wolfe, General James, 110–111

Worcester, J. E., *Elements of History*, 108–111, 130, 187–188

Wordsworth, William, 76, 78, 188

Young, Edward, *The Complaint: or, Night Thoughts*, 75, 188